O9-CFS-557

in both print and electronic media. He explains the mass market for information and popular art, thereby providing a basis on which to judge contemporary criticism of the content of mass media, and discusses changes in the moral web of the community which are relevant to an understanding of this criticism. He considers the effect of media content on society and reviews contemporary criticism. In conclusion he outlines a proposal for the application of the ethical principles of journalism in an organization designed to help the mass media meet the needs of a changing society while at the same time fulfilling their traditional role in the self-governing state.

J. Edward Gerald, a professor of journalism at the University of Minnesota, has been an active newspaperman, serving on both metropolitan and small-town newspapers. He is a former manager of the Missouri Press Association and is a past president of the Association for Education in Journalism. He is the author of two other books

THE SOCIAL
RESPONSIBILITY
OF THE PRESS

J. Edward Gerald

THE UNIVERSITY OF MINNESOTA PRESS
Minneapolis

© Copyright 1963 by the University of Minnesota. All rights reserved

Printed in the United States of America at
the Lund Press, Inc., Minneapolis

Library of Congress Catalog Card Number: 63-15503

Acknowledgment is made in the notes to many authors, publishers, and copyright owners who have granted permission to use quotations and references; among these, the following have also requested notice here:

Advertising Age, Chicago, Ill., November 9, 1959, copyright 1959 by Advertising Publications Inc.; *The Fading American Newspaper* by Carl E. Lindstrom, copyright 1960 by the author, quotations from pp. 99–102 used by permission of the publisher, Doubleday & Company, Inc.; *Jacobin and Junto* by Charles Warren, copyright 1931 by Harvard University Press, permission to quote from pp. 50–51, 71–96 granted by the President and Fellows of Harvard College; *The Responsibilities of Business Leadership*, Harwood F. Merrill, editor, copyright 1948 by Harvard University Press, permission to quote from pp. 5–12 granted by the President and Fellows of Harvard College; *The Daily Newspaper in America* by Alfred McClung Lee, published by the Macmillan Company, 1937, copyright by the author, who granted permission to quote from pp. 371–372; *Free Society and Moral Crisis* by Robert Cooley Angell, copyright 1958 by the University of Michigan Press, quotations from pp. 3, 9, 23, 29, 30, 34, 38, 39, 40, 82, 83 used by permission of the University of Michigan Press; *Social Progress*, March 1960, copyright 1960 by the Board of Christian Education of the United Presbyterian Church in the United States of America, permission to quote from pp. 5, 156–157 granted by the board; *The Story of Advertising* by James Playsted Wood, copyright 1958 by the Ronald Press Company, permission to quote granted by the publisher; *Advertising to the Mass Market* by James Davis Woolf, copyright 1946 by the Ronald Press Company, permission to quote from pp. 46–57 granted by the publisher.

PUBLISHED IN GREAT BRITAIN, INDIA, AND PAKISTAN BY THE OXFORD
UNIVERSITY PRESS, LONDON, BOMBAY, AND KARACHI, AND IN CANADA
BY THOMAS ALLEN, LTD., TORONTO

To Dean Emeritus Theodore C. Blegen

"There is as much sense in Hafiz as in Horace,
and as much knowledge of the world."
—Sherlock Holmes in *A Case of Identity*

ACKNOWLEDGMENTS

THE opportunity to gather and to organize the material in this book was provided at various times by the Graduate School of the University of Minnesota. The National Newspaper Survey, which the School supported in part, is the source of the information about the proprietor and the managerial function in mass communication. The opportunity to study the media as social institutions affecting the common values and moral web of the community came from a Graduate School summer fellowship.

Sincere appreciation is expressed for this help.

The specialist readers and the staff of the University of Minnesota Press have, by patient and self-effacing work, contributed to the integrity of the work as it stands.

It should be clear that the author takes sole responsibility for the opinions and recommendations growing out of the facts he presents.

J. EDWARD GERALD

Minneapolis, August 10, 1962

TABLE OF CONTENTS

The Social Responsibility of the Press

ˊ I

THE NATURE OF MASS COMMUNICATION

THE mass media of communication are social institutions that serve the society by gathering, writing, and distributing the news of the day. They take their character principally from our political and economic institutions, offering information and entertainment in the market place to uncoerced buyers. Uncoerced means that the diverse mass public is able voluntarily to choose anew each day the media it will purchase and to which it will devote its time.

This book intends to describe the market and its journalistic products, to observe their influence on other social institutions important to self-government, and to seek out ways in which the media may contribute more to the development of institutions that make up our civilization.

The effort to adjust our agrarian political institutions to the present industrialized community, which has been going on for some time, particularly affects journalism. The mass media have the whole people as an audience and this fact makes their social importance apparent. Cold and hot wars waged with mass populations require mass media of communication and the maelstrom of propaganda places a premium upon accurate information usable in making stable decisions. Communication usually arises outside one's immediate group and cannot readily be tested for error. The mass media provide nearly all of the information we receive.

Bedeviled as we are by the pedlars of bias, it is difficult for a citizen to seek out and to evaluate information about any country, including his own, particularly if he gives attention to information that differs either from the official propaganda line or the line advanced by a powerful group.

3

The Social Responsibility of the Press

The mass media, in theory, are expected to maintain freedom of speech and discussion, but they are also under heavy pressure from interest groups (the sources of diversified communication) to bolster and sustain bias as if it were truth.

In the strategy of communication, the masses in our society are deemed unsophisticated and easily exploited by demagogs. Systematic study of public opinion processes has proved useful to both the friends and the foes of democracy, and any distortion of information sabotages political processes based on reason and logic.

An important fact about the "age of the masses" is the large scale of the political and economic instruments being used by the community. Rivalry in trade, propaganda, and armaments is no longer between individuals and freely formed groups but between nations, and it is world-wide. The business enterprises developing the Tennessee, the Missouri, and the Nile are regional and official as well as private; labor activity is national and international in scope; merchants utilize a national and even international network of distribution, and they advertise over radio and television and through the networks of printed media reaching hundreds of millions of people. Teams in soccer, baseball, football, and other sports have international followings, and are watched in action by television audiences as well as by those present in person. Desegregation is a regional issue politically important all over the world.

When a leader speaks through print, film, or broadcast media, the effect on the masses, regardless of frontiers, is quickly visible; the impact excites those who wish access to these powerful agencies of influence and heightens the frustrations of those unable to achieve the results desired. Those who fail to persuade often blame the media rather than the message, and those who succeed often give the media more credit than they deserve.

It is hoped that when the reader has finished this book he can judge the performance of the media and proposals for improving them and that he also may be able to judge critics of the media, including the author of this book.

The material will be presented in this order:

1. The definition of society used in the book, making clear why mass communication is deemed to be important.

2. A review of the classical political theory of the self-governing community and the theoretical part mass communication plays in it.

3. A review of business history, the practical as opposed to the theo-

4

retical, to bring out particularly the course of events in which entrepreneurs worked out a theory of their own in the publishing and broadcasting business.

4. A description of the business of journalism adequate to keep the promise to make each layman well informed about the internal structure of the print and electronic media.

5. A description of the natural habitat of owners of the media so that the reader can see their environment and weigh its causal relationship to the content of the media.

6. An explanation of the mass market for information and popular art, furnished as a base against which to judge the contemporary criticism of content by persons who apply their own tests of value.

7. An insight into the extent to which nucleation of population and industry has damaged the moral web of the community, forcing us to knit a new one with the aid of social institutions not yet clearly understood or easily managed.

8. A review of the contemporary criticism of the content and the effect of mass communication.

9. The author's speculation that a new form of organization for the discussion and application of ethical standards of journalism might strengthen the mass media to meet the requirements of the new ethical community and the old self-governing state.

WHAT IS SOCIETY?

We can begin, then, by realizing that in social interaction words and acts draw their lively existence from one another. As with mind and body, it is difficult to separate them precisely and often impossible to determine the roots of words or actions. When students look at a social structure it is difficult to distinguish concrete forms from the words that describe them: forms and words appear inseparable.

The miracle of learning helps us round out, splice, and even extend structures that otherwise might not be seen as effectively complete.[1] When we learn upon authority that an observed object should look a certain way, or that a certain behavior is not to be evaluated in a particular way, we soon internalize the preferred meaning and are then its captives.

Learning is illustrated by the familiar sight of a mother instructing her toddler to stay out of the street. When the child, his mother's warning ringing in his ears, steps into danger, only a good strong pull can bring him back to safety; further words are waste and futility. But the memory of the word coupled with the emotional gesture registers its meaning, becomes internalized as a barrier in the mind which the child cannot cross. This is interpersonal communication, authoritative in the sense that the mother and child are in a particularly intimate relation and the child knows, or soon will know, the love and power behind the command.

Social communication in a democracy takes place between individuals or groups and the element of authority is not present or not dominant. When the communication is mediated through print or broadcasting, the relation between the communicators is relatively indirect and voluntary, the frame of reference is less intimate, and the messages are more generalized.

The interposition of mechanical media has changed communication in the same way that the orator is changed when, moved from the platform to the stage, he merges with the collective personality of the players. He still uses rhetoric, logic, and persuasion, but his words now are not necessarily his own, and his effect on the audience is dependent on the course of the action in the play, upon characters supporting and opposing him, and on the brooding omnipresence of the playwright.

Most students of communication seem to assume that the media can be separated from society and studied as if they had a virtually independent existence. Such an assumption creates a static and unreal field of observation. Thus the history of the Reformation and the Renaissance can be told as a history of writers and printers making use of Gutenberg's new movable types. Modern war can be seen as a struggle between rival teams of propagandists vying for control of the minds of men while cannon and bomb blast away indecisively. A political campaign can be pictured more as Rosenman (the speechwriter), Russell Davenport (the political idealist), or Batten, Barton, Durstine, and Osborn (the mass communicators), than as Roosevelt, Willkie, or Eisenhower. Such versions of events may be nearer to reality than the formal, full-length portraits of conventional political history. But more often they distort conventional political history by snapping the shutter on one instant of life and displaying the snapshot as typical of the whole. Separation is a device for directing attention to one part of social structure while neglecting its organic unity.

Society is the basic organization of mutually dependent family, kinship, and kindred-interest groups that provides for exchange of labor. Social organization has so grown in complexity that it is everywhere more visible

6

than the individuals caught up in it; we speak of the age of the masses and think of work and ideas as being the product of groups rather than of individuals. Communication has advanced from its interpersonal orientation in the family and small groups to the point where it also takes place on a national and international scale. The typesetting, printing, and broadcasting machines of the communications art have ended the isolation and separation of communities within particular societies. Cultural uniformity in such communities tends toward homogeneity, and society must deal with this sameness, as it did with cultural diversity, in terms of its impact on personal and group interests, upon social goals both sought after and in being.

The influence of social institutions. Mass-communications media are social institutions, the product of a social demand, even though they appear to be self-propagating. In the author's view, the human personality is shaped decisively by the family and by interaction with significant other persons in the community; particularly in infancy and youth, but all through life, the individual is sufficiently plastic that role, attitude, skill, and behavior alike can and do change. The individual has an influential original nature of his own; together, the original nature and the social environment constitute the matrix of personality, a matrix assumed not as a completed shape but as being built up gradually of units of experience. The acceptance by the individual of any one unit of experience leads to more formative interaction. When the individual becomes mature, that is, relatively habituated in the way he ingests new information and processes it, he can see the separateness of particular aspects of his personality and, if he has sufficient insight and will, can bring about further modifications and integrations. But for most persons the opportunity for self-analysis and for change is quite limited. Personality appears much more substantial than the will can easily alter. The individual, through his attitudes and beliefs, and particularly through his susceptibility to fear, is sensitive to the import of mass communication — though not so sensitive, perhaps, as in an intimate frame of reference. But when the opportunity for rational action comes, he responds to his knowledge. Significant others may channel and interpret information for him and persuade him to act in concert with them. If countervailing factors are present, however, he retains his freedom of choice.

The pressure of communicated demand or need helps create institutional forms whose purpose is to do the work of the group. Thus economic

7

institutions are constructed to provide food and physical facilities for life and political institutions take up the roles of rulemaker and arbiter. There are formal definitions of such institutions. "Any well systematized and effective social psychic mechanisms that satisfy basic, or what appear at the time to be basic needs, that enhance the ability of social groups to maintain themselves and persist, that control the individuals and groups within a society, whose demands are generally thought to be right and that have the power of enforcing themselves, are institutions." [2]

The mass communications and government. The mass-communications industries are institutions with functions located centrally in the network of social relationships, ranking very high in any arrangement of institutions according to social importance. The family, the institution which has grown up around the sex drive and the attendant task of rearing children, might occupy the first category in such an arrangement. The institutions of agriculture and business, satisfying the need for food, are on the same level as the family. Government is next, and language and writing, out of which the mass communications have grown, are either a part of government, as in totalitarian countries, or on a level of their own, in countries where society and government have separate identities and separable institutions. The labels "authoritarian" and "democratic" are loosely applied to governments. The function of the press in either system is to provide communication that establishes the reality of social institutions and facilitates control of them. In the authoritarian systems, journalists are under the discipline of the ruling group and willingly help shape and condition individuals according to plan. In systems that try to reconcile diverse groups and their different concepts of social function, the press is the agency by which the constituent groups in society become aware of their differences and are brought to accept intercourse based on the principle of toleration. When contending groups recognize the importance of public communication they want to use it for selfish ends, but if they are frustrated in this desire they then demand communication that is accurate and fair to all.

Government is in the same central position. Where the party system tolerates controversy it outlaws violence and lets the franchise depend upon peaceful activity. Like other social institutions, the political grew out of man's need to conventionalize differences and make possible orderly political action. Political history shows how difficult it is to confine parties to orderly procedures free of violence and how closely political stability

8

follows the fluctuations of economic well being. What we describe as stable government is the rather direct product of an economic situation in which individuals and groups eschew violent forays because their basic needs are met, or because the system promises fulfillment of needs in return for reasonable and non-violent effort. Struggle for self-improvement must be conventionalized.

Where authoritarian parties rule, the communicators, journalists, intellectuals of whatever kind, must accept the task of obtaining acceptance of the decisions of the ruling group. In much of the West the journalist is a collaborator with parties, groups, governments — a partisan and teacher of controversial ideas. He also, in some cases, aspires to be a reporter, a vehicle for the objective transfer of information, somewhat above the battle, equally important to all contestants because he serves all equally well, an instrument indispensable to modern civilization.

Political and social rights. The idea that the individual has basic rights, as well as duties, was articulated in ancient and medieval society as in modern. The state's claim on the people's loyalties is predicated on the benefits they get in return for performing duties assigned them by the state. The differences among political systems are qualitative; they concern the kind of relation between the individual and the state of which he is a citizen.

This theory originates in the experience of the people, in the interaction of the preferences and actions of the constituent groups in society. The role of the intellectual theorists is to provide options from which the people choose. Once the choice is made, the literary theorists describe and interpret it, law gives it stability, and education attempts to perpetuate it. The political theory of freedom of communication accepted in the United States originated in Anglo-Saxon tribal and village society and was developed by such cardinal social experiences as adjustment to the Norman conquerors and Parliament's successful efforts to subject king and bishops to the law. The question of the basic rights of the individual is in constant discussion and development. In order to deal with it currently we must first summarize the body of theory and note its origins.

⁊ LIBERTY UNDER LAW

The contribution to political liberty made by Anglo-Saxon tribal and village life was an understanding relationship between the citizen and the officials. Whether the leaders were elected, chosen, or accepted by the group in some other way, the continuity and dignity of tribal custom and common law was understood by both leader and led and there was opportunity for the people to utilize the prestige of law in opposition to the prestige of leadership, although the relative political strength of the individuals concerned may at times have put little restraint on the executive power. But the fact that law and leadership were recognized as community products and that they ran separate if parallel courses in the life of the community, provided the fundamental ethic from which all claims of men against the power of government developed.[3]

In the English-speaking world political and religious controversy, beginning with the conflict between English common law and William the Conqueror's concept of national landlordism, developed a system of politics and jurisprudence lodging sovereignty, or ultimate power, in the people. There are bright figures in the controversy: Sir Edward Coke, who upheld the common law as the law of right and reason in the face of royal prerogative; John Milton, whose plea for unlicensed printing was directed at a parliamentary dictatorship from the intellectual ground of a Greek temple of justice, the Areopagitica; John Wilkes, whose activities as politician and editor helped open Parliament to public reporting and gave greater security to the system of party government; Richard Carlisle and his family, whose unequal struggle with authority established the opportunity to sell and distribute printed matter as equal in importance to the right to print without prior censorship, and by thousands of writers, printers, and readers who stood in their time before authority, in the tradition if not with the same effect as did Coke before James I, to assert the supremacy of law. When James said to Coke that he, too, as well as common-law judges, had reason, the Lord Chief Justice replied that it was true that God had anointed the king with "excellent science, and great endowments of nature," but the king was "not learned in the laws of his realm of England, and causes which concern the life, or inheritance, or goods, or fortunes of his subjects are not to be decided by natural reason but by the artificial reason and judgment of law, which law is an art which requires long study and experience before a man can attain to a cognizance of it." James replied that it was treasonable to suggest that he should be under the law; the course of his action stemming from that attitude led to civil war, to the Revolution of 1688 and the supremacy of the views expressed by Coke.[4]

10

The Nature of Mass Communication

We can let our statement of the theory of political freedom begin with these men. Coke is a figure symbolic of the primacy of law interpreted by professional judges. Milton represents the ideal community in which controversial discussion proceeding freely among all who wish to speak was counted upon to facilitate a reasonable consensus. This model community, free to discuss and to decide, was secure in the faith that truth would win out over error in public debate. It was projected in the *Areopagitica, a speech of Mr. John Milton for the Liberty of Unlicensed Printing, to the Parliament of England,* published November 25, 1644. The book was practical in intent, for a complaint against Milton was on file in the House for a previous breach of the licensing ordinance, and Milton wished not only to escape punishment but to publish still more. In particular he wanted to agitate for reform of the laws of marriage and divorce, partly because under the influence of her Royalist family, his young wife was then living apart from him and he, a vigorous adherent of the Parliamentary camp, despaired of a reconciliation. He knew that the Stationers' Company, which had a government printing monopoly, was under the influence of the clergy and would not license a publication so heretical.

But the *Areopagitica* was addressed to broader and more general problems than Milton's domestic troubles. The country was in a civil war brought on by controversy over the role and power of bishops. There were at least three distinct parties with positions on this issue well defined and Milton was advising his own party, then in control of Parliament, that it could safely entrust its cause to unlicensed and uncensored public discussion. "Let Truth and Error grapple," he assured the parliamentarians, "who ever knew Truth to be put to flight in a free and open encounter?"

Does truth always win? — Gautama and Jesus. Since Milton's statement of principle was uttered in a controversy having religious content, it is appropriate to turn to the lives of two great religious figures for illustration of how this theory worked out in practice. Siddhartha Gautama, founder of the Buddhist faith, was the son of a king and designated heir to the throne. After a period as deputy civil administrator he found himself opposed by a faction headed by Prince Devadatta. Frustrated by this opposition and in disenchantment Siddhartha went into a nearby wilderness where, living as an ascetic, he worked out a philosophy and set himself up as a teacher. He had great success but old political enemies plotted against him. They left the body of a young prostitute beside his hut and

11

spread a rumor that he was her murderer. His disciples, ready in the human pattern to believe the worst, turned away from him indignantly. Rejected, deprived of mission, Siddhartha returned to his home city. Here he found that his enemies had preceded him and that they were sedulously spreading their false report. Moreover, to intensify the public's reaction to their great lie, they placed the body of the girl on a litter and carried it through the streets. To the litter a banner was attached naming Siddhartha as the slayer. Afterward, the body and the banner were transferred to a funeral pyre to await gathering of the village residents.

The people of Siddhartha's home city reacted in the same way as the colony of former disciples. As the people turned against him, Siddhartha was caught up in a raging encounter of truth and error; it seemed certain that error would prevail because he could not think of a way to communicate his case as forcefully and effectively as his enemies had purveyed the lie. The imminent victory of error through the use of an ugly, dark smear would make it impossible to gather another group around him to teach his hard-won philosophy. In addition, he faced loss of patrimony, exile, and rejection by the community he had sought to serve.

There was only one counter action he could take, to mount the funeral pyre and shout out the truth to the unbelieving crowd. As he summoned desperate courage for this act, he was rescued by the timely intervention of authority in the person of his father. Sizing up the situation at once, the father turned on Siddhartha's enemies and obtained the testimony of an informer and a confession from the principal. Truth was again in the field, backed by superior force. The chief conspirator was convicted and set off on a procession behind the same litter. The ugly banner was corrected to absolve Siddhartha and to identify the guilty.[5]

There is a parallel demonstration of the Miltonic theory in the life of Jesus of Nazareth, whose career illustrates how important a part friendly authority played in the experience of Siddhartha. On the day when Jesus carried the cross through Jerusalem, the political power and prestige necessary for his rescue was not in friendly hands. Recognizing this, Jesus occupied his final hours by setting in motion plans for continuation of the struggle the climax of which was a ritual of resignation and acceptance. The struggle was to continue beyond the grave.

Truth as a function of political control. The experience of these two spiritual leaders makes clear an aspect of the theory Milton understood acutely but which he neglected to make clear. Truth victorious is not pas-

12

sive; it is always at war, hot or cold, and those who wish to see truth succeed tend to come into action with all the weapons at their command. They can hope to win only if the centers of authority are in friendly hands. Effective truth is not mere communication, but the control of the state and of the machinery of enforcement of decisions. When the followers of Jesus organized and instituted teaching missions in an essentially hostile environment, they needed conventions that placed great charismatic value on tolerance and protection of the heretical individual. In needs also of agents and agencies of communication, the Christian protagonists used those they found — students, leaders, itinerant evangelists, housewives, all who showed interest. Where these agents of communication found it possible to go freely and openly about their work, they made friends and eventually challenged the special interest groups opposed to them. The threat of cunning and violent opposition always hung over them, as it did over Siddhartha, and when a community rebelled under the impact of the new ideas authority was called upon to decide between the antagonists; once force was used the opportunity for further discussion addressed to the issue was at an end. Others might later pick up and go forward with a similar discussion, but violence, as communication, is impossible to reverse.

Analysis of bias. Modern analysts seek to identify the motive of communication and to separate relatively truthful, disinterested communication from its opposite, the relatively biased self-serving message. This approach is justified by (1) the expectation that the agencies of mass communication will faithfully provide a trustworthy service of intelligence adequate to the needs of self-government, and (2) by the widespread change from selective to mass distribution of communication which makes it increasingly difficult to observe the effects of communication whether biased or not.

The theory of the tournament of reason assumed that anybody with an idea worthy of attention could get into the competition. The Miltonic ideal attempted to alter the violent game of politics so that government would abandon the coercive art in which it excelled and leave time for a clash of wits and words. This was and is a notion so appealing to humanists that they have used the ideal in their unceasing effort to erect an order based on reason and law able to harness brute force. Because the ideal was stated wholly in terms of restraining government, it cast a gentle literary fog over differences among the men who play the game, their physical strength,

13

The Social Responsibility of the Press

wealth, official status, leadership skills, ability to influence the grand marshal of the tournament, and their emotional and mental coloring.

The banners or placards mocking Gautama and Jesus were lettered by hand and circulated in a district small enough for most of the people concerned to have some primary knowledge of the controversy. Even so, the people were confused and civil authority was responsible for what happened. Many centuries later communication is accomplished through intermediaries who possess technical skills and who work with a mechanical apparatus of dissemination which they control. As a consequence, antagonists in today's disputes are concerned not only with the merits of an argument but with access to the industrial plant necessary to communicate with the members of society to whom the decision-making machinery is entrusted. The extent to which the industrial process has changed — and has carried communication with it — is glimpsed by noting that the affairs of once-isolated cities like Kapilavastu and Nazareth have become intertwined in those of the larger world and that it is difficult for any of them to manage their own affairs or control their destiny.

Residues of bitter partisanship. Milton's statement of the ideal community fits the needs of a society with multi-party government and diverse cultural groups and institutions. It has been elevated to the status of social theory in democratic societies and is constantly used as a benchmark by our courts in deciding disputes arising under the guarantees of freedom of speech and press. But it has not had the approval of those who prefer to influence a leader rather than to lead the people. For that reason, it must be constantly supported and defended. Hamilton called attention to this in the *Federalist* papers when he said that freedom of the press could be secure only if actively supported by the people. It was improbable, he said, that freedom could be protected by negative prohibitions on interference by government. How, for example, could the press be placed beyond the reach of the taxing power, a power fully able to cripple or to destroy it?

The first serious test of the open society came during the aftermath of the French Revolution when feelings ran high and American public opinion was split between Britain and France. It was this split that gave strength to Jefferson and his new political party.

Charles Warren, historian of the Constitution, tells us about the kind of political controversy which Jefferson faced and in which he took his decisive stand for political freedom. "Nothing could pass current without being stamped with Federalism" (the pro-British point of view), Warren explains.[6] "A man could hardly sell his bread, his milk, or his meat, without designating it Federal. If he wanted to hire a house the first question asked would be: 'Are you a Federalist or a Republican?' If a tavern was advertised in the paper to be let there would be a *nota bene* at the foot of it, 'None but Federalists need apply.' "

The language of the press during the Federalist-Republican controversy was a noxious amalgam of insult, invective, slander, malice. Its stench permeated the community like summer garbage.

What Jefferson taught us. Jefferson's decision in favor of open political discussion, stench and all, was taken when the federal government passed the now infamous alien and sedition laws of 1798. He and Madison denounced, through the Virginia and Kentucky Resolutions, the federal power typified by these laws, and the election campaign in which he won the presidency established an assumption, good for many years, that no central government could tamper with freedom of speech and the press, as the Adams administration had done, and survive. As Hamilton predicted, though, the assumption was good only for the memory of the generation that had felt the impact of the political warfare and made the decision at the polls. The political theory of communication in America, as differentiated from that in England, begins with these men.

The various newspapers making up the press were individually subordinate to the political leaders of the time. The political turmoil was akin to that which produced Milton's plea for unlicensed printing and only the strength of the British tradition of political liberty appears to have made possible the emergence of a stable government based on a free party system.

Jefferson's contribution to freedom of the press and political system deserves to be evaluated as greater than Milton's. Though Milton formalized a powerful idea he was, after all, primarily a man of words whereas Jefferson was a man with political power. He broke up the one-party system in government and developed an effective alternative to the philosophy of the Federalist party.

The press is an institution that learns from experience, just as individuals do, and learning tends to be passed by one generation of managers to the next. Since its experience during its identity with political parties was of formative significance, we should take a longer look at what happened.

15

The Social Responsibility of the Press

Jefferson's speeches and letters show a sincere belief in the open society. He believed that the people, if well informed, had common sense and reliable judgment. They might be led astray for a moment, he wrote, but will soon correct themselves. Politicians might offer wisdom, but the truest and best insight was to be found in the people themselves; even when they were wrong their authority should not be questioned. The way to keep the people from making mistakes was to give them full information about politics and government through the press; to this end he wished the papers to penetrate to the whole mass of the people. "The basis of our government being the opinion of the people, the very first object should be to keep that right; and were it left to me to decide whether we should have government without newspapers, or newspapers without a government, I should not hesitate a moment to prefer the latter. . . . But I should mean that every man should receive those papers and be capable of reading them." In a letter to Charles Yancy he stated this philosophy in shorter form: "Where the press is free, and every man able to read, all is safe." [7] His respect for information did not extend to unrestrained debate and one of his biographers says he "can fairly be said never to have made a speech," because he hated the morbid rage of debate. "He believed that men were never convinced by argument, but only by reflection, through reading, or unprovocative conversation; and this belief guided him through life." [8]

Morbid debate borders on violence. The morbid rage of debate that Jefferson disliked brought on a libel suit in which a Federalist editor was personally defended by Hamilton. From this trial another tenet in our system of press liberty emerged: truth told with "good motives and justifiable ends," is an adequate defense in suits for defamation.[9] This holding accorded with Hamilton's view, and a law making proof of truth a justification for libel was enacted in New York and spread to other states.[10]

The perfervid party press tested the patience of the country into the years of civil war and beyond. Hamilton's death by the pistol of Aaron Burr resulted from a quarrel abetted by unbridled newspaper vilification; the meeting took place on the same field where Hamilton's son had died in another political duel. These deaths were two among many. The hand of the political polemicist turned character assassin reached into city, village, and hamlet alike, taking away the reputations and sometimes the lives of editors, candidates, party officials, governors, even presidents. Rival teams of political journalists and traders collaborated in opening up the new country.

16

The Nature of Mass Communication

Party, faction, biased newspapers. Towns in the new states came to have three, four, and five newspapers, along with business allies engaged in land speculation; but this kind of diversity was hardly as enlightening as pure theory would require us to believe. A prejudiced journal read by a prejudiced mind is a far cry from the dream of many informative media in the market place of thought, for even if the people read, as Jefferson wanted them to do, how shall they understand? Jefferson's view of the blindly partisan press was that it canceled out its usefulness.

I have lent myself willingly as the subject of a great experiment, which was to prove that an administration, conducting itself with integrity and common understanding, cannot be battered down, even by the falsehoods of a licentious press, and consequently still less by the press, as restrained within the legal and wholesome limits of truth. This experiment was wanting for the world to demonstrate the falsehood of the pretext that freedom of the press was incompatible with orderly government. I have never, therefore, even contradicted the thousands of calumnies so industriously propagated against myself. But the fact being once established, that the press is impotent when it abandons itself to falsehood, I leave to others to restore it to strength, by recalling it within the pale of truth. Within that it is a noble institution, equally the friend of science and of civil liberty.[11]

The journeyman journalist and editor made the diversified party press possible. A close look at one such polemicist might help to show why party newspapers fell out of fashion and demonstrate that it was a miserable press produced by unhappy men not averse to finding greater security and satisfaction in different employment. Jefferson looked upon himself as a teacher of political ideology; his interest in the press stemmed in part from his need for assistance in spreading his ideas as far as possible. For this reason he supported the *National Gazette*, edited by Philip Freneau; the help he gave another journalist, James Thomas Callender, was similarly motivated. Callender was a penurious English political refugee resident in the United States, trying to make a living by serving whatever patron he could find. After passage of the alien and sedition laws he left Philadelphia for Richmond, thinking he might be personally more secure there while continuing work in his libelous art. He contributed to newspapers and wrote a political pamphlet smearing President Adams for which he was punished under federal law by a two-hundred-dollar fine and a jail term.

In jail or out, Callender had never earned enough to cover his living expenses, keeping up a stream of begging letters to his political patrons.

17

The Social Responsibility of the Press

Jefferson, a frequent contributor, helped again while the journalist was in jail. After Jefferson became president, Callender demanded a political appointment and when he did not get it he turned ferociously on his patron. His libels of Jefferson, when reprinted, resulted in the case against Croswell in which Hamilton contributed his services as attorney. But Callender's lot did not improve with the switch in allegiance; his family was dependent upon what he could wheedle and beg. Besides, he was by now a proved political renegade, considered unreliable by both parties.[12] The future, at best, promised only more of the same.

Such journalists and such journalism were only as secure as the political fortunes of their allies. These activities made up the competitive age of diversity and tarnished the bright hope for the tournament of reason held out by Milton. The principal social gain was that the frustrating of Callender's tribe served to turn journalists away from careers in the art of political vilification and lead them to search out a more satisfactory base for a living.

Control of the press by judges. One other major dispute with political overtones helped round out the political theory of freedom of the press in the nineteenth century. A federal judge in St. Louis, sitting in a dispute over public lands, was criticized by a lawyer living outside the jurisdiction of the court. The judge, in the usual hearing without a jury, punished the lawyer for contempt and was, himself, then impeached in an effort to remove him from office.[13] The effort failed, but the Congress and most of the states then made such use of the contempt power unlawful. The state courts gave up the authority grudgingly and took it back in a series of decisions only to lose it again in an opinion by the United States Supreme Court in 1941. The press has been vulnerable historically to the use of the contempt power and this is a critical area in the dynamics of government and press relations.

By 1941 the United States courts had undertaken to guarantee freedom of the press as "among the fundamental personal rights and 'liberties' protected by the due process clause of the Fourteenth Amendment from impairment by the States."[14] This left the press in a strong position so long as the federal government was more liberal than the states in its attitude toward freedom; if the situation were to be reversed, the press would be back to the conditions of 1798 when Jefferson took up its cause and saved it from repressive federal controls.

The one indispensable tenet in the theory of communication that flows

18

from this series of events is that the people must believe they have an irrevocable right to freedom of speech and press; and they must be willing to remove, by decisive political action, restraints upon their enjoyment of the right.

⁊ BUSINESS AND THE PRESS GROW TOGETHER

Milton's model of the society of open communication was incorporated in 1791, as part of the Bill of Rights, into our Constitution. The original Constitution itself had assured freedom for business, for it contained something of the spirit of Adam Smith's *Wealth of Nations*, published the year the American Revolution began. Smith applied the Miltonic ideal to relations between government and business, arguing that society would be better off if production of goods geared to bar subsistence gave way to wider opportunity to pursue individual economic aims. He advised free competition in goods as Milton had urged free trade in ideas. He trusted men as reasonable and ethical beings capable of learning from personal and social experience; he felt them inclined toward sympathetic consideration for others, and able to adjust their activities accordingly. This was the self-righting process of ethical society; it was the process that Smith, like Milton, counted upon to monitor competitive practices. The statement of the theory of freedom of information on the political and legal levels must, therefore, be supplemented by an examination of the economic level. The theory in the hands of businessmen is equally important, for the modern shape of journalism stems from the work of these men.

The majority of editors and publishers were content with neither the poverty nor the political misery of the Thomas Callenders and sought a greater degree of economic security. The natural and historic association of journalism with politics could hardly be abandoned at once, but the general growth of business, and the equally natural and historic association of the press with advertising offered a way to improvement. Business and politics were hardly separable or distinguishable, but the ideal of political and economic independence grew inside the press.

The discovery of mass readership. The first and second American dailies were business ventures hopefully designed to cater to the needs of business growing in the new climate of freedom. The second one succeeded where the first one failed; but it was not in an appeal to advertisers, but to readers, that the daily paper first found promise of new vigor and independence. The New York *Sun*, a penny paper published by a job

19

printer who had little interest in politics, and less in Wall Street, was the first to take hold of the general public. This paper was sold copy by copy on the streets directly to readers instead of by annual subscription payable in advance. In a year it had twice as much circulation as the higher-priced newspapers oriented to business and politics. Its focus was largely on plain people and the problems common to humanity, police-court cases, and the varied human tableaux of passion and violence. It had a feeling for adventure and escape that was rudimentary in form but appealing to the unsophisticated human heart. The *Sun* proved a true pioneer, the creation of an entrepreneur whose insight into the mass mind was fundamentally sound. Its success accounts for the first element in the new economic theory of the press: Go after wide readership. Mass-periodical circulation was built by assuming that most men live on the level of the senses and that to them the urges, needs, and frustrations of the self are the things of most importance.

When a businessman undertakes a venture involving trial, error, and risk — as Day and his imitators did — he follows essentially the procedures scientists describe as empirical and pragmatic. The important difference is that the scientist publishes a record of his experience and invites other students to improve on his procedures and broaden the predictive value of his results. The businessman does not. If the results of entrepreneurial effort are successful, if a satisfactory profit is produced, the information as to method, results, and the probable predictive value of the data is treated as secret and held in reserve for future struggles against competitors, present and potential. If the venture is unsuccessful, the entrepreneur sometimes has to reveal his data before a referee in bankruptcy; even so, only a few businessmen will attempt to evaluate unsuccessful experience and to make use of it in future ventures. Because much of the information upon which entrepreneurs base their strategy is circulated by word of mouth, the speed with which explanation of both success and failure is transmitted is slow. Moreover, the fate of nearly all business ventures is decided by the march of events rather than by the conditions at the time the original decision to invest was made.

The great journalistic innovators. The march of events from 1830 was favorable to the mass-circulation paper but Day's contemporaries soon saturated the market with their product. Technology produced the semi-automatic machines necessary for a large growth in circulation, with papers delivered to readers on the day of publication, and for a large increase

The Nature of Mass Communication

in the daily average number of pages. Another entrepreneur, the merchant, needed publicity to guide to him a tide of customers gradually rising with increases in population and disposable income. Thirty-five penny papers started in New York alone in the 1830's and only two survived.[15] But in spite of difficulties, the idea of the mass-circulation paper spread around the world.

James Gordon Bennett founded the New York *Herald* five years after the *Sun*. He took Day's human interest formula and developed it on a regional, national, and international level, gradually stimulating a public appetite for news as a viable commodity for which part of each day's pay had to be allocated. Merchants of many classes began to ask him for large advertising spaces and he was able, after a mechanical breakthrough in stereotyping and press design in 1854, to develop the *Herald* into the most profitable newspaper of the moment — a purveyor of news and bold reports of the excitement that human beings find in their common vicissitudes.

The *Sun* and the *Herald* were edited by Democrats and this fact made the field look attractive to Horace Greeley, a journalist and political writer allied with the Whig party. He established the New York *Tribune* in 1841 as a penny paper with opinions. He developed the editorial page so successfully that he is rightly credited as the inspiration of the leadership-page tradition in the American newspaper, a tradition of despair as well as glory, for while a journal may lead one willing segment of its readers who crowd close on its heels, it must suffer the disapproval of another segment, often larger than the first, that does not like either the ideas or the politics with which they are associated.

The financial success of the *Tribune* excited the interest of the men who established the New York *Times*, Henry J. Raymond, a former editor on the *Tribune* staff, and George Jones, a banker and former employee in Greeley's counting room. Greeley's style of thinking and writing, and the sensationalism of the *Sun* and *Herald*, left Raymond and Jones a market for content based on wide coverage of news, moderation in editorial opinion, and objectivity in place of sensationalism.

The competitive struggle following establishment of the *Sun* emphasized circulation growth. The daily newspaper press that emerged from the competition for circulation was oriented more to business, including its own economic welfare, than to politics. An eye witness was Frank Munsey, who assigned himself the role of broker and liquidator after

21

The Social Responsibility of the Press

mushroom overexpansion had put several of the most respected firms into difficulty. He wrote in 1898 that the development of journalism as a business was influenced most by James Gordon Bennett with his *Herald* and that the transition to the stage of big business was due chiefly to the impact of Joseph Pulitzer and his daily and Sunday *World*.[16]

Yellow Journalism. Edith Merwin Barstow says that the pressure the sensational newspapers put on the conservative publishers forced changes in content through heavy competition for mass circulation. She writes:

Leading the confused and bewildered conservative publishers were the yellow journals. Frenzied in their power, their unlimited fields for exploitation, and their determination to dominate competition, the converts of the Yellow Kid created and fed the hysteria that demanded more news, shocking news, improbable news, news with scareheads and banners and appropriate pictures. . . . Risk to invested capital multiplied with mounting costs of newsprint, presses, tools, talent, wire and feature services. Conservatism and caution were imposed on the press by hard facts, and puzzled publishers looking for guidance beheld success in terms so contradictory that confusion was worse confounded; the public granting life to newspapers was unfathomable, unpredictable, imperious, and inflexible.[17]

Helen MacGill Hughes adds further detail: because of the coverage of sensational human interest news by Bennett and others, she says, the circulation of the daily papers grew by 187 per cent between 1830 and 1840 while population was growing only 32 per cent. Bennett's popularity was "as natural as that of a talkative sheriff or coroner," Mrs. Hughes says, for in coverage of crime and murder stories he shared all the gossipy details with the public. His skill and boldness brought down upon him the wrath of the conservative newspapers of New York, who cloaked their envy in moral indignation. Even the archbishop of New York was moved upon one occasion to threaten Bennett with excommunication because of stories in the *Herald*.[18]

Human Struggle — The Greatest Story. The content of Bennett's paper might offend his competitors, as the relative size of their circulations declined in comparison with his, but though the elite groups may have objected, the masses did not. Instead, their purchases of the *Herald* raised its circulation to record heights.

The human-interest story soon had even a wider range than Bennett gave it. With Dana and the *Sun* it was gentler, often with a tinkle of laughter or a twinge of pathos in it; with Robert Bonner of the New York

Sunday Ledger, it had the big names of statesmen, ministers, and literary lights he obtained as contributors, and in the strong, simple appeal of love, struggle, and mystery in his fiction. With others, as for example the editor of the *Police Gazette*, the deviation was in the direction of crime and violence.

The success of Joseph Pulitzer encouraged imitators who saw only the *World*'s sensational material, not its effort at a balanced presentation of news and opinion. These imitators used extreme display of news of scandal, crime, and violence and won circulation in New York City despite the popularity of the *World, Herald*, and *Sun*. Proprietors throughout the country sought quick increases in circulation. "Eventually most newspapers recovered from the disease, but modern journalism has exhibited some of the effects of the curse of yellow journalism ever since." [19]

Business Competition. Munsey lets us see inside the counting rooms of some of the publications competing with leaders like Hearst and Pulitzer. From the owner's point of view, he said, the "most heartbreaking publication is the one which is almost breaking even. But it either should be enlarged in plant and facilities so as to become profitable or it should be discontinued at once." He estimated that a million dollars a year was being lost in New York from such publications' almost breaking even. The price at which these papers were sold to the public had to be the "lowest possible to discourage competition and encourage consumption," he said, for while readers are not slow to recognize extra value and to follow a new leader, they "won't follow anything but the successful journal." It makes no difference to them if the maker of shoes they buy is near bankruptcy, "but they won't follow the near-bankrupt journal." These economic facts accounted for the effort to build the human-interest type of content, for it was far more popular with the readers than more serious material. And it retains its popularity.

Scandalous Newspapers. Twenty years later, with competition still intense in spite of the closing of a number of newspapers, a new series of deliberate efforts was made to push human interest in the news well beyond the limits of good taste, and oftentimes beyond the legal limits of decency as well. This was the period of jazz-age journalism which began in earnest after World War I and was checked only by the great depression. One of the most successful of the practitioners of this brutal art was Emile Gauvreau, trained on the conservative Hartford *Courant*, but coming to prominence as editor of Bernarr Macfadden's *Morning Graphic*,

23

known in the trade as the pornoGraphic, and of Hearst's *Mirror*. Gauvreau said that in retrospect the yellow journalism of the early twentieth century was simply an exploration by the papers of the full possibilities of the vast new mass audience.

Not so jazz-age journalism. It was, said Gauvreau,

an offshoot from the parent stem, and was dedicated to the fullest extent to the primitive instincts of mankind. Its object was to attract attention at any cost, and the most intimate details of life, in a period noted for its excesses, appeared in the sensational press along with smashing displays of crime news and an occasional crusade for better conditions in local government.[20]

"The newsstands of the country at the time were swamped with sensational magazines, a large number of them of the art and sex variety." Gauvreau claimed it was to this audience that he appealed with his paper. *True Story* magazine had two million circulation and the sex magazines of other publishers had a combined circulation of nearly fifty-six million. Gauvreau estimated that publications of this category had at least two hundred million annual readers.

The sensational *Graphic* and *Mirror* attained large mass circulations but could not succeed financially because advertisers withheld their patronage.

The great depression followed close upon the experiment testing the profitability of sensational content. Like the jazz age, the depression was a symptom of problems men did not understand and could not discuss in wholly meaningful terms. Economic assumptions accepted on a wide scale had brought industrialization and great prosperity to urban areas. All at once the economic plan broke down. Why? Failing to find answers, governments in various parts of the world floundered and were replaced, but the same journalists struggled with the new problems in an effort to explain them to the people. Conscious of inadequacy, they introduced college-trained men whose numbers steadily increased until the old type of journalist-craftsman was no more. As new economic assumptions based on the Welfare State drove out the chaos of the depression, journalism turned seriously toward the new mass society and the age of big government to report incident and trend as meaningfully and as accurately as it could.

But the depression adversely affected the press by hastening the process of concentration of ownership. The newspaper count in the country dropped from 11,689 weeklies, semi-weeklies, and tri-weeklies in 1930

24

to 10,182 in 1960. Raymond B. Nixon reports that daily papers declined from 1,942 in 1930 to 1,763 in 1960. This left only sixty or so cities with competing daily newspapers and although radio and television established alternative channels of communication and undoubtedly reached a mass audience, their content was prevailingly entertaining rather than informational. The theoretical basis of the democratic self-righting process seemed impaired if not destroyed, and the New Deal years in which the press found itself in a politically weak position intensified doubts, aroused by consolidation, that a basis for diversity existed any longer.

⌐ SUMMARY OF BUSINESS PROBLEMS

All of these things — Greeley's great contribution as an editor using the exciting tools of reason and as the producer of a newspaper with cosmopolitan interests, the high news standards of the New York *Times,* the gentle humor of Dana, the composographs and lurid paragraphs of Emile Gauvreau — made up the reputation of the press, and as with all reputations the bad stuck more firmly than the rest. The twentieth-century press had tried out several ideas on the market and had a theory it thought would work. Together with the political theory of diversity, these findings constitute today's practical theory of the press system:

1. The form of association and of government developed by the community gives first priority to diversity of political and religious ideas and second priority to corporate unity. The system of thought assumes that institutions for cooperation and government can be constructed under conventions that will force compromises among competitors for political power.

2. The press system provides an opportunity for openness and diversity of communication in support of the political ideology. A diverse community is made up of innumerable special interests pressing their claims upon the general society. For a time, newspapers of general circulation were published by and for particular interests of one kind or another, but these publications proved poor competitors with others that provided information and entertainment as well as — or in lieu of — propaganda.

3. Owners of newspapers discovered that human-interest stories — news about the joys and tragedies of the human struggle — were marketable to a wider audience than was serious information. They used this discovery to build mass circulations. They also found, because many newspapers carrying it went bankrupt, that the market for human interest, like that

for information, was limited. Simultaneously, some of them learned to develop other devices for competition — crusading and muckraking, special correspondence from news centers at home and abroad, news enterprise and promotions, editorial pages, special features of several kinds.

4. The competition for circulation had one particular goal — sale of space to advertisers. This brought problems of content and standards which, on their own account, are still to be resolved.

⸢ II

JOURNALISM AS BIG BUSINESS

The industrial form of journalism was brought about by long-run changes in distribution, seasonal changes in styles of apparel, and the formation of large retail units, particularly department stores. The long-term static-to-downward trends in the price level, 1815 to 1863 and 1871 to 1914,[1] promoted apathy among consumers and opened the way for an aggressive and opportunistic kind of retail store. The Wanamaker store in Philadelphia and A. T. Stewart in New York City were pacesetters, with Wanamaker particularly influential because he used large amounts of newspaper space and frequent special-event promotion to build and sustain his volume of business. Stewart, Wanamaker, and other merchants who subsequently operated in the same pattern, were big centrally-administered buying organizations possessing far more than the average information about business conditions. For individual bargaining on price and for the traditional battle of wits with customers over quality of merchandise, Stewart, and later Wanamaker, substituted a policy of one price for all, plainly marked, and an offer of reasonable return and refund privileges. The two merchants limited credit to a monthly basis and encouraged transactions for cash. The tightening of credit and its reduction from an annual settlement to a monthly basis gave the department stores a substantial cost advantage which they passed along by selling goods at lower prices.

Wanamaker's view of advertising was that it should help people buy, not help the store sell. He insisted that it be attractive in form, "first to get the attention of the reader, second to get her interest, third to get her confidence, and fourth, to get her into the store."

The Social Responsibility of the Press

It is worth noting that Wanamaker spoke of his clientele as female and this point of view in the trade was also an innovation. His interest in publicity extended to founding and publishing such magazines as *Everybody's Journal, Farm Journal, Ladies Journal,* and *Book News Monthly* to advertise his business.[2]

Distribution is speeded up. Frank Munsey says that advertising broke up the vicious circle by which the manufacturers and producers marketed their products only through brokers who were virtually in control of the market, fixing prices and terms. "The producer was absolutely at the mercy of the jobber. The latter could make or break him." Advertising brought the consumer and the producer together and the jobber's hold on distribution was broken. The wholesaler remained but he could not control the manufacturer. Advertising ended the dependence of retailers on big markups and a small volume. "Talking to the people, that's the idea. . . . It is the very bedrock, the substratum of modern business," Munsey wrote in 1898.[3]

The department store from the beginning had to stress rapid turnover in contrast to the attitude of merchants who could put surplus merchandise in storage between seasons and bring it out again with fair assurance that it would still be acceptable. For example, before the retailing revolution and before the development of paper patterns for dressmaking and pictorial reproduction in books and magazines, fashions were demonstrated by dolls dressed in London and Paris and imported to America. Dressmakers made up dress forms for each of their clients and made clothing to order from materials selected in market centers. The wide manufacture and sale of home sewing machines by Singer and others opened a new popular market for dress and fashion goods — a development later enlarged by improved processes of making halftone and line engravings.

Rewards of publicity. The importance of publicity and active selling practices in developments of this sort is crucial. The home sewing machine is but one example: it is clear that the device developed by Barthélmy Thimmonier in France and patented in 1830, and the device developed by Walter Hunt in New York around 1834, were as much subject to development and wide sale as the machine patented by Elias Howe in 1843. The Singer machine, although the basic patent was adjudged an infringement on Howe's, soon came to be the best known and largest selling machine because its advertising and selling practices fitted new conditions in society.[4]

Sewing machines could be advertised and sold over a wide area and did not greatly affect the income of any one newspaper. But the department store sold thousands of items from one location and newspaper advertising was the logical means of building a steady publicity pressure for a firm. The legend of Wanamaker is dear to the hearts of advertising men, for he is reported to have invested $24 out of his first $24.67 in sales in newspaper advertising. By 1879 he had launched a program using full pages of advertising; the modern industrial newspaper may fairly be said to have stemmed from his pattern of advertising. His success commended his methods to others. He corrected a business slump with a promotion device that soon became an American institution, the clearance sale. By the time the President of the United States personally appeared in 1911 at the dedication of his new Philadelphia store, his place in the history of advertising and publicity, as well as in the list of multi-millionaires, was long since assured.

Even before they discovered the mass market for readers, the newspapers gave great emphasis to advertising. Lee notes that daily newspapers gave five-sevenths of their space to advertising between 1830 and 1860. Although some merchants established guarantees of money back on goods returned, newspapers continued for a time to place on readers all of the responsibility for discriminating between honest and dishonest advertisers and between news and advertising matter, but the same forces were at work in both advertising and merchandising. With the aid of legislation the situation generally improved.

Out of the volume of advertising a partnership developed between business and journalism which became the most distinctive characteristic of the communications system of our dynamic society. The theory by which the partners operate became identical and they grew to be the most powerful influence group in the community.

✓ MORE ADVERTISING, LARGER NEWSPAPERS

As advertising volume grew and papers became larger, publishers gradually adopted a fixed allotment of space for news regardless of the number of pages in an edition. Jason Rogers of the New York *Globe* thought sixty columns in a metropolitan paper was about right for news but he trimmed this to between forty-five and fifty columns when newsprint became dear in 1917.

Lee shows how the space for advertising varied. In 1878 he found 21.5

per cent advertising in representative metropolitan papers and ten years later advertising occupied 29.8 per cent of all space; in another decade it was 28.2 per cent. A group of 147 dailies in twenty-one cities gave 32.1 per cent of their space to advertising, but there were wide fluctuations, from 25 to 70 per cent advertising, because more advertisers wanted space on the best shopping days. An advertising–reading matter ratio of 50–50 came to be a vague ideal before World War I. Afterward, the proportion of advertising began to increase; Lee reported it at 63 per cent in a group of evening papers in 1923. There was a reduction in volume during the great depression, but since World War II the space for advertising in 101 morning newspapers, 151 evening newspapers, and 141 Sunday newspapers published in 132 cities, as measured by *Media Records*, has averaged around 60 per cent. At this average, of course, many papers carried 70 per cent or more. The remainder of the space is not to be taken as the amount of news because features occupy a substantial portion.[5] The increase in advertising gradually enabled firms to look to it for 70 per cent or more of their income.

The growth of newspapers over the country was due to increased demand for advertising. Newspapers in 1958 employed 294,000 persons and 52 per cent of them were in production departments concerned more than half of the time with advertising, as the proportion of space used throughout the industry shows. Not only did retail merchants in the large cities, relying on the same faith that sustained Wanamaker, greatly increase their demand for space, but national or general advertisers made major contributions to the growth of newspapers and magazines. Purchasers of classified advertising in newspapers also proved to be substantial consumers of space. By 1929, when the disposable income of the country was $82.5 billion, advertising expenditures totaled $2.34 billion. Newspapers received $760 million of this amount, magazines $210 million, and radio $35 million. In 1956, total advertising expenditures were about $9.9 billion and were divided $3.3 billion to newspapers, $782 million to magazines, $565 million to radio, and $1.2 billion to television.

As a result of this growth, newsprint consumption virtually doubled between 1941 and 1956, rising from 3,922,000 tons to 6,802,000 tons. During the same years, the proportion of paper used for news and editorial content declined 21.4 per cent. In the last year of the interval the newspapers sold 61.5 per cent of their space to advertisers, and daily papers with more than 100,000 circulation averaged forty pages a day, compared with twenty-seven pages in 1941; Sunday papers averaged a hundred and thirty-five pages per issue against eighty-eight in 1941.[6]

The cumulative effect of these figures shows that, because of the growth of advertising, the industrial and manufacturing aspects of newspaper (and magazine) production greatly outweigh the news and editorial process, although the public tends to judge newspapers in particular as publications designed primarily to report information and express opinion on current affairs. Leaving aside printing and distribution, the cost of the news and editorial activity for newspapers around 100,000 total circulation is about 16 per cent of the total expenditure of newspaper firms reported in annual surveys of the business.

It is common knowledge that the income from sale of newspapers and magazines to the public is insufficient to cover the costs, and that no successful newspaper in the twentieth century has ever been published without advertising. The lesson of experience, such as the failure of adless newspapers, including Marshall Field's *PM* in New York, is that a mass-circulation newspaper cannot be published without a substantial subsidy from advertising. Neil Borden, in his *Economic Effects of Advertising*, said that in 1935 65.6 per cent of the expense of publishing the newspapers he studied was attributable to operations other than advertising. He used accounting procedures to allocate production expenses, but had to be content with data from a small and perhaps unrepresentative group of newspapers. He calculated that after all expenses chargeable to advertising were deducted, 50 to 54 per cent of advertising revenue was available to pay other costs and profits. This meant, he said, that in 1935 advertising subsidized the news and editorial function to the extent of $250 million. If the same ratio may be assumed to have prevailed in 1956, when newspapers received three and a third billions from advertising, the subsidy contributed to the news, editorial, and entertainment portions of the newspapers in that year was more than a billion and a half dollars.[7] Borden also estimated that advertising, after paying all expenses attendant upon its preparation, publication, or broadcasting, contributed in 1935 $380 million to newspapers, magazines, and radio, or 25 per cent of the total cost of all advertising.[8] No later estimates on the same base are available, but Cooke Coen, a Chicago accountant operating a newspaper analysis service, reported two examples in 1956 of the extent to which income from sale of copies to readers fails to cover the total expense of newspaper publishing. Coen did not represent his two cases as typical, but said the figures were well within the range he had observed in his extensive experience. Leaving both advertising income and expense out of consideration, Coen said the two newspapers in 1955 had costs per hundred subscribers amounting to $1,814.45 and $1,702.60, and that these costs exceeded income from subscriptions and sales by $564.30 and $695.95 per hundred subscribers. In percentage terms, 30.5 per cent and 40.8 per cent of the expense was left to be made up, in the two cases, by net income from advertising.[9] This bears out Borden's conclusions. Moreover, since Borden's survey, television has developed into a nearly two-billion-dollar industry and the amount paid for advertising to the mass media has been substantially increased. If Borden's 1935 proportions were assumed to hold, in the absence of proof, the contribution of advertising in 1956 to all the mass media, above its costs, would have been more than two and a half billion dollars.

ꜰ ADVERTISING PRACTICE AND MONOPOLY TRENDS

The dependence of journalism upon advertising is built into the pricing formula introduced by the first successful penny daily, the New York *Sun*, and continued in principle by the industry ever since, subject only to such modifications as the absence of local competition allows. The paper is furnished to readers at a nominal price and all competitors in the mass market must meet the price. The real competition between printed media is in the arrangement of content so as to achieve the largest possible appeal and consequent circulation. This circulation can then be sold to advertisers and differences in advertising rates that are related to differences in circulation can be sustained competitively. Magazines have an additional competitive opportunity in the sense that they can cater to sections of the mass audience, identified in part by sex or age or special interest. Some few daily newspapers — for example, the New York *Times* — select a particular class of readers even though their price per copy may be the same as or close to other newspapers in the community. When two newspapers print about the same kind of news, feature, and editorial content, the readers and advertisers together determine the survivor, but the advertisers have by far the more persuasive voice in the outcome, since the revenues from readers never cover the cost of the service.

Advertisers soon developed formulas by which rate for advertising is expressed in terms of the quantity of circulation; these formulas were either used to select one newspaper or magazine in a market or, more

32

frequently, to give the publication with the most favorable combination of rate and circulation the largest order. When all or many advertisers followed the same order of preference, the publications in secondary positions were made more vulnerable to depressions and to annual increases in wages and salaries and other costs of doing business set by leaders in the market. In communities where competition has been intense, such as Philadelphia, Chicago, New Orleans, Boston, Birmingham, Los Angeles, Detroit, Cincinnati, Columbus, long-established papers have recently been discontinued or merged with others. Cumulatively, over the years, this mode of selection has been the principal cause of the fluctuation in the number of daily and weekly newspapers and magazines in the twentieth century. Radio and television stations, and even networks, appear to be operating in the same economic pattern and the total number of firms no doubt will follow a somewhat similar course in the long run, although major efforts to differentiate programs, and thus to preselect special sections of the mass audience, may prove competitively helpful.

Local advertisers get lowest rates. Another impediment to the security of newspapers in particular is the tendency of large local advertisers to engage in collective bargaining, openly or secretly, for the most advantageous rate. Secondary newspapers in a market suffer in such business negotiations. The national advertiser seldom deals directly with the medium, but purchases space and makes most business contacts through agents. The local advertiser, on the other hand, deals almost daily with members of the newspaper staff, often with the publisher or general manager, and has a more direct opportunity to discuss rates. Such individual contact is sometimes bolstered by tactics and agreements worked out by representatives of big retail advertisers in conferences to which the newspaper is not a party. One obvious consequence is that on the average the rates of daily newspapers for national or general advertisers are considerably above the highest rate to transient local advertisers, who pay the highest local rate, and this basic charge scales down sharply for large local users of space on monthly or other contract basis.

The difference among charges to local retail stores has been conventionalized in rate schedules incorporating discounts for volume purchases of space similar to those of the electric power companies. But off-the-card arrangements are common enough in the industry that no realistic analyses of rates have been published by trade associations and professional analysts. Instead, after years of delay, the problem has been attacked by

33

newspaper trade associations who have commissioned time-and-motion studies of advertising composition designed to establish norms which can then be shown to large advertisers when bargaining on rates is found necessary. Newspapers justify the difference between rates for retail and for general advertising by saying that the total circulation is useful to a general advertiser but that a portion of the copies is distributed outside the trade territory of even the largest retail stores. Direct bargaining between the medium and the customer, on the local level — as explained above — must also be persuasive, since local radio and television rates tend to adopt a similar differential pattern of rates.

For two or three years after World War II, the newspapers, the magazines, and radio and television stations enjoyed record profits according to reports published by trade associations, by *Editor & Publisher* magazine, by the Federal Communications Commission, and by accountants and others who make special surveys. (The profit record is dealt with in a subsequent chapter.)

Bargains for big users of space. Don C. Seitz, business manager of the New York *World*, wrote in his story of Joseph Pulitzer that the New York newspapers had to recognize and deal with a group of merchants that bargained to force down rates and was extremely difficult to deal with. At the time, according to Lee, a group of twenty merchants placed half the retail advertising in New York newspapers.[10]

Such tactics forced newspapers out of business in New Haven, Pittsburgh, and elsewhere, Lee reports, the seven newspapers in Pittsburgh being reduced to four between 1923 and 1927. Twelve department stores simultaneously pulled their advertising from the New York *World Telegram* in 1932 when a rate increase was announced, and subsequently the paper had to reduce the increase by half. The Justice Department filed a complaint at the end of World War II against a similar combination of New York *Times* advertisers and won an order breaking up for at least that one occasion the coalition against the newspaper. The American Newspaper Publishers Association found the pressure of merchants worth attention in its annual meetings.

Response of rates to economic conditions. In times of business depression, when newspapers are particularly vulnerable because a part of their manufacturing capacity may be idle, associated merchants or powerful firms acting alone organize free-circulation publications in imitation of newspapers and distribute them from house to house. Emery says that

34

between 1921 and 1933, merchants cooperated in the establishment of 187 such shopping newspapers in 154 cities. Advertising rates of newspapers decline more slowly in depressions than the cost of living and commodity prices. Charles V. Kinter calculated the relative changes for the great depression and reported that in 1933, for example, the cost of living index was 57 per cent of 1929 and the commodity index 69, while the rate per line per million circulation for evening and Sunday newspapers stood at 114 per cent of 1929.

Advertising volume and rates also lag behind when disposable income starts rising on the upswing of a business cycle. In 1941, for instance, the index of disposable income was 111 per cent of 1929, but the total volume of advertising was 69 per cent.

Newspaper rates tend to lag in still another way, as the experience between 1945 and 1956 — a time of rapid growth in circulation and money volume — shows. When the cost of living index for those years is compared with an index of retail and general advertising rates adjusted to the same base, it is apparent that newspapers gave away to advertisers 15 million extra circulation they had added between 1940 and 1950. An index where rate per line is expressed in terms of one million copies, usually termed the milline, stood in 1950 at 103.5 per cent of the 1935–39 average when the cost of living index on the same base was 171.2. The milline rate index had moved no higher than 126 per cent by 1956. Newspaper rates in absolute terms increased almost exactly in line with the cost of living index, at least to 1950, but circulation gains were not charged for, perhaps because for the moment labor and materials charges were just emerging from wartime controls, volume was up and earnings appeared unusually good. Cost studies published since 1950 show that the lag in local advertising rates has caused a progressive shrinkage of profits, as a percentage of gross sales, since 1950. The consolidation of publications, and the discontinuance of magazines such as *Collier's*, *Woman's Home Companion*, and *American*, were also linked to problems of advertising support, but much more closely related to competition between firms in the same advertising market than failure of the management to fix rates appropriate to conditions.

Dimensions of advertising business. The growth of advertising in the printed media had its parallels in the electronic media — radio and television — and although there are relative year-to-year changes, the $9.9 billion total in 1956 was distributed in this way: newspapers, 32.66 per

35

cent; magazines, 8.02 per cent; radio, 5.72 per cent; television, 12.18 per cent; all other media and forms, 41.42 per cent. By 1959 the total had reached $11 billion and newspapers had lost 1 per cent in their relative position while television had gained more than 3 per cent.

Advertising is a business receiving annually nearly three cents out of each dollar of disposable income, that is, three cents out of each dollar of gross national income less taxes. In 1954, when advertising totaled $8.1 billion, about $3.1 billion went through the hands of advertising agencies and an additional $200 million was handled by other firms intermediate to the media. The business had a $400-million payroll and 73,206 employees. In addition, there were 6,744 proprietors of unincorporated businesses. Agencies handled most of the business volume — 91 per cent — and had 61 per cent of the employees and two thirds of the 6,744 unincorporated businesses.

In addition to being a big business, advertising is also an unusually important business, one which employs experts privy to the public's innermost thoughts and attitudes and which seeks, tests, and uses techniques for identifying opinion and bringing about changes in attitude that are usable in the marketing of goods and, at election time, in the sale of ideas to the voters. Though government is committed to freedom of the press, actually advertising makes possible whatever political freedom the press enjoys by furnishing a substantial base of support. Moreover, although there are giants among the advertisers, and their potential influence cannot be ignored, the $11-billion size of advertising expenditures means that thousands of firms make individual decisions about the purchase of advertising space in the media and the largest firms tend to deal with the media through middlemen who have ethical standards of their own and considerable stake in an orderly system throughout the business. The net result is that the owners of the media have come to enjoy a considerable amount of elbow room in which to maneuver, when it comes to holding to their own opinions about and ethics in what they publish, and that they are at least as well off in this respect as the institutions of the country as a whole.

⁊ ADVERTISING SELLS GOODS

The relation between advertising and the media is one of the problems to be examined here and the topic might well be opened up by a look at general advertising, that category which is largely placed by national and regional firms through agents and which is the portion of advertising that has had to bear most of the criticism of the business.

The purpose of advertising is to attract attention, create an interest in the product or service being advertised and an appreciation of its desirability great enough to generate an impulse to possess or to buy in the individual reader, listener, or viewer. Since attention is prerequisite to everything else, overemphasis and exaggeration have been associated with advertising since its beginning. Early advertising overemphasized the many virtues of coffee and the concealed or doubtful virtues of folk medicine. Early English-language periodicals used heavy type faces and intricate ornament in advertising to support the enthusiastic language already there, and whenever new devices for getting attention, or new versions of old ones, were developed, advertising soon made use of them.

The spirit of the pitchman: Barnum. P. T. Barnum (1810–91), who had a knack of understanding human credulity and human interest, raised the art of advertising to a new peak of effectiveness, and to a seldom-matched level of insincerity, humbug, and ballyhoo. His success emboldened others during his lifetime and since, particularly the vendors of patent medicines, and fitted in nicely with the commercial ethic expressed in the phrase, "Let the buyer beware." But not all advertising, indeed only a small portion of it in terms of the total, deliberately schemed to take advantage of the buyer.

Some of the biggest and most consistent advertisers used copy that gave publicity to the product without resort to emotional involvement and certainly without the kind of exaggeration associated with medical advertising. A few such advertisers, representatives of hundreds, can be cited at random: RCA Victor, Uneeda Biscuits, Dutch Boy Paints, Smith Brothers Cough Drops, Old Dutch Cleanser, Fisk ("Time to Retire") tires, Kodak, Wrigley's chewing gum, most automobile companies, the Borden Company, Sears, Roebuck, and Montgomery Ward. The last two companies at one time carried patent-medicine advertising in their catalogs; but reference here is made to their performance as general merchandisers.

Insight into Human Nature. Barnum's gift to the advertising business is his extraordinary insight into human nature. The worst of his blatancy and exaggeration could be tamed, in time, but not his discovery that human beings never grow up and can be manipulated like children. Barnum viewed the human being as a docile and friendly animal, living in a barely-alert mental state, who could easily be attracted to join crowds in which he lost his identity and his skepticism. When he chose to make suckers of gullible humans, Barnum always bragged publicly about it afterward, and thus his manipulations, being out in the open, were fairly benign. He apparently had no sinister aspirations for power, but was quite well satisfied with exhibiting himself, his freaks, and his great artists alike, to the multitudes for a fee.

Important national advertisers of food and drugs, from the beginnings of that kind of business down to passage of the Wheeler-Lea act in 1938, were free to mislead the public and some of them did so.

Abuse of Public Confidence. National advertising got its start in peddling drugs to the public with the patter and ethics of pitchmen and, until the 'thirties, when sixty-seven deaths were blamed on a sulfanilimide mixture sold by a Tennessee medicine-man, no laws existed under which the federal government could really protect the public. The Tennessean, for example, paid a fine of $200 as his debt to society. J. P. Wood, author of a recent critical history of advertising, aptly characterizes the typical patent medicine as "valueless if not pernicious. Advertising alone gave it value." [11] Advertising had been given such a bad name by the patent-medicine men that for a time it was little used by reputable business firms, who thought advertising not only controversial but an unnecessary expense. The pioneers like Wanamaker on the local level and Royal Baking Powder and Sapolio on the national had to overcome public distaste for advertising that had by no means disappeared when, in building the New York *Times*, Ochs sought to persuade his news staff to accept the growing volume of advertising in the paper as a service to readers.

Wanamaker, evangelist of enterprise. What should be the obligation of the advertisement writer to the public? For a time, Wanamaker employed as advertising manager John E. Powers, a man famous for his skill as a copywriter and for his straightforward approach to the public. Powers' work typifies informative advertising copy; he sought to describe merchandise accurately and to help people make rational choices in buying, a motive which — up to a point — Wanamaker apparently shared. In method and outlook, Powers was akin to the writers of catalog advertising who, aided by a favorable and relatively truthful illustration, describe merchandise in enough technical detail so that differences in quality between similar items are apparent. Though Powers was honest to the point of stubbornness, Wanamaker was not averse to some of the tactics of the pitchman. On one fateful occasion Wanamaker ordered labels on a consignment of Ameri-

38

can-made men's hats changed so as to indicate English origin. Powers, in an advertisement, revealed the switch in labels, and in a discussion of the advertisement with Wanamaker he was fired. Later in his career Powers was displaced as copywriter for Bissell carpet sweepers by Claude C. Hopkins, who had served his apprenticeship in the medicine-man school of advertising. His defeat at the hands of Hopkins was symbolic, for advertising was undergoing a transformation during which it appropriated the skills and techniques of the dramatist and playwright. The reasoning of the advertisement writers was much the same as that of the literary men: make up the actors with grease paint and costumes so that their personalities become more definite and can be projected more easily to the audience; remove them from commonplace surroundings onto a lighted and well-furnished stage; add music, color, motion — and above all else, imagination — to the scene and bid the players make the best of their parts.

Powers used fact too much unadorned to survive this kind of competition, as it turned out. He sought merely to accomplish in low key the classic maneuver of advertising men — to get attention, to arouse interest, to promote an understanding of the product, and to tell the reader where he can buy. Venturesome copywriters, in light of the demonstrated fact that Powers-like simplicity was not the most successful advertising policy, developed a new salestalk, or pitch.

Lasker and the elastic truth. The patron and saint-elect of such venturesome writers was Albert D. Lasker of Lord and Thomas, Chicago, who employed, at different times, among many others, both John E. Kennedy and Claude Hopkins, who turned their pitchman talents to the sale of a great variety of merchandise. Lasker said in later life that the two most important things in the history of advertising copy were the dramatization of appeal already referred to and the injection into copy of themes tapping sex and love interest. Thus, when another advertising man, Victor O. Schwab, came to select five advertising headlines he liked, four of them used varieties of this approach: "How Five Out of Seven Women May Win New Loveliness in Three Minutes." "How to Give Your Children EXTRA IRON Three Delicious Ways." "I Lost My Bulges — and Saved Money, Too!" "New Shampoo Leaves Your Hair Smoother, Easier to Manage." [12]

The line that, in Lasker's opinion, epitomized the contribution of J. Walter Thompson Company to advertising was "The Skin You Love to Touch." Copy appropriate to such a headline was not difficult to drama-

39

tize and held its own in competition with hundreds of other advertisements appearing simultaneously in the various printed media.

Herald of a new mass culture. The advertising men developed a full-scale methodology for manipulation of the consumers, starting from the premise that advertising must compete with the sex, love, and excitement content of the mass media in order to win readership. This methodology still permits the presentation of facts, as John Powers would have found them, but only after a dramatic scene during which the reader's attention has been firmly secured by an emotional appeal. This kind of advertising enters the personality of the reader and plausibly suggests that she can buy new beauty for ten cents a cake. In such an intimate and subjective concern, who is to argue with her and deny her hope? By attaching itself, piggyback, to the main sensory syndromes of the human being, advertising gets through the logical pickets of reason to the innermost part of the personality where it enters into the persuasion process. "The body of a sale comprises both flesh and bone, the flesh of an emotional response and the hard bone of fact to support it," Mr. Schwab explains. This kind of advertising was used most often by products in highly competitive fields where there was little or no price competition and where almost any of the products was a true economic substitute for any other. Advertising and salesmanship had to take on the burdens that competitive differences in price and quality had once assumed. It was from this merchandising situation that a copywriter, knowing that virtually all brewers cleansed their empty bottles with live steam, conceived an advertising theme which ascribed this hygienic precaution by implication exclusively to Schlitz and in which Lucky Strike's famed slogan, "It's Toasted," equally appropriate for many large cigarette manufacturers, helped achieve temporary national leadership in sales.

Appeals to the man in the mass. James Davis Woolf, one of many former vice presidents of the Thompson company, explains the methods and thought processes of men who, like himself, set out to dramatize advertising and to put its appeal on the emotional level of the mass media and their great audience. The methods were derived in part from evidence produced by social scientists and widely discussed in press and pulpit. They involved pressing home in the copy themes conceived in terms of basic changes taking place in the culture. These changes are now visible to everyone, but the advertising man discovered them and correctly appraised their utility. In sensing and riding the wave of social transition he

40

sided with the revolutionaries rather than the standpatters and found himself blamed for contributing to changes in the old order which he may have helped along but did not initiate.

Old Values in Decay. The mass market, and the mass advertising audience that goes with it, arose during a period of two great wars that greatly increased the mobility of the people and placed in the hands of the labor force, whether blue or white collar, billions of dollars in new money available for consumer goods, automobiles, and household appliances. Advertising men sought out this human market in terms of its own values, needs, and aspirations, and addressed it with words from its own vocabulary. Nineteenth-century middle-class values such as personal integrity, self-reliance, self-discipline, thrift, and simplicity came tumbling down, Schwab recounts. Society apparently regards it as more important for a man to be successful than to maintain a nineteenth-century integrity, and if a man is successful the second question is not always asked. Children were taught to adjust themselves to the new conditions, to ingratiate themselves with others without accepting responsibility or raising the question of moral principle. Salestalk in which pitchmen alone were once skilled invaded the home, and every man with something to sell faced a competitive climate in which, short of bringing down the law, success rather than integrity was the criterion. The mothers who followed the lead given by pediatrics and psychology indulged their children lest their competitive spirits be lamed by inhibitions and unnecessary self-restraint. Woolf says the solitary fisherman, as an icon in the culture, gave way to the gregariousness of the group and the mob at the beach; there was everywhere a dizzy demand for the novel, the new, the sensational as a reaction against the commonplace, the tried, and the true.[13] Young women first, in their dress and cosmetics, and automobiles next, led the way in the revolt against simplicity in design. In the 1950's the chromium-toothed snout, pushed through the crowd by overwhelming power, became the ego cage of the unhorsed American.

The startling success of Barnum and the patent-medicine men had already revealed the basic mass design of simple human nature. Advertising men like Lasker and Thompson tested marketing ideas by trial and error with the millions at their disposal as well as systematically with opinion and attitude research. Both methods quickly developed successful guides to procedure well within the tolerance limits of error allowable in the fast-moving advertising business.

41

New Views of Human Nature. And what is this human nature?

As a conditioned animal living in the company of others, man is insecure and carries constantly a burden of psychic anxiety. Is he secure in his job? Do his associates like him, and will they support him or talk about him behind his back? Will he be able to make the grade in his place of business at promotion time? What do women think of him? Why is he so ill at ease? Is that uneasy feeling under his left ribcage stomach gas or is it a symptom of real illness? Will he be able to make ends meet this month? If not, where can he borrow? Does the family insist upon a vacation this year just to keep up appearances? Are the children normal? Are they doing well at school?

Or perhaps the clarity of mind implied by the clear statement of these perceptions is misleading. Do not the factory girls of our cities live from day to day in a dream? Could there be any lot more cruel than that of woman, required by the mores to be modest and flirtatious at the same moment, demure but provocative, intelligent and discriminating yet compliant, waiting, always waiting for the male to take the initiative in overtures of friendship and love? In such a daily whirl of contradictions, how could anyone avoid escape into dreams?

And when in the evening the door closes and solitude sets in, then what? Is not the modern American wholly without personal resources for constructive individual or small-group use of leisure? Must he not contribute himself, for better or worse, unquestioningly to a group and accept its trend, its movement, its direction, as his own?

And what of the level of individual comprehension of the problems of this group? Library-card holders are a splinter group; the preferred fare of the readers is comics and magazines and books dealing with love and adventure as seen in the leading western shows on television. The feelings to which they react are on the sensory level of the self. In the language of Woolf, the advertising veteran, and in the milieu of the *Reader's Digest*, they "like their literary corn shelled and predigested. . . . Do not ask them to think too hard." [14]

Explaining the advertising appeal made famous by the J. Walter Thompson Company, Woolf says that in communicating with the mass public just described advertisers can provide a crutch for fears. At the same time, the suggestion that arouses the fear must be gentle enough not to trigger reactions of frustration and anger. Gerard Lambert was among the most famous of the advertising men to use this approach, selling a mild antiseptic, Listerine, for halitosis, colds, sore throat, and dandruff. The underarm deodorants for the most part take the same approach, raising fears which can be silenced by promises of security. Closely akin to the fear approach is advertising that substitutes a feeling of friendship and approval for vague uneasiness. Man believes what he wants to believe, says Woolf, and there is security in the use of products in which men have placed their faith. Rinso, reaching for that friendly feeling, taught American housewives to escape the drudgery of centuries by singing a happy washday song.

These examples explain why advertising has become Barnum's successor as ringmaster of the greatest show on earth. It is competing for readers, listeners, and viewers in the mass media, and in these move all events both great and small that make up the glamorous pageant of mankind. Faint heart never won fair reader. Advertising often is too nice, Woolf assures us, and "good taste is what sells goods to the mass public."

✟ CONSERVATIVE REACTION: ANGER AND PAIN

Meanwhile, the great body of advertisers has lagged behind the pace set by the many impresarios in the advertising show, and leaders of the conservative group have raised on several occasions mighty cries of anguish at the methods used to compete with them. When Lucky Strike hurt the makers of sweets by suggesting that its cigarettes would better serve the high-fashion feminine figure than candy, the injured businessmen were not passive. When copywriters out of the same school told the mass public that all cigars — except a brand they were selling — were contaminated by the spittle of the workmen who made them, property rights as well as public rights were involved in the reaction. When obviously insincere testimonials boom the sales of amoral advertisers, are competitors to be hounded into the same silly antics, or is law to provide a better, more sensible defense against unfair competitors?

The struggle against loss of business to the impresarios and ringmasters who practiced the most successful forms of dramatic persuasion proceeded on two fronts: attempts to establish private professional standards and to strengthen federal and state laws so that sanctions could be applied under laws of fair competition.

On both fronts, the effort was motivated by the general outcry against amorality and corruption in business and politics stemming from the crusades of the muckrakers in journalism and their fellow travelers, the re-

43

formers in politics. The movement had considerable depth and duration and is noted in political history for its association with Theodore and Franklin Roosevelt. It had great impact within business, where it was manifested extensively in legislation and in efforts to formulate professional creeds and codes of business conduct, as well as in other parts of society. S. S. McClure, in the magazine that bore his name, Cyrus Curtis, in the *Ladies Home Journal,* and editors of newspapers like the New York *Times,* the St. Louis *Post-Dispatch* and the Scripps-McRae group, printed extensive information critical of patent medicine advertising. A federal food and drug act was passed in 1906, but the courts held that Congress had not intended this act to give powers adequate to the cleanup task.

Curtis used the influence of the *Ladies Home Journal* and *Saturday Evening Post* in another way, to stabilize the advertising agency business and to reduce the pressure on the media for rate concessions the agency could keep for itself or pass along to the client. He offered agents a ten per cent commission in 1901 on business placed in his magazines and an additional five per cent discount for prompt payment. Less than two decades later he and other publishers increased the commission to fifteen per cent and allowed a cash discount of two per cent. The advertising agencies and the media, together with their respective trade associations, incorporated fifteen and two per cent discounts in contracts and in the rules for credit recognition of agencies. The American Association of Advertising Agencies wrote into its membership standards a pledge against rebating any of the earned discount to clients, and over the years this rule lent further reliability and professional spirit to the agencies.

However, the anti-trust division of the Department of Justice broke up all these agreements by a series of consent decrees in 1956. The basis of the action was that the agreements to maintain uniform rates and discounts for customers of the same class tended to restrain trade. The effect of the decrees was to increase the pressure of the clients on the agencies for additional services and for rebates from commissions, thus weakening the professional attitudes built up since 1919 when Curtis first gave them an opportunity to install a system of self-respect in their business.

The advertising practice codes. It remained for the crusading zeal of F. J. Schlink and Arthur Kallet, aided on one occasion by the scholarship of Stuart Chase, to revive public agitation for the protection of consumers beginning in 1927; as noted, this drive culminated in the Wheeler-Lea act of 1938.

44

Journalism as Big Business

The Advertising Federation of America and its predecessor organizations drew up a code for members in 1911. *Printer's Ink* magazine, whose editors appeared prevailingly to be motivated by strong moral principle, criticized charlatans in advertising and began successful national agitation in the same year for state-by-state adoption of a model advertising law under which offenders in obvious cases of fraud could be prosecuted.

Inside the advertising business reform was pushed as a means of preventing unfair competition, and the suggested performance codes had the same general purpose. In the wake of Schlink and Chase, and ahead of a major reform effort begun in the Congress in 1933 by the Roosevelt administration, a copy code was adopted in 1932 by the Association of National Advertisers, the American Association of Advertising Agencies, and the Advertising Federation of America. This code denounced unfair advertising practices in seven categories as follows: (1) False statements or misleading exaggerations. (2) Indirect misrepresentation of a product, or service, through distortion of details, either editorially or pictorially. (3) Statements or suggestions offensive to public decency. (4) Statements which tend to undermine an industry by attributing to its products, generally, faults and weaknesses true only of a few. (5) Price claims that are misleading. (6) Pseudo-scientific advertising, including claims insufficiently supported by accepted authority, or that distort the true meaning or application of a statement made by professional or scientific authority. (7) Testimonials which do not reflect the real choice of a competent witness.

This copy code was the culmination of several persistent efforts within the advertising business through the years to express ethical principles and obtain sponsorship of a code of practice incorporating such principles by leading professional organizations. Though widely publicized in the trade press, these activities did not often come to public attention. They lacked the spectacular news interest and appeal of the activities of the amoralists and were also couched in the business context of fair competition as often as in the more popular terms of consumer interest. As was the case with nearly all the efforts at code-making, the industry decision on this occasion placed the care and development of the code in the hands of an enforcement committee. No professional powers or legal sanctions were provided, however, and the committee found itself helpless to agree on criticism of borderline cases of unfair competition such as the Listerine and Lucky Strike advertising. The enforcement committee soon lapsed, but the code remained and its principles were applied within the limits of the activities

45

of the local and national units of the Better Business Bureaus. These were concerned mainly with warnings to the trade and to the public and, in occasional exaggerated cases, requests for prosecution.

The general ethics of the business community frustrated in this way were stated by Clarence Francis, while chairman of the board of the General Foods Corporation, in an appearance at a Harvard University seminar.[15] He said that improvement of ethical practice in business waits upon an agreement by business leaders who have the will and the competence to define and meet their enlarged responsibilities and that public reaction to business operations made it apparent that the profit motive alone was not enough to justify freedom of business operation.

In the United States, he went on, after a period of expansion in which the interest of the stockholders was neglected, business was required to mend its self-control structure. Then consumers called for and got an acknowledged voice in the operation of industry. Employees next asserted their claim through unionization which was recognized by law. Finally, "during two great wars we found that government can exert a claim on industry's energies that transcends all other claims." At bottom, Francis said, there must be a will to make business work in the public interest, and this must be preceded by an agreement on motives.

A creed for business leadership. What are our motives? "We work for our families, to educate our children, to acquire comforts, leisure and security." But most of all, "I believe we are working for freedom. . . . I believe we are making a system work because without it neither we nor the others can be free. I believe we are proving every day of the world that the American way of operating industry is the best way."

In the hope that a way could be found in which young businessmen could be dedicated to management's responsibilities, Francis suggested a pledge modeled after the Hippocratic oath for that purpose. With responses omitted, the pledge is as follows:

I believe that a business must be run at an adequate profit and must hold its own in fair competition with other businesses.

I believe that business must serve employees, stockholders, consumers, and government and that management must keep the interests of all these elements in balance.

I believe that management's operating goals are continuously improved productivity and growth, in order to provide jobs, reward investors, attract capital, and provide more and better goods and services at lower costs.

I believe further that the greatest assets of a business are its human assets and that improvement of their value is both a matter of material advantage and moral obligation. I believe, therefore, that employees must be treated as honorable individuals, justly rewarded, encouraged in their progress, fully informed, and properly assigned, and that their lives and work must be given meaning and dignity on and off the job.

I believe that a reputation for integrity is another priceless asset of any business and that management must deal fairly with customers, competitors, and vendors, advertise truthfully, fulfill its commitments, cooperate with other managements in betterment of business as a whole, and oppose any artificial restriction that may limit production, fix prices, or restrain trade.

I believe that the future of the American economic system depends on the confidence, good will, and understanding of the people and that business leadership must make itself a responsible part of the human community by participating in worthy activities locally and nationally.

I believe that whenever business has earned a hearing, it has not only a right but a duty to ask for public confidence and that it must speak freely, give information gladly, and answer the attacks of those who seek to undermine American freedom under democratic capitalism.

I believe, finally, that business leadership is nothing less than a public trust, that it must offer a message of courage and hope to all people, and that it can help an economically strong America to lead other nations to lasting prosperity, freedom and peace.

I will work not only for the advancement of myself, my family, and my country, but for liberty and democracy for America and for the world — now and in the years to come.

"This is not a perfect code, I know," Francis said. "Perhaps no one of us is humanly capable of living up to all these principles. Yet I shall always believe that it is far better to fall short of a high standard than to accept and live by a low one. Moreover, I don't think the public demands or expects perfection of us. People simply want to know that leadership is conscious of, and trying to meet, responsibility."

Preconditions for the effectiveness of a code. Francis urged that businessmen reject cynicism in all its forms. It is in the realm of moral principle, he said, that their real responsibility will be discharged. "The test of leadership is its capacity to lead. We know the principles to be sound. We need the faith and the will to make them work."

Francis introduced his statement of ethics by stipulating the conditions under which it could have significance: the participants in the system must have the will to define and to meet responsibilities. Without the element of will ethical statements serve to confuse the community as well as to

47

guide it; in the absence of will the often-made charge that pious statements of principle can be used hypocritically to mask selfish motive and action is pertinent and applicable.

The Better Business Bureaus. The National Better Business Bureau had been formed and branches established in major cities by the vigilance committee of the Associated Advertising Clubs, the forerunner of the Advertising Federation of America, in an effort beginning in 1912. The bureaus — occupied particularly with investigating fraudulent advertising and selling schemes and maintaining a national warning service to keep media and associations alert — are financed by the advertising associations and local business organizations. They can give advance notice of itinerant teams of salesmen who violate laws or mislead the public, and can call attention to doubtful advertising claims. The help of the Post Office Department, the Federal Trade Commission, and state officials is sought in punishing and preventing fraudulent activities, but legal enforcement naturally comes too late to prevent some abuse of the public's confidence in advertising.

Federal Trade Commission regulations. The Better Business Bureaus also investigate advertising claims of legitimate sales organizations that appear unfair to competitors, but remedial steps are confined, after the fact, to negotiation and publicity. Federal Trade Commission actions since 1938 have done much of the work the bureaus could not accomplish by negotiation. The FTC orders also tend to build up case law that can serve as a guide to all advertisers.

The Better Business Bureaus and the advertising associations have looked to the media to provide a substantial share of the effort at enforcement of standards for advertising copy and sales practices. The state laws based on the *Printer's Ink* model statute settled on the media a substantial part of the responsibility for policing unfair advertising claims. In one of the periods of futility, between a crippling court decision in 1932 and the Wheeler-Lea act of 1938, the FTC also called on the media to exercise a militant police function. This insistence from advertisers and government so alarmed media owners that they asked for and received specific exemption from liability for advertising claims when the Wheeler-Lea act was drafted, seeking to put the responsibility on the sellers and advertisers.

The owners of the printed media actually had few if any facilities for testing merchandise to detect misleading claims. They felt they had lost national advertising, in particular, to radio stations because important magazines and newspapers enforced copy requirements that interfered with national distribution of the sales appeals of some of the leading amoralist advertisers. Besides, they had fair warning from the futility of enforcement efforts inside the advertising business that no real help would be forthcoming from that source. The license to exaggerate claimed since time immemorial by those with something to sell made particularly difficult the construction and application of any tests for fact or truth in advertising copy. Advertising, as a rule, arrived in publication offices only a few hours before the time scheduled for its appearance, and since the planned use of advertising in the printed media usually was integrated with similar schedules for outdoor, poster, and direct-mail advertising, the media did not have in their hands all of the elements needed for control. Radio and television station owners had no opportunity to audition network advertising and no remedy except outright rejection of recorded salestalk received for scheduled local broadcast. What made the situation even worse for the media, the request by government and the advertising associations for more vigorous enforcement seemed to be an appeal to challenge and defy some of the largest advertisers in the country in an arena from which all others had fled.[16]

The consumer movement and other critics. With the advertisers, the advertising associations, the media, and the government before 1938 unable to regulate the substantial quantity of misleading advertising, the consumers supported a movement of their own sparked by Schlink, Chase, Kallet, women's clubs, and groups like the American Home Economics Association whose programs stressed consumer interests. Schlink founded the Consumers Research organization with the idea of filling the need of the consumer for information upon which to base judgment in buying. Advertisers and most marketers up to that time provided no information upon which a rational choice could be made between competing products, and Schlink sought to provide testing services and to distribute his findings to members. Leaders in the consumer movement taught their followers, without significant contradiction, that price competition was discouraged by the big producers and marketers in the country. It was also said that advertising conveyed an illusion of consistency in quality of branded products which enabled the sellers to vary quality to compensate for any changes in price due to competition.[17] The consumer groups got aid in this argument from an unexpected source, the chain grocers such as A & P and Kroger, who introduced grade-labeling of their private-brand canned foods and advertised them in local newspapers until World War II at com-

49

The Social Responsibility of the Press

petitive prices. This action helped explain the grade-labeling controversy to the public and put claims of the national advertisers of ungraded foods into perspective.

Advertisers came to fear government regulation as a result of the success of the consumers' organizations and they reacted by subjecting the product test reports of Consumers Research and Consumers Union to analysis, finding sufficient error to serve as a basis for counterattack. They also moved to discredit authors and teachers whose fiction and textbooks attributed to advertising an uneconomic if not baleful influence in society. Pease says the authors criticized included Walter Lippmann, Thorstein Veblen, Sinclair Lewis, Sumner Slichter, Robert S. Lynd, and Gilbert Seldes, and while the textbook writers were less well known, they were considered even more damaging to advertising because their criticism reached young people just forming social attitudes. Harold S. Rugg of Teachers College, Columbia University, was one of the teachers whose economic and social studies textbooks came especially under the fire of the Advertising Federation of America and its special textbook department. The same machinery that had been assembled to identify and intercept the crooked advertiser and salesman was now turned locally and nationally to the task of preventing the use in secondary schools of textbooks that the committee had found, upon unilateral examination, to be unfair to advertising.

Pease says the critics of advertising at this time were men in professional careers not closely wedded to business: writers, journalists, teachers, economists, technicians, engineers, scientists, and salaried officials of the government. In the main, they professed orthodox visions of the good society, but were zealous in presenting their views in writing and speaking. Some of them recommended specific controls on advertising, and all of them favored extensive education of consumers in the techniques of advertising and merchandising and in the selection of goods. They charged that what the advertisers called enthusiasm and salestalk was really misrepresentation and added that most advertising was economically wasteful because consumers had to pay for it and, in addition, were often misled into purchasing an advertised brand when another was a better value.

Does advertising create demand? When advertisers replied that their activity created greater sales volume and made possible lower unit costs through mass production, the critics usually agreed that, theoretically, lowered prices could result, but that the facts did not fall into this pattern.

50

Instead, they said, unadvertised products of equal or higher quality were the ones lowest in price.

Pease explains that the critics — following John E. Powers, perhaps — often assumed that producers should first determine what the consumer wanted and then use advertising to state plainly what the product was, when and where it could be purchased, and how much it would cost. But for their part advertisers wanted to change the preference of consumers and to persuade them by any device short of overt misrepresentation. Until recently, when behavioral science was applied to merchandising — and even now — advertisers have only one dependable way to determine what the customer likes, and that is to put the product on the market and advertise it for sale. As the followers of Albert Lasker would say, the assumption that consumers will make rational choices does not lead to business success.

The battle between the advertisers and their critics was called off by the outbreak of World War II and the attendant rationing and price control of food, clothing, and toilet articles. Since the war, the strengthened Federal Trade Commission, using more of its Wheeler-Lea authority, has restrained some of the worst misrepresentations of merchandising. But when, at the outbreak of war, the fight between the amoral advertisers and their critics died down, the advertising business as a whole was holding its ground, asserting that its service had economic and social value, particularly as the creator of the mass market, and that such weaknesses as appeared merely reflected the state of the business world. To the assertions that advertising was using its great mass-communication expenditures to misshape American ideals and mores, the advertisers replied that though they used the configurations of human nature in sales strategy, they did not create man. Pease said in summarizing the advertisers' view,

In all cases, the criterion for acceptable advertising should be nothing less than the limits of public tolerance. . . . Advertising deserved to remain free from all external coercion or controls. Advertising was always signed and was the most honest form of persuasion. . . . No other business had gone so far to protect the public. . . . The best check on a fraudulent claim was the claim of a competing firm and the best check on any advertising was the common sense skepticism of the average reader.[18]

51

' III

THE NATURAL HABITAT OF THE PRESS

W E MAY safely assume that the business institutions in a community are important constituents of the culture, that the association of the owners and managers on the basis of common interests separates them from others in the community sufficiently that they become members of a subculture, and that their performance cannot be explained except by the logic arising within their own frame of reference. Accordingly, we must look at them in the context of the activities in which they are caught up.

The newspaper is the archetypal institution engaged in gathering and interpreting the news for mass distribution and for that reason we are justified in giving primary attention to it. It differs from radio and television, as is explained elsewhere, in that the newspaper workers have better control of content than their counterparts in the newer media. All three media are in the business of mass communication, but the newspaper gives great weight to the informational function; the electronic media, while undergoing significant development in the field of public affairs, mainly emphasize entertainment.

The basic goal professed by newspaper owners is to operate at a profit with honor. They have many other related goals and values, and these are dealt with herein, but profitable operation — or lack of it — governs the degree and the kind of attention the newspapers can give to any other consideration. The problem of making ends meet can be explained, for newspapers of all sizes, and without oversimplification, by a description of the simplest of them, the weekly and small daily. The example chosen combines the case histories of more than one newspaper so that stages of growth, which are a function of time and economic expansion, can be presented simply. The student of the newspaper business soon learns that the pattern of operation is closely similar regardless of size; a small firm may struggle to pay for a thirty-five-thousand-dollar press, but its problem is the same as that of a larger concern making a two-million-dollar addition to its pressroom — to get the volume needed to pay all expenses, and to spread it through the day and the week so that the work force can be utilized efficiently.

The 1961 financial statement of the New York *Times* stated the problem in this way:

In the years 1953 through 1958 the *Times* was successful in stabilizing but not in reducing unit costs. In 1959 and 1960, these costs increased as a result of the strains imposed by shifting part of the operation to the new plant and the sharp increases in volume which temporarily dislocated scheduling and created costly bottlenecks. In 1961 improvement in productivity was achieved and continuing progress is being made in 1962.

Paraphrased for emphasis, this paragraph says that in producing a newspaper of premier quality, the *Times* has incurred costs that seem fantastic to publishers of newspapers less interested in excellence and more determined to make large profits; until 1961, there seemed to be no way of cutting costs, but productivity agreements with unions and the installation of new machines now give some hope. Differences in size of firm and volume of output mask the essential kinship of all of the firms in the industry.

Here, with a view to explaining general principles, we shall give attention to a newspaper office where, in the first stage, the proprietor is the principal workman. His basic tools are a cylinder press imprinting four newspaper-size pages at a time, a linecasting machine for putting into type reading matter and parts of advertisements, handset types in a variety of sizes for headlines, advertising, and job printing. In addition, the owner has a machine that will fold the printed newspaper from its size of four pages to a sheet down to the one-page size seen by the reader, a simple foundry for melting typemetal so that it can be poured into matrices to make printing plates of photographs and line drawings for advertising and news, and a variety of small presses and other job printing equipment.

In capital invested, the business is small, no more than $10,000 perhaps; half of that is borrowed. The machinery is auxiliary to the proprietor's skill. What he sells in a firm of this size is mainly his own labor.

When he must hire help he seeks workers whose fairly low skill he can upgrade, through his supervisory and teaching ability, with simple machines. Otherwise he could not sell his product at competitive prices. In a business of this size the newspaper is produced in less than three working days. The equipment would be idle the rest of the week except for job printing, and additional business has to be brought in by active solicitation in the community.

News as a commodity. Newspaper readers would not alone absorb all of the overhead charges of a firm in which no other printing was done. Run-of-the-mine news just does not have that much appeal in the market. When a time of community crisis arrives, the people want to know all the news; they will pay for it and ask for more. When the news is critical and controversial, they may even seek other sources of information so as to compare one account against another. The physical plant necessary to provide communication adequate to a crisis will gather cobwebs during times of public apathy unless the proprietor has something to sell in addition to the current of news. In order to see himself through periods of apathy, he has learned to offer his paper on an annual subscription basis, for in this way the few periods of crisis-born interest can be made to justify a long-term purchase. But the principal way in which he carries the costs through periods of public indifference is in the sale of advertising and job printing.

If the proprietor of this business is asked to identify himself and describe his calling he will say that he is an editor-publisher. If asked what he does, his answer will reveal that he is a printer. He is skilled in the trade and the ability to supervise others is based on or derived from his printing knowledge. His assistants take their pace of work from him and his standards are theirs.

Struggle for economy of scale. In order to get at his problems and motives, let us begin our observation of the proprietor at a moment when he is making a meager living from his business and would like to do better. He must turn over a larger volume of work, that is, expand his business in scope. He needs more help and must either hire a man for the work he himself likes least, or, if that seems impractical because of the cost, to relieve himself of low-skill work for which he can obtain a substitute at a cost that will not come out of his own return on his labor. This may mean that he will bring in his wife for part of each day to keep books and collect bills from customers and hire a boy or girl just out of high school to write local news. This arrangement will give him more time to sell advertising and job printing. Soon he is running an average of ten pages a week and, if he had more help, could easily run twelve. A ten-page paper is awkward to handle and he would prefer to run twelve, for a paper of this size could be produced in sections of four pages in about the same time as the ten-page edition. The proprietor decides to employ an additional man in the shop who will divide his time between job printing and newspaper printing. He does not earn enough on the present volume of business to pay the wages of the new man, but he is willing to risk getting the money through extra sales effort once he can manage free time for that purpose. However, when the extra man is employed the proprietor cannot find time himself during the business day to bring in sufficient business volume to use the full labor and machine capacity he has for sale. He is paying for labor not sold.

Cut Back or Expand Again? His dilemma now is whether to lay off his extra man and cut back to his former scale of output, or to hire an advertising salesman who will bring in the new volume needed. He finds no satisfaction in the possibility of returning to the first operations base, for he was not making an adequate living. The only way out seems to be to expand again. The facts he needs for judging the probable effects of the move are plain: He can pay up to $75 a week for an advertising man if the man, in turn, can sell an average of 336 extra inches of advertising and extra job printing valued at $50 or more each week. On such an enlarged scale of activity the proprietor could make money for himself. So, he employs the advertising man and sets his sights on a sixteen-page newspaper each week.

In operating on the new basis, he finds that he is more and more confined to the shop in the production of the paper and that the employees on the street are carrying the main responsibility for representing the firm in dealings with the public. He does not enjoy the hard grind and long hours on the floor as a journeyman printer. He now carries a considerably increased administrative burden which is incompatible with his production obligations. He feels that he must have another printer so as to be free for the supervisory duties and to make calls on customers himself. The additional volume of work has created a variety of new individual tasks. Not only must the type be set, but proof must be pulled and read, taken to advertisers, and brought back to be corrected in the shop. More bookkeeping entries are needed, bank deposits must be made up more frequently, and at month's end there are more bills to mail or to take personally to customers. The owner's wife can absorb some of the extra work, but she insists on being at home to care for the children when school is out.

Great contrasts are observed in the skill required to set type and to pull proofs, and mark proof for correction, on the one hand, and simply to carry it to the customers for approval, on the other; it seems common sense to bring in not only an extra printer but low-cost help for the unskilled tasks. So a printer is employed and a boy is added for routine tasks.

Higher Volume, Sharper Pace. The business now has a new pace and new level of overhead. The point at which the business broke even when only the proprietor was employed resulted from the sum of the money he expended for his basic personal needs — these were somewhat flexible — and the amount required to amortize his investment in machinery and equipment, to pay rent on the building, to buy necessary supplies, and to pay for power, light, and water. But now, as a result of additions to payroll, the proprietor finds himself with a serious new problem, one which comes to a crisis each week: he must have enough cash on hand to meet his payroll and, at the end of the month, to pay his bills. If he can meet his quotas of advertising and job printing, he can meet expenses and include a salary for himself and his wife, and it also appears — though this will have to be determined later — that his direct operating expenses will use up about fifty cents out of each dollar he takes in. Out of the margin he must meet indirect costs, make the payments on his loans, set up modest depreciation reserves against the day when he will need new machinery, and pay his taxes. After all these charges are met, he can determine if he has made a profit.

In his original situation his motive was to make a living for himself and this he could do with little risk and only the effort normally expended in a 48-to-56-hour week. The basic nature of his problem changed when he took on his first employee, for from that time on the business had to operate at a volume adequate to take care of both of them. In time of difficulty he could release his employee and do the work alone, but by now this step is unthinkable. He has grown accustomed to the new division of labor and pace of operation; the product he puts on the market is much more attractive than formerly. Neither he nor the readers would want to go back to the former situation. Instead, he must go forward, build up volume and hire more men as needed for the work. Already it is clear in the proprietor's mind that the next addition to the staff must be a competent news and editorial writer.

The benchmarks available to him in planning ahead are based on fragments of data and he regards them as unreliable, but they promise reward for expansion keyed to correct estimates of community demand for his products. In a recent year the small establishment with a circulation under a thousand copies paid its owner $5,885 in salary and dividends, and the next five hundred added circulation and was worth $2,000 more in net income. Proprietors with papers up to two thousand circulation made nearly $9,000 a year and those with three thousand circulation kept as much as $15,000.[1] There were comparable rewards for establishments of larger size, $52,000 for fifteen thousand daily circulation, $400,000 for fifty thousand daily, $700,000 for morning, evening, and Sunday operations of about a hundred thousand circulation.

Working together, he and the advertising salesman have built up eighty to a hundred active customers. The biggest of them, a small departmentalized store, accounts for 12 per cent of the total income from advertising and a substantial additional amount in job printing — stationery, advertising circulars, business forms. His ten best customers provide 42 per cent of his advertising income and 71 per cent comes from the top quarter of his advertising clients. He derives some income from subscribers and substantial receipts come in from job printing, but he cannot help but be aware that a few customers furnish the bulk of his income and he strives to give them good service and to develop a lasting and friendly relation.[2]

⚊ DAILY NEWSPAPER OPERATION

The publisher of a daily, large or small, faces similar problems, though they appear more acute because of the size of the sums of money involved. A heavy increase in capital is required when the small daily changes from a flat-bed web press to a rotary press requiring plate-making equipment. Though the differences in capital investment may not appear to the layman large on their face, they can be understood in terms of the average household budget by assuming that each $1,000 of a four-year installment debt for equipment will cost at least $25 a month. A $25,000 second-hand press with stereotype and plate-making equipment would thus represent an increase of $625 a month in cash payments if financed on this time period. This sum of money, which is an extra cost not borne by the firm previously, must be secured by a complex series of activities: personal visits to advertisers to increase the space used by regular customers, and calls on a number of prospective new customers. The salesman at each point must make a specific request for business and run the risk of a turndown; in fact, many more turndowns than acceptances are met. When an order is received the advertisement must be painstakingly set in type and then printed and distributed. Out of each dollar in receipts at least eighty cents will be used to pay manufacturing and distribution costs of the newspaper. Out of the remaining twenty cents must come taxes and also the profits that will enable him to make the payments on the new physical equipment.

Publisher against critics. Since these facts are here exhibited to show how they impinge on the performance of the editor-publisher, it is within context to say that the difference in the orientation of the publisher and his non-journalistic critics is greatest at this point, for it is here, particularly, that the task of the critic is to manipulate words while the publisher must manipulate people — customers and employees — to get the desired result. The critics have developed the concept of social responsibility to help put pressure on the private entrepreneur at the moment when he is evaluating their proposals for reform. As the publisher would certainly point out, the critic would expect him to finance, at his own risk, the recommended controversial public policy information campaigns and extensive additions of content in support of cultural objectives. This is a particularly sensitive point when the critic, though motivated by the highest ideals, asks the publisher to assume a reformer's role which would put him in conflict with important parts of the community. The publisher, assuming he is sympathetic to the goals of his critic, must weigh the probable amount of work involved inside the firm in achieving the goal against the probable benefits to be obtained in the event of success. He and his employees are selling a service, advertising, the benefits of which are sufficiently intangible that it is difficult to see a clear cause-and-effect relation between advertising and the business that comes in. The advertiser, when he confronts the salesman from the medium, always must balance negative against positive factors in his impelling need for publicity with which to inform his customers of what he must sell. This long-term need for publicity is not likely to change, but the merchant's decision as to what to buy on a particular occasion when the newspaper salesman calls is influenced by mood. It is of considerable importance to the daily success of the association between the salesman and the advertiser to avoid new tensions or disturbances, in addition to those normally present, in evaluating the probable effectiveness of advertising. The long-standing effort inside the newspaper office to insulate the advertising and news departments from each other comes from the willingness of the advertising salesman to look for scapegoats when unforeseen and unresolved tensions arise in his relation with the client. The utmost skill is required in introducing new elements of tension in such a way as not to affect the relation seriously; but an ameliorating fact is that in interest and attitude merchants have many differences as well as similarities. This helps the media keep the tensions arising in their association with their customers well dispersed and diverse in origin. Though merchants need newspaper advertising, substitute media are available and it does not take much difference of opinion, where advertising cost is high in relation to sales, to bring about retaliatory switches in the choice of media or reductions in normal purchases. McEvoy shows that in the communities he studied 66 to 78 per cent of the merchants did not buy any newspaper advertising.[3] The newspaper always runs a risk of financial reprisal in taking positions of strong leadership; it usually finds the financial benefits of such activity, if any, in the prospect of long-run growth of the community.

The advertiser's frame of mind. At any rate, each separate solicitation of advertisers must be presented in terms of a promised benefit, for the customer must believe that his purchase is directly related to the volume of traffic through his store. Merchants also confront variables of weather and public mood. A rainy day can cut the volume of business to the point where the money spent for advertising appears wasted. A wet and cool period may increase the sale of raincoats but leave on the racks much more profitable clothing that would turn over rapidly in a season of normal weather. A drop in employment on account of a strike or a downturn in the pace of business may greatly increase the normal difficulties of merchants, and of advertising and circulation salesmen. It should be clear from this account that the extra $600 per month needed for the new press must be obtained by confronting merchants every day, in a situation which the merchants control, to ask for business. It may be assumed that the newspaper owner would not buy new equipment unless he had good reason to believe the community would enable him to pay for it, but hard work is required under the best of conditions, and the degree of uncertainty is such that even a small decrease in business can force reductions in payroll or other adjustments.

The Social Responsibility of the Press

The next natural stage in the business growth of the newspaper to which we have been giving attention requires, as noted, a news and editorial employee and sets up a new and higher point of activity at which the business can break even.

The new scale of operations is successful in the case at hand and has its advantages for the firm. The proprietor now becomes completely free of production duties, though he may still help out in a glut of work. He gives more time to administrative work, cost accounting, and the pricing of individual jobs of printing. He is out of the office more with his customers and with members of the business community. He works with committees of the Chamber of Commerce and service clubs, is a member of the school board. He begins to feel responsible not only for the success of his own business but for the showing his town makes in competition with others in the area. He wants the prosperity of his firm to be based on a healthy, expanding community.

Eventually in his increased levels of operation the publisher comes for the first time into contact with government regulation of his business. Aside from taxes, his first such experience is when the Wage and Hour office of the Department of Labor requires him to keep records of the hours of his employees and of the rate of their pay. He must now, under the law, pay time and a half for all work over forty hours a week; the minimum wage law also applies to the schoolboys who put in twelve hours a week mailing papers and doing janitorial work at the plant after school. This first experience with regulation, about which he has read so much, is not particularly expensive, but it is annoying to see outside authority available to referee disputes with employees over rates of pay and to find that the government is apparently committed to giving employees the benefit of the doubt while assuming guilt on the part of the employer, at least to the point of conducting an investigation.

The second experience with an outside economic power comes when the typographical union begins to organize his printers. Soon the printers ask him for a contract which would bring into the shop the working rules of the union and a scale of pay as high as that received by men in the nearest city locals. The proprietor looks at the faces of the men with whom he has worked but finds no sign of the spirit of comradeship he thought they knew. They appear friendly, but they want higher wages, clearer definition of the work that they can be assigned to do, and apparently they

60

welcome a chance to pay dues to the union in return for its promise to back them in disputes. Finally, a new scale is worked out which adds only 20 per cent, rather than the 40 per cent asked, to the total rate of pay. He can see that in the showdown the men have sided with him on a compromise proposal against the union business agent, for they believe him when he says he cannot afford to pay more. But the 20 per cent increase in wages and fringe benefits is not to be related in any way to an increase in output. He gets nothing for his extra trouble and may earn considerably less after he has tried to pass the extra expense along to his customers. The old friendship between him and his employees is changed. From now on he will find them friendly only up to a point — and they will decide where the point is.

Publishers of established daily newspapers went through this psychological experience with printing trades unions many years ago, largely before World War I. Their more recent experience with the American Newspaper Guild resulted, for them, in a real crisis of the spirit. The psychological relations of top management with journalists were different than with printers. The reporters participated with management in planning how to get out a good paper. They provided management with intimate knowledge of the community as well as with ordinary news. Moreover, they were doing work that many of the executives in their younger days had done themselves and this shared experience helped to cement feelings of common interest. Nevertheless, management consulted journalists about policy only when it wanted to. Its decisions represented the views of men in charge of advertising, circulation, and physical production, as well as of news, and were not always acceptable to journalists. The skill of the journalist was one in which all literate men had some competence. The esoteric vocabulary by which medicine and law separated their practitioners from the general public and made control from outside centers more difficult existed only to a limited extent in journalism and quickly yielded its mystery to outsiders who wanted to learn it.

The tools of the journalist were a typewriter and a pencil, far from impressive in comparison with the linotype, casting boxes, and presses used by the printing trades. The advantages the journalist enjoyed over laymen who could read and write were those of the craftsman over the neophyte: he could work rapidly and with reasonable accuracy and dependability; he knew the personalities, values, systems, and history of the organizations about which he wrote. He was self-reliant and versatile.

The Social Responsibility of the Press

Competition for Jobs. But would-be journalists in considerable numbers were always knocking at the door; many liberal arts graduates just out of college wanted to write or to apply their knowledge in a socially useful way; the difference between a story produced by the skill and insight of an able journalist and by a willing neophyte was not readily apparent to the public. It was possible to downgrade a job, so to speak, by hiring a man with less skill and still get out the paper. The public lacked the sophistication to spot the missing professional values and would not care, anyway. Only the elites of sports and business investment depended on the newspapers for primary information and both had roving teams of specialists whose work was distributed by syndicates controlling the supply of information and they also contributed to other publications or services that represented adequate substitutes for the newspaper report.

Journalists as Members of the Firm. The journalists were not always earners in the corporate system of publishing, but they were always spenders. Circulation revenues never paid the cost of production. The heads of news departments could not project a future budget and stay within it; something was always happening, either in Timbuktu or Kalamazoo, that was unexpected and for which no budgetary provision had been made. When journalists traveled on business, they wanted to do so in a hurry and sometimes haste increased the expense. Moreover, they were careless about expense accounts. Now, thanks to labor unions and the New Deal labor laws, they were going on a fixed work week, like the printers, with time and a half for overtime.

⨍ PUBLISHING COSTS INCREASE

When it found its journalists arrayed against it inside the firm as members of a labor union — a union that on election day usually backed the opposition candidate — management not only suffered a crisis of the spirit but went to court with its doubts and fears about being deprived of control of the news. When the courts assured management that it still had complete control of content, but not of labor's right to bargain collectively, it solved its isolation within the firm by paying a few men above scale to fill the policy positions on the news staff and editorial page and went forward as best it could. But the burdens of the extra payroll, as the pay of the journalists and the printing tradesmen gradually was equalized while simultaneously being increased, plus the preference of advertisers for the paper with the largest circulation, was more than the weaker papers could meet. The pace of concentration and consolidation increased, and because their demands were the latest to be expressed, journalists got the blame for some of the suspensions.

⚘ THE LEADERSHIP GROUP

But we must return to our composite publisher. Now that he has his time under better control, he joins a small group of his fellow businessmen meeting for coffee at ten o'clock each morning. Out of these meetings grow plans that are taken to the Chamber of Commerce. A retail division of the chamber is eventually formed, and it undertakes activities inspired by the coffee club. Special-value advertising days are planned by the stores and the newspaper is extensively distributed for the occasion in tributary villages and towns and to farms. A regular pattern of community showmanship and entertainment is developed to give the town an attractive personality.

One of the coffee club's discoveries is that health care is a principal source of dissatisfaction with the town as a place to live and trade. Sums of money quite large relative to available resources are spent annually outside the community for health care. The publisher and his friends inspire the formation of a committee within the Chamber of Commerce to organize a hospital and to find medical specialists who will move to town. It is hoped that they will draw patients and their families from the tributary area as well as provide for local needs.

On one occasion the coffee club invites the president and the secretary of the public school board to talk about school needs and from this conference plans eventually develop for the newspaper to print a series of articles on the public schools and their problems. The club acts upon its assumption that schools are associated in the public mind with progressive community spirit.

The coffee club constitutes a leadership group. The substance of its continuing conversations concerns building business volume. The merchants long since have found that the job is too expensive for two or three firms — that it can be accomplished, if at all, only through wide participation.

The members of the leadership group fall into two general categories, those who started in business as teenagers and, through ability and knowledge of how to save and invest, have become owners, and those who, entering after a period of higher education, have had the financial backing

63

of family or friends. Regardless of education, all of the merchants are in the same trial-and-error situation in identifying and catering to public demand. The basic choices of what to produce are made by designers and manufacturers in large cities; local merchants must select what they can sell locally.

The coffee club includes veterans of chain-store sales organizations who have chosen to set up for themselves, and one member who manages a local chain unit. Chain-merchandising experience principally provided them with a knowledge of how to adapt to the price requirements of the community and a pattern of promotional and merchandising activity within a store which enables a firm to bring itself repeatedly to public attention.

The members of the coffee club talk about the price lines of merchandise that can be sold in town, about the effect of the general improvement of economic status on merchandising strategy, and plan the community promotions which are intended to make the town a lively center of its territory. When the club members talk about advertising and selling they agree that good advertising informs customers about values. "You can't kid people; they won't bite on a phony offer more than once, and in a town like this, why try?"

Price is important in getting customers into the store, but the skillful merchant can usually bring about a switch in attention from price to value when he talks with a customer. Community promotions, the club members agree, are useless unless each major retail store makes itself particularly attractive for the occasion; this seems to lead to the conclusion that display within the store and special-event merchandising are really more important than community events.

The coffee club complains to the publisher that the price of his advertising for the special shopping days is too high, so he solicits subscriptions in the fringe areas to see if costs cannot be cut by putting distribution on a regular subscription basis. In time, he increases coverage in the new areas and then raises the regular price of his advertising space. The coffee club greets the rate increase ruefully, but added distribution is in their long-run interest and they pay the bill.

The conversation upon occasion turns to the "red fronts," stores operated by persons representing capital brought in from outside the community. These stores have a knack of finding substitutes for standard-brand merchandise at competitive prices. Can anything be done about them? After a time, the club agrees that much of the business the red fronts get is from customers brought to town by the appeal of low prices; the members do not like the competition, they do not invite into their circle managers of red-front stores, but they look with general favor at the evidence of increased traffic into the community. The grudging cooperation between the old-line merchants and their red-front competitors gives the community an outward appearance of business harmony.

We can leave this particular proprietor at this point, but we do not mean to imply that he has reached a condition of security. He still has to meet his customers in the market every day and ask for business which they are free to withhold or give. His labor costs are increasing; he must recover them from advertisers and readers, through rate increases or increased volume, or by a mixture of both. It is clear that if he is turned back by customer resistance he will have no choice but to reduce his level of operation until such time as general improvement in the local economy again makes it feasible to try for an increase in volume. His freedom is solely to meet other free individuals in the market and negotiate transactions acceptable to all.

The fact that the proprietor described is the owner of a small newspaper must not mislead the reader: his problems and the events of his daily life are representative of the experiences of the general run of publishers large and small. The chief owner of a large newspaper will have department heads and to them he will delegate the routine of running his business. His lines of presses may dwarf the small shop used here in almost allegorical fashion. But when he can, he, his manager, and the department heads will turn, as did our symbolic small publisher, to a coffee club or to other leadership groups in the community, of which there is a considerable variety. If the business is large and prosperous, the chief officers may meet some of the members of the coffee club during the winter in Phoenix or Las Vegas, the Bahamas, or Puerto Rico. But wherever the club members gather, they are still interested in building the community so as to enhance the security and development of their individual investments. Their shops may employ hundreds, but the task is still to achieve economy of scale and a dignified place in the community. Their trades days may bear festive names, such as the Orange Bowl, the Cotton Bowl, the Rose Bowl, the Fiesta, the Veiled Prophet Parade and ball, or Aquatennial.

Some members of leadership groups respond to the challenge of building the community by dedicated and purposeful study of the community's problems; they are well read and conscious of world problems as well as the state of local trade. A few tend to take upon themselves leadership burdens of the larger community. But most do not.

In the main, the problems of the representative publisher here are the problems of the mass-communications business, large and small. The materials presented were chosen because it was possible in this way to state the principles in terms common to the industry. As will become clear, the social problem of journalism is that a majority of its owners are engaged routinely in business and are too little involved in understanding the cardinal problems of the time. Our next chapter may help explain why that is so.

' IV

THE PROPRIETORSHIP ROLE

W HAT is the economic state of the mass communications industry?

It is widely assumed that newspapers and magazines are declining, and that television's rapid rise has left radio stagnant. What are the facts?

The facts are that growth and readjustment are taking place all around the industry and that the American economy is big enough for all the media. The readjustment is serious and the growth is relative.

Newspapers, despite the fact that there are 837 fewer of them than in 1909, sell sixty million copies daily and their total volume of business is still growing. They have become local monopolies in all but sixty or so cities, and the economic balance counted upon to support political diversity and freedom is gone, but newspapers are still growing.

Magazines — general mass-circulation magazines largely catering to the "play, fun and escape" market — have lost both circulation and advertising volume. Other magazines, particularly business magazines, are prosperous and growing; as an industry, magazines are still a growing, potent and aggressive advertising medium.

Radio has grown in the sense that hundreds of new stations have been established and found new acceptance and revenue in local business communities not previously touched. The old pre-television volume has not returned, but radio and television are the same industry and together they are growing strongly.

Television, the great new mass medium for advertising and entertainment, has created an entirely new force in the world because of its ability

67

to evoke an intimacy in every living room in the land. Under criticism for programing too much trash, it has turned determinedly toward improving its news and public affairs reporting and, in so doing, has demonstrated its very real power to communicate ideas as well as to sell goods with soap operas.

The newspaper business is prevailingly private, not public, and industry-wide analysis of its financial position is not possible. The author has tried on several occasions to get reports from a national sample of papers and has been successful only outside the big cities. The earnings of the big dailies, with few exceptions, are not known; only thirty-eight newspaper companies were listed in standard financial reporting services in 1946 and data about some of these have since become private.

Occasionally, a dispute among the stockholders lifts the counting-room curtain of one of the old and well-established firms, as when a court was asked to establish a market price for A. S. Abell Company (Baltimore *Sun*) stock in 1959. It was learned, on that occasion, that net earnings per share in 1956 were $17.25, or about 26 per cent return on capital. Earnings on sales, before taxes, were about 18.6 per cent. Accountants specializing in newspaper practice say that newspapers need at least 20 per cent profit on sales before taxes in order to pay reasonable dividends.

Earnings of public companies. The public companies owning news-papers, according to the author's compilation from their annual state-ments, earned from 7.25 to 21.59 per cent just before World War II. The smallest figure in the range is that of Hearst Consolidated Publications, which has improved its position in recent years by mergers and discontinu-ances of newspapers. Profit after taxes ranged from 5.67 per cent on sales for Hearst to 17.50 per cent for the Hartford *Times*, a Gannett newspaper. The Boston Herald-Traveler Company earned a net after taxes of 11.28, the Brush-Moore Newspapers 16.39, the Chicago *Daily News* 9.09, and Federated Publications of Michigan and Indiana, 11.41 per cent.

The five newspaper companies listed can be compared with firms in steel, chemicals, tobacco, and retailing. When this is done, the newspapers are found to have the lowest current ratio of assets to current liabilities, 1.3, while five steel companies have the highest, 4.4. The newspaper mar-gin of operating profit, 24.5, is well ahead of the other businesses selected, five chemical concerns being next with 17.0. The figure for times interest earned, which is derived by dividing operating income — that is, total reve-nue less total operating expenses — by interest paid, finds newspapers at

23.4, very much on the same level as chemicals and steel, while retail firms report 42.7.

The price-earnings ratio on common stock finds newspapers and retail stores virtually even at 8.7 and 8.8, whereas chemicals (14.0), steel (10.6) and tobacco (18.0) do better. The percentage return on common stock shows the newspapers leading at 6.5. Chemicals earned 3.7 per cent, steel 5.6 per cent, tobacco 4.6 per cent, and retail stores 5.2 per cent.

After World War II all the firms shared in the generally increased prosperity. The author's National Newspaper Survey showed, for the 1947–49 period, that newspapers under ten thousand circulation earned generally between 13 and 20 per cent on sales, before taxes. Papers in the twelve thousand to twenty-five thousand bracket did better, and only larger papers, those around a hundred thousand and above, remained on the average under 15 per cent. The median profit figure for all groups was 16.8 per cent. The rate of profit has declined somewhat since 1958, but in 1960 and 1961, years in which many newspapers had difficulty holding advertising volume, the papers were reporting profits ranging from 8.6 per cent on gross sales to 16.5 per cent.

In 1961, the newspaper business reported to the United States Census total advertising receipts of $3,630,000,000, which is 175.9 per cent of 1950. In the fifty-two large cities where the newspapers are measured by *Media Records* the lines of advertising printed in 1960 were only 118 per cent of 1950, but the rates were higher and the money volume much larger. For purposes of comparison, the gross national product in 1958 was 122 per cent of 1954, so even with television taking one and three quarter billion dollars in advertising, the newspapers did not perform badly.

Record of the advertising industry. The newspapers had 281,000 employees in 1954, 294,000 in 1958, and only 6,000 of the extra workers were in production jobs, although the consumption of newsprint increased 23 per cent. In terms of value added by manufacturing, output in 1958 was at 117 per cent of 1954, and the Department of Commerce found that circulation of newspapers per family had declined from 1.23 copies to 1.12 copies between 1950 and 1960. The papers lost 6.5 per cent of their share of total advertising expenditures between 1949 and 1961, but in dollars their share increased by $1,725,000,000.

Magazines, in 1960, in spite of hard setbacks among general weeklies and monthlies, reported their business at 186 per cent of the dollar income of 1950.

69

The Social Responsibility of the Press

Television stations and networks in 1953 had revenues of $592,937,000 and the total revenues of the industry were $793,915,000. This figure passed the billion-dollar mark in 1955 when the chains and stations had $1,137,581,000 income. By 1958 this had risen to $1,723,987,000.[1]

When all these figures are added together the mass communication industry total (newspapers, magazines, radio, television, books and bookbinding) is $4,587,000,000. Table 1, showing how advertising is distributed among the media, would indicate that this figure is too low, since advertising totaled nearly $12 billion. However, it is based on gross billing for space and includes auxiliary costs, such as art work and engravings, talent costs, advertising agency commissions, earned rate rebates to advertisers, and so on; moreover, 42.3 per cent of the advertising was placed in other than mass newspapers, magazines, and electronic media.

Newspaper income and expense. William M. Layman, a professional accountant with a large newspaper clientele, gives the figures in Table 2, based on 1961 averages, for a group of morning and evening newspapers between 80,000 and 130,000 circulation.

The Census of Business gives averages in 1954 for all newspapers which may be compared with Mr. Layman's group. These show that newspapers received 28.7 per cent of income in that year from subscriptions and sales, and 70.3 per cent from advertising. An additional 1 per cent of gross income was not distributed to either advertising or subscriptions. Periodicals

Table 1. Advertising in Selected Media as a Percentage of Total Advertising Volume

Year	Total (millions)	News-paper	Maga-zine	Radio	Tele-vision	All Other
1949	5,202.2	36.6%	9.5%	12.2%	1.2%	40.5%
1950	5,691.3	36.3	9.0	11.7	3.3	39.7
1951	6,548.2	34.0	8.6	20.5	7.4	39.5
1952	7,156.2	34.6	8.6	8.7	6.3	41.8
1953	7,809.2	34.1	8.6	7.9	7.8	41.7
1954	8,164.0	33.0	8.2	6.8	9.9	42.0
1955	9,194.0	33.5	6.8	5.8	11.1	42.5
1956	9,904.7	32.6	8.0	5.7	12.1	41.4
1957	10,310.6	31.8	7.8	5.9	12.2	42.0
1958	10,301.8	30.9	7.4	5.9	13.1	42.4
1959	11,090.0	31.7	7.8	5.7	13.7	40.9
1960	11,931.7	31.0	7.9	5.8	13.3	42.0
1961	11,996.0	30.2	7.7	5.9	13.9	42.3

Source: *Printer's Ink* from McCann-Erickson. The percentages do not add to 100 because of rounding. The 1961 figure is preliminary.

Table 2. Distribution of Income and Expense for a
Group of Morning and Evening Newspapers
(80,000–130,000 Circulation), 1961

Operation		Percentage of Total
Income		
Circulation		25.65
Miscellaneous		.45
Advertising		
Local display	49.65	
National	9.36	
Classified	14.24	
Legal	.65	
		73.90
Total		100.00
Expense		
Administrative and general		19.06
Advertising sales and service...........		6.77
Circulation and mail...................		12.04
News and editorial.....................		15.14
Composing (typesetting, make-up)........		16.07
Press and stereotyping		6.93
Newsprint		22.39
Supplements		1.60
Total		100.00
Net profit....................10.74% of sales		

reported 37.1 per cent of income from subscriptions and sales and 61 from advertising; the remainder, 1.9 per cent, was not distributed between the two categories. Table 1 shows advertising growth since 1949.

Changes in the size of metropolitan newspapers have been great. Bennett started the *Herald* in 1845 with thirteen editors and reporters, twenty compositors, and sixteen press hands. Jones and Raymond started the *Times* with a capital of $60,000, and only paid $13,000 in news staff wages in the first year. Today the *Times* employs more than fifty-two hundred people and its payroll is in excess of $49,000,000. The $40,000 spent for newsprint in the first year has become $35,000,000.

The *Times* printed 62,545,996 lines (4,467,142 column inches) of advertising in 1961. Space given to news was not reported in 1961, but four years earlier it amounted to 11,000 pages (1,892,000 column inches) or 33.6 per cent of total space. Weekday circulation had risen from 24,000 copies in the first year to 713,514 and Sunday circulation was 1,348,220. In contrast to the stock-watering practices of some financiers of his time,

Ochs, owner of the *Times* from 1896 to his death in 1955, put two thirds of the earnings back into the firm to pay for its rapid growth. The company's statements show that from 1934 through 1961 no dividends were paid on the common stock but $32,720,088 had been reinvested in the business.

The net income of the company after taxes in 1961 was $2,212,709; of this amount $597,986 came from newspaper operations and $1,237,723 from Spruce Falls Power and Paper Company Limited, in which the *Times* has a 42 per cent stock interest. The mill is operated and controlled by Kimberly-Clark Corporation. The *Times* had a working capital of $12.9 million on December 31, 1957. The 1961 statement showed total assets of $57,878,491. Net profit in 1953 and 1954, years of slight business decline, was $71,985 and $61,346, more than $3,300,000 less than simple 6 per cent interest on invested capital today.

The *Times* is not represented as typical, but its growth is not unusual among metropolitan newspapers. The point is that it and all other major papers have become very large business corporations employing thousands, and news-reporting is only one of the many tasks performed.

Television's competitive achievement. In noting television's growth and comparing it with radio and the print media, the figures prepared by A. C. Nielsen Company show that it was in 46.9 million homes, 88 per cent of the total, by 1961. It was viewed in the average home at least six hours and four minutes a day. Another researcher, Sidlinger & Co., Philadelphia, counts an audience of 93,257,000 people over 12. In the evening hours of an average day, 50.2 per cent to 64.5 per cent of the home sets are tuned in.[2]

In 1958 the median profit of ninety-three television stations that existed prior to the freeze ordered by FCC while it was trying to decide on division of channels in the available broadcast spectrum, was $930,000 before taxes and the top eight stations earned more than $3,000,000 each. Half of them made more than a million. The networks and the nineteen stations they owned got 50 per cent of all television profits, $43,000,000.

Post-freeze stations were less profitable, a hundred and ninety-one of them averaging $98,000 in 1958. Fourteen pre-freeze and a hundred and four post-freeze VHF stations were unprofitable. Only twenty-three stations on the ultra-high frequency range, reception of which required alteration of the standard home receiver, reported profits.[3]

Networks reported to FCC that they lost $9,300,000 in 1958 from radio operations but they earned $5,700,000 before taxes on their radio stations. From television operations they had $34,000,000 profit and their stations paid an added $43,000,000. The networks had earned more in 1956, less in 1957. In 1960, the three networks, including fifteen stations they own and operate, reported $95,200,000 profit, and ninety-three pre-freeze television stations made $98,500,000. Post-freeze VHF stations, three hundred forty-six in number, reported profits of $50,100,000 and seventy-six ultra-high frequency stations shared a profit of only $300,000 among them. The radio and television profit in 1960 was $244,100,000. Radio's total volume of advertising started to grow again, after the setback from television, in 1959, and the gain over 1958 was 12.5 per cent. By this time there were four hundred seventy-two licensed television and four thousand forty-four licensed radio stations, and radio's share of the advertising was $609,114,000.[4]

Radio data distorted by small stations. Rapid growth in the number of stations since 1946 makes FCC figures on average radio station earnings largely meaningless. Thirty-four per cent of the stations reported an operating loss in 1958. The figures show that radio has made strong gains in local advertising, even while national advertising revenues were declining, and that it outsold television in local markets $323,200,000 to $181,300,-000. The FCC reported that sixteen hundred eight stations earned less than $25,000 before taxes, two hundred thirty-seven stations were in the $50,000 to $75,000 profit bracket, and a hundred and forty-one reported earnings of over $500,000. The clear-channel stations averaged $200,763 profit. Because of the increase from nine hundred thirty-six on the air in 1945 to four thousand forty-five in 1959 the stations had fragmented the advertising coverage in a way reminiscent of the days of heavy competition among the printed media. The losses reported by 34.6 per cent of all radio stations indicate that eventually concentration and consolidation will become manifest as in the case of the printed media.

The FCC explained the hazards of station ownership and operation in a special study for investors in 1947 when the post-war rush for new licenses became sizable; in part it has kept the basic data revised.[5]

Post-war financial condition of radio. The standard broadcast stations emerged from the war in an excellent profit position; aggregate revenues of all stations were 212 per cent and expenses were 187.5 per cent of 1940. In ratio of income to investment the AM stations increased threefold during the war. Local stations with unlimited broadcast time were the most profitable. When key network stations are excluded, the average ratio of revenue to expense for all stations in 1945 was 30.9 per cent and had been as high as 35.7 per cent during the war. Even at this profitable time, 1945, fifty stations reported losses, and four hundred fifty-seven were losers at one time or another between 1939 and 1945.

Half of the new post-war stations lost money during their first year of operation. FCC found 287 communities where more radio stations existed in 1945, or were authorized, than in any city of the same population in 1939. These communities had one thousand sixty-three stations in existence or authorized and the FCC estimated that a 56 per cent increase in aggregate station revenues would be required to make all of the new stations profitable; reports filed by two hundred fifty stations in 1947 showed that half were profitable, averaging about $1,200 a month. A new station in a community with existing stations had a 50 per cent greater chance of losing than those in non-competitive communities. In that year the average construction costs of a hundred and twenty local unlimited stations in towns under 50,000 population was $34,107. Regional unlimited stations cost an average of $91,011 in towns of this size and $133,000 in larger places. The new stations making a profit found that they began to break even in a month or two, but of course half of them had not yet turned a profit by 1947 and in 1959 losses were reported by one thousand thirteen or 34 per cent of the stations. The median loss was $15,000 a year and 84 per cent lost less than $25,000. Earnings of profit-making stations before taxes were distributed as follows in 1958: 1,608 earned less than $25,000, 237 $25,000 to $50,000, 67 $50,000 to $100,000, and 141 over $500,000.[6]

The impact of television on radio. The impact of television on radio has been greatest in its loss of listeners and a correlated reduction in national advertising (Table 3). The increase in local advertising in the face of substantial losses in station audience reflects the pressure of salesmanship hinged on better local programing and the fact that local unaffiliated stations gained rather than lost listeners. In 1949, the four radio networks sold 90 per cent of daytime hours but in 1956 only 51 per cent; in the same years the networks sold 74 and 30 per cent of evening time.[7]

There are two or three conclusions to be drawn from the radio data: First, having lost heavily in the sale of national network advertising, radio has made large gains in local advertising at a time when newspapers, large and small, are also turning more directly away from national advertising

Table 3. Changes in Percentage of Families Listening to
Radio Stations (1949 and 1956)

All Network Stations	Percentage of Families Listening		
	1949	1956	Change
NBC daytime	87.4	54.7	−32.7
NBC nighttime	91.2	36.6	−54.6
CBS daytime	86.9	60.0	−26.9
CBS nighttime	89.4	37.2	−52.2
ABC daytime	81.8	47.6	−34.2
ABC nighttime	84.3	29.2	−55.1
MBS daytime	80.2	47.8	−32.4
MBS nighttime	77.8	29.4	−48.4
Non-affiliates, daytime	26.0	36.0	+10.0
Non-affiliates, nighttime	15.0	33.0	+18.0

Source: *Editor & Publisher*, March 23, 1957.

to sell intensively in the local field. For the first time the two media may feel direct competitive rivalry that hurts. Second, the radio stations now in operation have fractionized the audience and it is difficult for most stations to solicit business on promise of heavy or dominant market coverage.

Third, half of the stations in operation are losing money, a condition which could usher in a trend toward consolidation. The cost of production facilities and the costs of operation so far give the radio stations a better chance to survive than newspapers had in a similar situation of overcompetition, but there is one important limiting factor: a station must fill out its broadcast day whether or not advertising support is available. The advertising not only brings in revenue but program material designed to attract an audience — material likely to be more attractive to a general or special listenership than sustaining programs put together as cheaply as possible. Thus a station deficient in advertising patronage is losing not only revenue but audience.

ᵼ THE NATURE OF FINANCIAL SOLVENCY

Newspaper proprietors stress the need for keeping solvent ahead of all other normal business considerations and the blunt statement of such a determination is often misconstrued as denial of an obligation to serve the community. The real import of the profit consideration is to be seen in a balance sheet such as that shown in Table 4, furnished to the National Newspaper Survey by the publisher of the newspaper concerned.

The business described in Table 4 appears to be insolvent. It has no

75

The Social Responsibility of the Press

Table 4. A Balance Sheet Showing Why Proprietors Stress Solvency

Item	Amount
Assets	
Current	
Cash in hand.....................................$	168.71
Accounts receivable	13,898.43
Inventories	614.25
Prepaid charges	695.71
Total	15,377.10
Land, building, and equipment at net depreciated value...	50,682.79
Good will and circulation structure....................	67,217.21
	$133,277.10
Liabilities	
Current	
Bank (overdraft)...............................$	734.99
Accounts payable	2,276.91
Notes payable	86.48
Accrued payroll	90.00
Accrued taxes	5,569.78
Accrued interest payable........................	1,370.84
Prepaid subscriptions	5,048.10
Total	15,177.10
Long-term indebtedness: mortgage..................	32,900.00
Fifteen-year bonds	75,000.00
Net worth	
Capital stock	5,100.00
Surplus	5,100.00
	$133,277.10

working capital and has overdrawn at the bank to meet current payroll. The listing of "good will and circulation structure" at $67,217.21 is a gesture, under the circumstances, that would be controversial in accounting practice; $1 would be a more appropriate value for the item, for there is no good will or circulation value if the business cannot be operated at a profit with normal application of energy and judgment. In fact, this publication has liabilities slightly more than twice its assets. Subsequent to the compilation of this statement, the nominal owner abandoned the business to his creditors and it later was conveyed to a buyer who did no more than assume the indebtedness; he, in turn, after five years of deficit operation, turned it over to a competitor who discontinued it. But the last owner was demoralized by his five-year struggle, and his ability to borrow money impaired; as a consequence he left the managerial class in favor of wage-earning status. This is the defeat which proprietors seek to avoid when they stress solvency of their firms.

This condition has been duplicated in newspapers going out of business over the country since 1909. The Los Angeles *Daily News* ceased publication in December 1954, trying to raise $113,000 just to keep the doors open a few days longer; already it had incurred deficits of $2,600,000 and no one, not even for the sake of political diversity in the community, would make new loans. When the world-wide Thomson Newspapers discontinued their St. Petersburg, Florida, *Independent,* they said the publication had incurred "fantastic losses"; only the great resources of the parent organization had kept the news of its distress from the general public. So it was with the Chandler family's *Mirror* and Hearst's morning *Examiner* when, in 1962, they followed the Los Angeles *Daily News* to limbo.

The publishers of all these papers made decisions identical with those made by our quasi-allegorical character, the publisher in a previous chapter, expanding their scale of operations hoping revenue would come in to meet the expenses. It never came.

✓ HOW ADVERTISING AFFECTED NEWSPAPER ECONOMICS

The special importance of full utilization of printing plant grows out of the pricing problem. The original discovery of the mass market by the New York *Sun* was accomplished, as has been explained, at a time when advertising was less important than the sale of news and when low manufacturing cost derived from an early form of high automation made it feasible to sell each copy cheaply and to depend upon volume of sale to recover costs and earn a profit. The theory of publishing prior to 1830 called for a high price on each individual copy and New York newspapers such as the *Courier* and *Enquirer* sold for six cents. Introduction of the low-price, or penny, papers created heavy competition and the papers used various mixes of content and price in the struggle for advantage. Readers were wooed by famous works of fiction, by popular contemporary authors writing exclusively for one publication, by sales promotions presenting a variety of inducements in addition to the intrinsic value of the product, by the development — prior to the general use of the telegraph — of various systems of getting the news in print first, by features such as comics and Sunday supplements, and by the exploitation of special writers on assignments that appealed to the curiosity and interest of readers.

Milline rate formula. Newspapers used magazine techniques — fiction; specialized news and features in food, fashion, homemaking, business, sports; special investigations akin to muckraking; reports by journalistic globe-trotters and adventurers — to supplement the news which was the hard core of their content. One newspaper competing with another tried never to allow a rival to enjoy a unique advantage, and once a feature was added to the paper it was not given up until interest in it ceased. This kind of competition was limited only by resources, and eventually a circulation leader or leaders emerged in a community which offered, or was willing to offer, anything save perhaps its own opinions, in order to hold its dominant position. The competitive struggle was made decisive, shaking out all but one newspaper in most American towns and cities, by the decision of advertisers to give preference to mass-circulation newspapers with the most favorable price per thousand readers. This relation is commonly expressed in the milline rate formula, the rate per agate line (14 such lines to the inch) in one million copies, or to put it another way, the rate for a 1,000-line advertisement in 1,000 copies. In the struggle, the circulation leader, other things being more or less equal, would always have an edge in selling to advertisers and, therefore, an edge in resources with which to cater to readers and advertisers alike. When the time came to bargain with unions, this advantage enabled the leader to settle for a wage higher than competitors could comfortably pay and each new contract multiplied the effects of such small but significant disadvantages until, one by one, the rival newspapers came either to final defeat or an opportunity to sell at a good price in an uncertain profit situation. In the few communities where competing newspapers likely will remain in business the resources are adequate for advertisers to buy space in more than one paper. Dominance in such communities is still to be won but some competitive papers have learned to divide the market among themselves by specialization of content and point of view. Thus in New York the *Times* and the *Herald-Tribune* compete, and so do the *News* and the *Mirror*; but the latter pair do not really compete with the first two. In the evening field the *World-Telegram and Sun* and the *Post* work from unlike points of view that give readers a fairly sharp impression of separate identity and advertisers a feeling that there is little duplication of circulation. The *Wall Street Journal* has largely removed itself from competition by a high degree of successful specialization and the same might be said of the *Morning Telegraph.*

Specialization of content aids security. The survivors in competitive fields, print or electronic, must find a way to specialize if each wishes to maximize its security. There is no security when competitors fight for the same readers and the same advertisers. Although New York and London are cities of somewhat the same size, all the morning newspapers in New York have less circulation than either one of two great popular morning newspapers among eight in London. Moreover, the New York papers appear to have lost nearly 300,000 circulation between 1950 and 1960. This phenomenon is sometimes explained by saying that London papers have a national circulation; this is true, but they first developed individuality and character — specialization — in ways that made them attractive to readers of the classes they wished to cater to. Whether the readers of the New York papers are paying their fair share of the cost of production or not, it is apparent that in a period of declining sales the publishers will find it difficult to persuade them to pay more without some change in the product.

Trends in circulation. Outside the New York area both the competitive and non-competitive monopoly papers also felt the need for establishing a mix in sales revenues from the joint products, advertising and news/entertainment, that would give assurance of security for the firm. In general, papers that have increased prices to readers above five cents have encountered sales resistance for a time and at ten cents per copy the losses have been serious; papers that have raised prices slowly, if at all, have had different individual experiences but the circulation total is lagging behind the rate of population growth. *Editor & Publisher* showed total daily newspaper circulation in 1962 approaching 60,000,000, an all-time high. But four years before, a cross-section list, 134 morning newspapers and 194 evening newspapers, had losses respectively of 1.09 per cent and 3.14 per cent from 1957 to 1958. A Sunday group, 182 papers, was down .91 per cent. The record of individual papers was uneven: 73 morning papers gained while others lost, and 85 evening papers gained while 109 lost.[8]

Advertising support for news. A managerial goal expressed by Lisle H. Baker, general manager of the Louisville *Courier-Journal and Times*, is for the readers to bear that portion of expense attributable to news and features and for advertisers to pay for selling, printing, and distributing the advertising portion. This apportionment of charges already is fairly well achieved in daily newspapers of sub-metropolitan size. M. S. Kuhns and Company, Chicago, reported in 1958 the experiences of seven firms publishing morning, evening, and Sunday editions from the same plant and for eight such firms in 1959. The papers all had a circulation range from 50,000 to 100,000.[9] In 1958 advertising paid all allocated costs, leaving an average margin of $374,063 for use in paying taxes and for profits. The subscribers also paid all costs allocated to them and a margin of $120,777 remained for taxes and profits. However, advertising's contribution to net income was only $1,734 more than its share. In 1959 the advertisers paid all costs allocated to them and $422,702 toward taxes and profits. Their share would have been $1,738 less.

Since the morning, evening, and Sunday combination in the same plant is the most efficient type of unit in the business, comparison with firms publishing single morning or evening papers gives a useful perspective. The same special reports of M. S. Kuhns and Company concerning papers with 35,000 to 50,000 circulation show that in 1948, for the average newspaper, advertising paid 72.37 per cent of all revenue and that it paid $75,044 more than its share of the net profit. The subscribers also paid costs allocated to them and $82,073 toward profits. For a similar group of papers in 1959 advertising paid its own way and $65,776 more than its share of the net income; but the subscribers paid $83,759 toward net income, or $2.05 each.[10]

The papers discussed here cannot be regarded as typical; they are better off than the average and have excellent managerial direction supported by expert consulting accountants. Not all newspapers are so fortunate in this respect. However, the industry's figures also show that the manager who looks to his subscribers to pay the costs that his advertisers should bear, but don't want to bear, may lose a substantial number of readers and have to go back to his advertisers for the money to pay a profit after all. There is no evidence here, from the cost-allocation point of view, that subscribers are not paying their fair share of the costs.[11] The same allocations formula might show different results from metropolitan newspapers, but it can be assumed that as a newspaper increases in bulk the advertisers will be allocated an increasingly greater, rather than a lesser, share of the costs. City readers in the immediate metropolitan area are almost certainly paying their share, as well; outside that area prices have been differentially increased by many newspapers in an effort to meet extra costs of service.

The cost allocations information brought out so far ignores the almost universal pattern of varying rates for advertising customers according to the volume of space used in any month. If we were to go back to the M. S. Kuhns data and note the distribution of income from advertising into appropriate rate categories we would find a large spread between the biggest local advertisers, the department stores, and the national advertisers who place their orders through the agencies and pay the top rates. In fact, despite the use of printed rate cards supposedly covering customers of all classes, most large newspapers keep off the card the rates paid by department stores. A former director of the Bureau of Advertising, American Newspaper Publishers Association, Harold S. Barnes, says he thinks department store rates ought to be raised 25 per cent. If the papers lose some of the present volume of business as a result, they would save money in the long run, Barnes thinks. A leading advertising agency executive, Norman H. Strouse, president of J. Walter Thompson Company, says the national advertisers paid newspapers over 50,000 circulation 55.9 per cent more than average published local rates in 1954.[12]

If the lowest retail rates were compared with the national rate, as Mr. Barnes meant to suggest, the difference in rates is considerably larger. Mr. Strouse suggested that impartial arbiters work out an equitable rate adjustment between advertisers of the several classes and that the newspapers put the new rates into effect over a period of several years to cushion the adjustments.

On the basis of what Mr. Barnes and Mr. Strouse say, we would not change our conclusion that advertising is paying its own way; but we would now see that smaller advertisers and national advertisers are paying a much higher proportion than others, a fact that some experts regard as against the best interests of the newspapers — and other business as well. The difference between local and national rates has forced large amounts of national advertising into a semi-contraband status in which local advertisers carry national advertising as their own and then sell the space back to national advertisers. Mr. Barnes estimates that 35 to 40 per cent of department-store advertising is paid for in this way; further, he reports assumptions that some of the stores even make a profit on this rate-option procedure. Max Ascoli, publisher of the *Reporter*, says that the papers are caught between the pressures of advertisers and of the unions: "the advertisers strengthen the newspapers that are already strong while the labor unions weaken those that are already weak."

A scapegoat is sought for costs. Newsprint-makers are sometimes substituted for advertisers as one of the millstones between which newspapers are being ground, because of the increased cost of paper. Mr. Barnes visualizes newsprint price as one of the grinding surfaces, but he observes that an increase in the department-store rate would soon ease off this pressure.

He is also fearful that some publishers will try to increase volume to get the money they need without significant rate increases. This tactic would simply accelerate the cost spiral, he says.[13]

Even worse, Barnes says it would probably cut the amount of time spent in reading each individual advertisement because readers apparently allot a relatively inflexible fixed time to the papers, whether they are thirty or sixty pages. He thinks publishers should emphasize profit on a manageable volume rather than a large number of pages and heavy advertising linage. In view of the largely uncritical pursuit, since the beginning of the popular press, of volume production, Barnes's fears are well grounded. The late George C. Biggers, president of Atlanta Newspapers, Inc., while serving as president of American Newspaper Publishers Association, expressed the popular philosophy in this way:

Let's remember always that newspapers are a mass medium. When we no longer deliver our market — every income bracket of it — to the advertiser, we are heading into difficulty. The retail stores of this country were built on fast merchandising, big sales, lots of advertising. Merchandise is manufactured fast and sold fast. To move it requires advertising, lots of advertising, frequency of advertising, multiple pages of advertising. And let's never delude ourselves with any occasional thought about our newspapers being too big, about advertisers getting along just as well with less space. American business wasn't built on reduction of volume.[14]

Mr. Barnes spoke up only three years later, after a term as the chief space salesman for ANPA, to say that the reader could not be taken for granted, the popular mythology notwithstanding. Ascoli, looking in the same direction, said "the situation in America can become hopeless if only a few good dailies go down, and if the most successful [news] weeklies remain just as they are." [15]

The newspapers expanded greatly to care for the increased volume. They reported $140 million in new plant construction during 1958. In the process more than six hundred papers equipped themselves to run more than one color. A firm of methods engineers surveyed the newspaper industry and said that under the swell of new business 50 to 75 per cent of plants were in need of expansion or replacement.[16] Advertising dollar volume virtually doubled between 1950 and 1960, from $5.7 billion to $11.1 billion. Newspapers got 36.4 per cent of the 1950 total advertising revenue and 30.2 per cent of the 1961 total, amounting to $3,630,000,-000.[17]

Since the ruling price theory in the business did not permit publishers to recapture added costs by forthright increases in price, a series of expedient compromises evolved. The pre-war price of newsprint was based on an abnormal surplus mill capacity that persisted from 1930 through 1944. Canadian mills went into and emerged from the price stabilization period of the war with a low average price. The psychology of the industry and of investors was derived from the costly experience of overextending production capacity prior to the great depression; therefore, the mills were slow in responding to the world-wide post-war demand for paper and paper products. The consequent rapid rise in costs hit the American papers at a time when they were expanding their advertising volume and circulation alike and they did not increase their prices fast enough to compensate for both the increased use and the increased cost of paper. In fact, they gave away about 12,000,000 increase in circulation subsequent to 1947 in the sense that the charges to advertisers did not reflect this increased distribution.[18]

Devices to save newsprint. Since advertising rates were not raised fast enough to compensate for costs, the proprietors made other efforts at economy. Page margins and page sizes were reduced, columns were set on narrower measure, page matrices for use in making plates for the press were shrunk more than usual so that columns appeared in print in smaller space than that occupied by the original type, and regular features such as comics were reduced in size. The result, in a period when competition with television for the reader's time and interest was keen, was a much less readable paper and some proprietors, upon coming to this conclusion, increased the size of the body type so that the reader would be less affected by the shrinkage. Readership of classified advertising slipped at one time from 40 per cent of the readers to 26 per cent, in part because of nine-column pages and type shrunken below the level of optical comfort.[19] Newsprint mills struggled with a host of new paper specifications resulting from the manipulation of column width. The Newsprint Information Committee reported that by reducing columns from twelve to eleven picas in 1959 newspapers saved $42,000,000 in newsprint but had spent large sums in making the change.[20]

Publishers who analyzed the cost of modifying equipment necessary to reduce page sizes were not so sure they were on the right track. Earl L. Deal of the Norfolk Newspapers, Inc., said it cost his firm $100,000 to reduce the columns by one twelfth of an inch; another reduction cost $250,000. Then it became apparent that the public was not pleased with the changes and, in Norfolk at least, the proprietor decided to get the extra money needed from advertisers and readers.[21]

Typesetting from tape. Another nation-wide change in the pursuit of economy was the adoption of the Teletypesetter, an auxiliary to the standard linecasting machine by which newspaper copy is set into type. The Teletypesetter, and similar machines, perforate a paper tape from a typewriting keyboard and the tape then actuates the linecasting machine. Where the unions permit, the keyboards can be located outside of the composing room and operated by clerks who are not printers; one printer or printer-machinist could then oversee the operation of a battery of linecasting machines on tape operation. This effort to save money was impeded by the capital investment for Teletypesetters and for the necessary modification or replacement of linecasting machines. New and specially designed machines had to be installed to use the speed potential of perforated tape. Moreover, in shops having agreements with the International Typographical Union, the union sought and got assignment to operate the perforators as well as the linecasting machines and the saving in wages was reduced. Many large newspapers, including the New York City general-circulation dailies, had no Teletypesetter units until 1961 because they could not agree with unions on their operation. Others, such as the Miami *Herald*, have for some years had tape-actuated machines.[22]

National and regional news transmission by teletypewriter circuits was reorganized so as to produce simultaneously a typescript and perforated tape ready for linecasting machines. More than half of the non-metropolitan newspapers used the tape system but adapted it to individual needs as best they could. No systematic study of the relative costs of the Teletypesetter and conventional systems has been made and given general circulation. The tape was usable mainly for tabular material, such as stock market reports, and for straight matter; headletter and advertising had to be handled as usual.

Cost analysis as an economy tool. Two related efforts at reducing costs, analysis by accounting techniques and a search for substitutes for letterpress printing, have received the attention and support of the industry.

The accounting analysis has been made by trade associations and by public accountants catering to a newspaper clientele. The approach is to departmentalize the newspaper office according to function and charge to each department the direct costs of its operation. By this means a firm can compile a historical record of its own operations and, if it cares to do so,

84

make corrections for changes in the value of money and other conditions outside the system of direct control. One group of trade associations has provided accounting comparisons for more than forty years, figures that have been influential in policy decisions. However, since the studies emphasized costs without reference to content or quality of production they tended to transfer attention from the needs of readers and advertisers to the mechanical aspects of manufacturing and distribution.

Weakness of Cost Analysis. One of the country's best-known general managers of a large metropolitan daily newspaper, giving his opinion of cost analysis under a promise that he would not be identified, said that cost analysis of advertising, without simultaneous rate analysis, is meaningless and perhaps misleading, and that the method ignores or depreciates all of the considerations of quality on which newspapers lay claim to preference by readers. In the case of his firm, comparative costs are high for such reasons as these:

1. The pension plan is generous rather than niggardly and it is supplemented by provisions for group insurance and sick benefits.

2. The firm places great store on having the best possible news report and this policy means a late press time. A late press time forced the purchase of additional press units and the employment of printers and pressmen at premium, that is, overtime, rates. If the decision had been taken on cost considerations alone the editions would have been sent to press five hours earlier and almost nobody would have known the difference except the editor and his staff and the press-room payroll would have been 40 to 50 per cent less.

3. The editors stress quality and should not be required to revise their judgment by comparing costs with papers that have lower standards or none at all. Information costs money to get and to print in meaningful form, and page costs increase as quality standards go up.

4. The firm can sharply cut its costs if it fails to put value greater than money income on modern buildings adequately maintained, air-conditioned, and serviced. Excellent library facilities and a diversified range of news reports from sources at home and abroad also increase page costs.

News Already Near a Minimum. Poynter McEvoy, a specialist in cost analysis, studied the progress of the art of cost comparison and, evidently in the hope of bringing an end to reduction of space for news as an economy measure, asked how much money proprietors could save by cutting down further on news. He found that in practice there was a point beyond which proprietors hesitated to go in replacing reading matter with advertising and that 69 per cent advertising was the highest proportion used by large newspapers in the group he surveyed. Further, 26 per cent of firms printing up to twenty-six pages daily were already at or near the maximum; the median newspaper could have saved only a page a day by adopting the maximum proportion; only 9 per cent of the papers had quality standards that represented two to three pages of reading matter above the minimum. Moreover, 91 per cent were operating within two pages of the minimum. McEvoy said his criterion in the study had nothing to do with the "rights of readers" but resulted from practical considerations — inability to place more advertising on pages because of its variety in size and the attitude of advertisers themselves toward position on pages with less reading matter.[23]

Time-and-Motion Study. Time study of standard typesetting motions was undertaken by the American Newspaper Publishers Association in an effort to arrive at norms. The method previously described compared firms and departments within firms, but gave little or no opportunity to pinpoint costs in relation to specific workers, equipment, or task. The ANPA contracted with Johns Hopkins University to set up the norms, but the standards arrived at have not been put to general use as yet in newspaper publishing. When they are, the post-war lament about the decline in productivity of printers will undergo systematic scrutiny for the first time. John Cowles, Jr., of the Minneapolis *Star* and *Tribune*, for example, reported that between 1947 and 1954 total newspaper payroll per employee went up 17 per cent in 1947 dollars and that the product increased only 8 per cent. The Johns Hopkins study found that advertisers in some cases were making extensive changes in proofs and demanding extra services that increased costs. Analysis thus pointed to several factors, in addition to work output, that account for the decline of newspaper profits.[24]

Experiments in cold type. Cold type as a panacea for rising costs has had about it some of the interest that attaches to a pioneering technology. The goal has been to eliminate one of the steps in the present printing process or to devise a complete substitute system. Various forms of the typewriter have been used to prepare copy for offset printing, rather than letterpress, or for engravings compatible with letterpress. The variety of headletter and display type available on these machines is limited, but auxiliary type-on-film machines have filled the gap, though not inexpensively. Letterpress typecasting machines have been adapted to film com-

86

position, but not always at great improvement in speed. New electronic photosetting systems have been developed, using magnetic tape and matrix discs, and, although the price is high, some of these devices have much higher capacity and flexibility than linecasting machines. Typesetting by high-speed electronic computers, reading directly from typescript, is in use in newspaper offices.

Martin M. Reed, president of the Mergenthaler Linotype Company, estimated that by 1958 manufacturers had spent more than eight million dollars in developing phototypesetting machines. Experimentation is showing how and to what extent the two processes can be profitably mixed in newspaper offices.[25]

When it comes to evaluating the new processes, each is found to have its partisans; but factual comparison cannot be conclusive at this time. Because the letterpress method is integrated from linecasting through the finished product, a substitute for any one step in the process is difficult to evaluate; substantial savings have been reported by some newspapers that have converted to offset, but so far the sum of the advantages and disadvantages has not been totted up. The rapid spread of offset printing showed that many firms were not waiting for a precise cost comparison to be available.

Welfare legislation. Because of the close margins on which many newspapers are operating, trade association committees are on the defensive against changes in unemployment compensation and social security laws that would increase costs without improving productivity. The committees are fearful lest the carrier boys and the large number of independent contractors doing circulation work be brought under social security and other governmental programs that are charged largely to employers. Already, newspaper controllers say, fringe benefits add one fourth to newspaper payrolls, as against one fifth for industry as a whole.[26] This figure applies only to the newspapers that have pension plans in addition to social security. ANPA surveyed 434 papers in 1955 and found 175 with pension plans, 85 per cent of them begun after 1940.[27] No information has been found about the other 1,300 newspapers.

Why rates are not increased. Two main causes underlie the psychological reluctance of newspapers to raise advertising rates and turn them to all sorts of alternate or substitute activities that seem easier. The first is the volume-production and low-rate theory of operation that has caused the average newspaper, large or small, to outgrow the trade territory of all but the largest advertisers. The second is competition. The two will be discussed separately.

As to the first, it is customary for the users of the largest volume of space to get the lowest rates.[28] They have sufficient bargaining power, because eight or ten of them account for 20 per cent of the average newspaper's advertising income, to resist efforts to raise their preferred rates out of proportion to others. The users of less space, assuming they have a smaller business volume and draw trade from a smaller segment of the newspaper's intense and widespread circulation, find themselves inevitably buying circulation of marginal value to them along with that which reaches their best customers. Each advertiser can buy newspaper space of a size consistent with his income, but because of the large circulation, the expense seems heavy and the smaller firms feel at a disadvantage in competition with users of large space. Since this is their state of mind, the publishers feel keenly the situation of individual advertisers and their pressure of opinion against rate increases. This pressure is renewed every time a salesman reports difficulty with a customer in this situation.*

Rate changes through zoned editions. So long as customers were concentrated in a central business district not much could be done about the advertisers with a sectional or district trade. Since 1940, however, the central cities have been losing population to fast-growing suburbs and peripheral growth became a factor much earlier. The Chicago *Tribune* started three zoned Thursday editions in 1949 after zoning its Sunday circulation since 1927. The Chicago *Sun-Times,* the Minneapolis *Star,* the Los Angeles *Times,* the Newark *News,* the Cleveland *Press,* the Detroit *Free Press,* and many other newspapers also publish either zoned editions or split runs one day a week. The zoned editions cater to readers as well as to advertisers. The papers mentioned maintain separate staffs of reporters, editors, and photographers to handle suburban news.[29] Although additional advertising is sold for the limited circulation, the zoned editions, in the early stages at least, did not pay their way. The proprietors count on growth to make them profitable. In the meantime, covering the news of suburban people, problems, and government helps the metropolitan

* In twenty-five cities in the United States and two in Canada the pressure on rates has led to joint ownership and operation of a central printing plant by two or more daily newspapers since 1950. Competing newspapers in such a situation usually consolidate their advertising departments but retain separate staffs for news and editorial work. See "Joint Printing Plant Kept Some Newspapers Alive," *Editor & Publisher,* April 19, 1958, p. 26.

newspaper circulations keep up with, or grow with, the suburbs. Covering such news is no small task. The Minneapolis *Star*'s suburban staff, for example, has twenty-nine city and village council meetings to report the first week of each month, twenty-three the second week, twenty-five in the third week and thirteen in the fourth week. In addition to councils there are school boards, planning boards, courts, athletic events to be reported; and, because of the closeness of the events to the people concerned, the job must be done with as much care as news of the central city. The penalties for failure to report suburban news range all the way from stagnation or loss of circulation to growth of suburban daily papers which tend to bottle up the central city daily in its own restricted area. New York City suburban and fringe area daily and Sunday newspapers gained 935,654 circulation between 1950 and 1960 while Manhattan dailies were losing 2,794,144.

Competition by statistical interpretation. As to competition, the second reason inhibiting higher rates, the principal antagonist in recent years is television and the most acute conflict is over which medium reaches the public at lowest cost. Before the competitive claims can be appreciated some background explanation is desirable.

Boastful claim of coverage is as old as advertising. Newspapers, while still competing almost solely among themselves and with magazines, developed conventions by which all claims of circulation could be settled through the Audit Bureau of Circulations, which was developed jointly by advertisers and the print media to verify claims and settle disputes. ABC counted only the number of copies printed and provided detailed reports on where these copies were sold to the public. It was left to the advertising trade to project census figures so as to estimate the probable number of readers. Field research, which was applied widely to the mass media after George Gallup led the way with his pioneering doctoral dissertation at the State University of Iowa, gradually developed a new set of estimates derived from home interviews. Upon them new claims of total readership and new definitions of readership were based. The typical readership study of a newspaper makes use of interviews of a statistically or randomly derived cross-section of the public and reports the number of persons who "saw" each item on the page and the number who "read" each item. There is a different traffic count for each page, each item of advertising, and each item of reading matter. An editorial-page cartoon, for example, may have 70 per cent readership whereas the best-read editorial may get less than

40 per cent. Readership of individual advertisements varies, even on the same page or in the same column, according to the general interest in the subject. A timely department-store advertisement for children's school clothing, even if lacking in some desirable typographical or copywriting features, may attract half of the readers, while a premium-grade motor oil advertisement, produced according to Madison Avenue standards, may attract 6 per cent or less. Cartoons scattered through a magazine or newspaper draw heavy readership and stop readers long enough for them consciously to select or reject material on the same page. In short, the print media sell space and an opportunity for advertisers to enjoy high readership if the subject matter and the manner of presentation are of interest to large numbers of people. The number of persons who read advertising is clearly visible and clearly separated from the number that reads news, features, and editorials. The number of readers of "any item on the page" and the number who read any individual advertisement can be clearly separated. Advertisers many times have the satisfaction of outpulling readers in competition with non-commercial matter, but the usual result is the opposite. Moreover, the actual audit of readership is done by methods well tested in psychology laboratories.

Radio and Television Surveys. Radio and television are up against a more difficult problem: they have largely been unable to deal with the question of who sees or hears what advertisement and, instead, can report only the number hearing or seeing the program or the number of sets turned on and tuned to a particular station at the time. The result is that the print media find their competitors comparing the number of persons seeing or hearing, or in a position to see or hear, anything on their program with readership of the average advertisement in an issue. This is as if one publication compared its highest page-traffic count with the average reading of all of the advertisements in a rival publication, omitting entirely the readership of editorial matter. The result of this strategy is that several commercial schemes for checking radio and television are in operation; the results do not agree, but program reputations are nevertheless made and unmade by them and accounts switch from one network to another or from print to electronic media on the evidence they present. Robert Feit, a New York University observer, reports the two leading rating agencies, Nielsen and Trendex, came up contemporaneously with these figures: the Columbia Broadcasting System had a 43 per cent larger audience than the second-ranking network; the National Broadcasting

Company has an audience 6 per cent larger than the Columbia Broadcasting System. A comedian, Red Buttons, was rated by one service third in size of audience and twenty-fourth by another.[30]

Professor George Gordon of the New York University Communications Arts Group gives his opinion: "The ratings people haven't got the answers. They can't measure the emotional impact of the advertising message on the viewer. Are they motivated enough to go out and buy the sponsor's product? All that rating services attempt to supply is the number of viewers who had an opportunity to see the message." [31]

Firms owning print media have diversified by heavy investments in radio and television and, as the record on legal action to diversify ownership shows, the newspapers own nearly eight hundred AM, FM, and television station licenses and permits.

These facts, added to the others brought out, have furnished the competitive pressure against increase of advertising rates to large newspaper advertisers.

Labor problems. The extra money needed has not come from successful bargaining with labor unions because for the most part the printing trades are old and well established; as a consequence they reserve the right to give central-office approval to contracts agreed to by locals, and they maintain a staff competent to analyze contracts and advise local bargaining committees. The International Typographical Union, oldest of the printing trades unions, is militant in the sense that it tries to enforce its claims by strategy that includes strike action and establishment of competing newspapers in key situations where settlements are difficult or delayed. In 1956, for example, members reported to ANPA fourteen strikes affecting twenty-three newspapers and sixty-seven instances in which disputes went into arbitration. During the eleven-year period 1946–56 ANPA members reported two hundred sixty strikes and four hundred sixty arbitration awards in dealing with all of the printing trades unions.[32] At the end of this period sixty-six strikes against ninety daily newspapers were continuing, although in most cases the papers were being published.

The ITU found itself in conflict with the Taft-Hartley law because its contracts called for a closed shop and required the foreman to be a member of the union. It rejected the jurisdiction of the National Labor Relations Board and its officers gave effect to the policy by refusing to take one of the oaths required of them by the law. Contracts incorporating closed-shop agreements were invalid, but the union sought to maintain its customary rules by informal understanding with the proprietors. In Chicago this effort provoked a unilateral strike of the printers for more than a year. The papers published by composing straight reading matter on special typewriters and then engraving the newspaper page for stereotyping. The other printing trades unions continued at work.[33] The closed-shop ban was the union's main objection to the Taft-Hartley law, but Woodruff Randolph, the president at the time, listed other objections in a request that Congress amend the law: the NLRB should be deprived of its power to fix the scope of bargaining; secondary boycotts aimed at workers who in effect are doing the work of men on strike should again be legalized; the NLRB should be deprived of the opportunity to ask court injunctions against unions.[34]

The publishers' associations customarily state that the wages paid to the printing trades are the highest in industry. Such claims are borne out only if sections of the newspaper business are compared with averages of all industry. The average weekly earnings of production workers in manufacturing industries in 1958 was $88.62, for the newspaper printing trades, $103.43. But the averages of workers in six large industries — blast-furnace operation, flat glass contract construction, industrial organic chemicals, petroleum refining, tires and tubes, tin cans and tinware — are higher than the printing trades, though when printing-trade hourly rates specified in individual contracts are multiplied by the hours to be worked earnings appear higher. The 1959 typographical scale for newspaper workers in the city in which this book is written, as an example, was $125.48 for a thirty-five hour week and mailers, who are not highly skilled, earned $115.53 for a thirty-six and a quarter hours of work. When 1945 is taken as 100, the 1959 gross average weekly earnings of all production workers was 199. It is apparent that the ANPA papers reported are paying above the average for newspapers and are basing their complaints on their individual situations.

Daniel H. Ridder, co-publisher of the Long Beach *Independent and Press-Telegram* observed after settling a strike:

"It is true that nobody ever wins in a strike. The employees lose their wages and . . . it takes years to get back what they lost. The company itself, of course, loses its revenues. It creates problems of ill will with employees and in many instances with the public. [Yet] you just can't say 'yes' to the unions and go out and raise the advertising rates or your circulation rates and expect to get it all back. You have to absorb some of that." He looked toward increases in productivity as the only way in which both the firm and the employee could prosper.

Objection to Union Rules. The mention of productivity raises another issue between the two parties, whether or not labor should accept new machines and processes even when jobs are lost thereby. A long-standing issue between the proprietors and the typographical workers is union insistence that type going into newspapers be locally composed. If newspaper copy of classes specified in the labor contract comes into the shop already set, or in such form that local labor will not be used, union rules require that it be reset, proofread, and made ready for publication. Afterward, of course, there is nothing to do with it but to dump it into the remelting furnace. The newspapers, complaining for many years, went to court after passage of the Taft-Hartley law in an effort to have the practice declared illegal, but the United States Supreme Court held for the union: the Taft-Hartley law forbade only collection of wages for work not performed. The court termed the union contract requirement, negotiated and enforced under threat of strike action, a "frivolous make work exercise." Justice Douglas additionally offered the opinion that the requirement was a new form of "oppression," but all the justices said the Congress had to outlaw it before the court could grant relief.[35]

New employees harder to find. The difficulty in raising rates for large local advertisers had one other consequence: the proprietors of the nonmetropolitan papers have found it hard to recruit college-trained personnel for the news and advertising departments and those of metropolitan newspapers have had to contend with heavy turnover because of ceilings they imposed on wages of experienced journalists. This has resulted in a crisis of the spirit as well as of the purse, for journalism considers itself one of the chosen callings and its practitioners take pride in the exceptional demands made upon them by the craft. Enrollment in journalism schools turned down after the post-war bulge and has since been static. Although newspapers continued to hold first place as employers of journalism graduates, public relations firms, advertising agencies, magazines of the several kinds, and merchandising departments of large business firms competed for graduates. The average starting salaries of graduate engineers, accountants, and salesmen were reported 36 per cent, 20 per cent, and 19 per cent, respectively, ahead of graduate journalists.[36] Several hundred staff members of high school publications attending a meeting at Columbia University in 1959 ranked journalism second only to medicine as the

93

most interesting profession, but six out of ten were not thinking of it as a career because they regarded it as a low-paying occupation lacking in prestige and not conducive to good family life.[37] The findings as to prestige are not borne out by other surveys of what the general public thinks about journalism,[38] but the other findings are confirmed. High school counsellors in the Pacific Coast area, classing journalism as one of the five occupations most appealing to students, ranked it last among the five as to security and next to last in financial rewards "for able young men." The counsellors were found to be grossly misinformed, principally by the United States Department of Labor handbooks, on the opportunities in journalism; but it could not be denied that students had picked up from them and other sources new attitudes toward journalism.[39] The emphasis on security was particularly galling to editors and publishers who had established themselves competitively with no more security than their wits, personality, and an occasional fortunate marriage could afford. Thus Norman E. Isaacs, managing editor of the Louisville *Times*, is disturbed because the first questions able young college graduates ask him concern pay, days and hours of work, and pension benefits. Isaacs blames the schools of journalism because their graduates are more interested in work conditions than in a place in an important public-serving profession, but he also finds forces inside the business working toward the same minimum goals, particularly the trade unions and the publishers' organization, ANPA.[40] "I would hazard the guess that out of every 100 in newspapering only ten really belong. They are the ten who do not fear the drudgery of getting the vital statistics; these are the ten who have a deep respect for the printed word and who love newspapering deeply."

Turnover Rate for Newsmen Is High. The press is by now well aware of the shape of its recruitment problem and realizes that it is not alone in such perplexity. A committee of the Associated Press Managing Editors Association headed by I. William Hill of the Washington, D.C., *Star* in 1959 surveyed the college graduates who entered journalism in 1953. It was found that two thirds of the journalism graduates of fifty-two colleges went into print-media work but six years later only 51 per cent of them remained. George J. Kienzle, Ohio State journalism director, gathered information for the committee from 185 graduates of the class of 1953. He interpreted the returns to mean that public relations work and editing for industrial firms were serious competitors with the mass media for experienced and inexperienced talent alike. Beginners in these tangential pursuits received salaries 9 per cent higher than those for comparable posts in news-room jobs; six years later they were earning 20 per cent, about $1,247 per year, more than journalists. Seven out of ten of the journalists in news rooms after six years were making $135 a week or less ($7,000 a year), and 11 per cent received between $8,000 and $9,000 a year, none over $9,000. In non-media pursuits, 3 per cent were making $15,000 to $20,000 or more.

Why Journalists Change Vocations. An inquiry into the motives of experienced men leaving journalism, made by the writer with a sample of forty-five men in two communities shows that money is only one side — but an important side to a man feeling a gradual increase in the cost of a growing family — of the problem. Many of the leavers are casualties of the struggle to get ahead within the organization employing them — men who found themselves unwilling to compete for preferment by a supervisor they regarded as whimsical, illogical, or tempestuous. The employer appeared oblivious to their need for emotional attachment to the organization and for appreciation or recognition for quality of services performed. Sometimes the rivals moving ahead of them had separated themselves from the others on the staff by becoming specialists in science, politics, economics, city and community planning, social welfare, education, or foreign affairs and the leavers had no money to return to school to build a specialty of their own. Without distinctive training and the recognition that goes with it, they came to feel rejected.

When the employers of these men were consulted they were largely unaware of the individual problems revealed. They explained that their system of promotion gave preference to the outstanding generalist and specialist alike. They did not have the money to pay the others as well as the outstanding men; competition for self-improvement and general excellence would disappear if they did. They also pointed to the men who remained in journalism and asked that their satisfaction be considered, along with the complaints of the leavers, in judging journalism as a career for persons of ability. Some evidence for that inquiry is available, but social research workers tend to study maladjustment rather than adjustment, abnormality rather than normality, and in that way build an involuntary pessimism into their work. Kienzle found that 69 per cent of his 1953 graduates were willing to recommend journalism to their children as a career and that 75 per cent of the leavers said more money was the main reason for moving on. Alvin F. Austin of the University of North

Dakota reached the same conclusion in a more comprehensive study made for the Newspaper Fund, a non-profit foundation established by Dow Jones & Company. He found also that because of this one consideration, money, boys had deserted high school newspaper staffs.[41]

Job-satisfaction statistics. Robert M. Pockrass of Pennsylvania State University questioned the graduates of his school and emphasized in his report the returns from former students who are satisfied with their jobs: 25 per cent of the satisfied group are in daily newspapers, 10 per cent in public relations, and 9 per cent are in advertising. A third of the satisfied group were advertising specialists as undergraduates. The typical respondent liked his job and thought he had a good future. All were above average in scholastic achievement. They found nothing seriously wrong with working conditions and had good morale. They look forward to doubling their present income and they are enthusiastic about their work. Typical comments from them: "I don't believe I could ever be happy in any other work even if more pay were involved." "I love the work. I should pay them. It is stimulating, satisfying and financially rewarding." (This respondent is an industrial writer.) "I enjoy the job very much. You feel you are contributing to the community on a small newspaper. Doing a bit of everything, you feel that part of you goes into every issue." [42]

Austin got similar reports of which these are examples: "No two days are alike. The work is stimulating, creative, and every situation is different. Boredom is impossible! The people themselves are exciting and congenial, too. Everyone seems to be closely knit and working for a common goal." "I feel as though I belong, and often get satisfaction out of the idea that at least a few souls in our area honestly depend on my newsgathering and writing for information on subjects vital to them." "I relish the opportunity to raise hell, poke fun at 'stuffed shirts,' laugh at the ridiculous occurrences, weep at tragedies, and be forever startled by the obvious." [43]

Recommendations to employers. The recommendations of the Associated Press Managing Editors Association appear to cover the ground of several sets of such advice given by other organizations. These call for (a) a plan to provide superior young people to fill vacancies; (b) a system to train staff members to fit their jobs; (c) a policy that will insure a climate of good morale in which competent persons can and will do their best as each plays his part in a two-way flow of information and ideas.

Proprietors were asked to realize that young people were looking for training on the job, for better pay, and a better chance for advancement.

96

Editors were also advised to place greater reliance on women and make a special effort to understand them and help them succeed as journalists.[44]

Experience of the schools of journalism. The reasons why bright young employees are more difficult to recruit are a bit more complex. The hundred and five schools of journalism reporting to *Journalism Quarterly* enrolled 11,766 students in 1959 and 11 per cent of this enrollment was at the graduate level. The state universities and, in general, the schools away from the eastern seaboard, developed journalism education and introduced it into the four-year arts curriculum as a major subject — that is, a subject in which work could be concentrated during the junior and senior years. The schools of business administration, education, and the engineering sciences developed their specializations in the same way amid a general lament from those who saw special merit in reserving four years for explication of cultural, aesthetic, and moral values and wished to delay vocational training until graduate school or job training. Traditionalists in education particularly objected to journalism schools because for a time they merely taught writing, editing, and press history — and what the classicists regarded as corrupt versions of those arts. As journalism education developed, its teachers drew upon the methods used by the established fields, history, government, law, literature, sociology, business administration, statistics, to create their own special subject matter — a procedure that accounted earlier for the emergence of government from history and philosophy; sociology from psychology, anthropology, and history; economics from history and statistics; and business administration from trade practice and economics. Business had never claimed professional status and organized education settled for legal controls on certification of teachers, yielding to local school boards the opportunity to set standards. But journalism, as this book has made clear, talked about itself as a professional calling and sought recognition as such. While law, medicine, dentistry, and engineering sciences were lengthening the period of preparation — and obtaining monetary rewards from society adequate to maintain the new requirements — schools of journalism were held back in their drive for graduate preparation first by the long period of competition which rendered newspapers unable to raise wages, second by graduates of high schools and liberal arts colleges willing to take apprenticeship-type jobs on newspapers at very low rates of pay while learning newspaper writing and editing, and, finally, by the inability or unwillingness of newspapers, so far, to establish advertising rates able to nourish a professional class of journalists. Unlike law, medicine, and education, journalism was beyond legal help in providing minimum standard of education because an open job market is regarded as indispensable to diversity and competition — even though these cardinal qualities have pretty well disappeared in the print media businesses themselves. To put it another way, as long as journalism kept any remnant of its old ideal of diversity in communications its practitioners were likely to be selected on the basis of economic considerations rather than on the assumed need of the community for intellectual and moral leadership. The press in its present situation preferred college graduates as journalists and 71 per cent of those responding to an inquiry sponsored by the Dow Jones Foundation favored journalism-school graduates and 8 per cent more had no preference. The papers that could not get them were hiring high school graduates and training them on the job, hoping they would be less transient than the college-educated persons.

Publishing problems and prospects. We set out in this chapter to get better acquainted with the newspaper proprietor and his management problems. The business challenges dealt with, the difficulty of making a satisfactory profit, the adjustments made inside the firms, and the consequences, make up the minds of today's newspaper managers as revealed through the proceedings of their trade associations and their own speeches and writings. Since they have talked about their problems, rather than about their accomplishments, it is too easy to overlook the fact that the problems arise largely because the standard concepts of daily newspaper operation and control were conceived in a time of competition and that they are now to that extent anachronistic. Though it may have been necessary in competitive circumstances to knuckle under to merchants resisting advertising rate increases and though it may be difficult now to realize the seller's market which local monopoly has provided, the strength for tougher bargaining is at hand.

At the same time, it would ignore the intrinsic reader interest in department store advertising itself to think that the stores are without recourse. If they decide the price of newspaper space is too high they can put their advertising in circulars distributed house to house, diverting subsidies received from national advertisers to that purpose. Their present concentration in newspapers is a habit of convenience that fits promotions based on price and price-lining; it follows an established pattern. But they have enormous financial resources to experiment with if they come to believe that increased advertising rates tend to limit their own profits unduly. They will not have to worry so long as newspaper firms sit piggyback on a huge typographical and printing complex designed for volume production and likely to go broke if the pace or the volume slackens. Modern businessmen have long since become the prisoners of the machines they own. As John S. Knight told the Inland Daily Press Association after selling the Chicago *Daily News*, "the danger signals are up for all newspapers — large or small — which fail in the management, sales, distribution and product tests."

The newspaper that survives, he says, must be bright and interesting, distributed so that it is easily available to all potential readers, containing advertising that is resourceful, creative, and aggressive. Its business management must be truly informed about costs, personnel problems, and labor contracts, able to cope with problems that did not exist twenty-five years ago. He goes on:

The newspaper has lagged behind all other industries in research and technological advances. There is continuing publisher inertia to advance in new printing, stereotyping, engraving, composing room and mailing room improvements.

We have failed to convince unions that we have a mutuality of interest. A new approach is needed to the problem of personnel. It is much too costly these days to be careless and casual in the hiring of new help. Once on the payroll, they have a way of staying . . . since terminations are expensive and department heads dislike admitting mistakes.

Finally, he said, newspaper selling and promotion leave a lot to be desired.[45]

The difficulties outlined promise meaningful careers to bright young men interested in solving problems in a business intimately linked to the public welfare. The fates of democracy and of public communication appear to be closely intertwined.

MASS COMMUNICATION CONTENT

W HEN journalism abandoned politics for business as a way of making a living it switched its personality from that of crusader trying to organize, teach, and change the people and the community to that of entrepreneur trying to make a good living with a minimum of trouble.

Except for uncharacteristic reaction to the regime of Franklin D. Roosevelt — which was motivated by unaccustomed government regulation of business — passive non-involvement in critical problems is journalism's outstanding quality. Few of the editors of mass-circulation newspapers since 1830 have risked their careers to exert strong leadership in the community, though Greeley and Pulitzer were activists who departed from the pattern. As a consequence Greeley's life is a model of knight-errantry and political frustration. Pulitzer was at war with evil — as he defined it — from beginning to end, but no one would argue that he was a happy man secure in the bosom of his community. McCormick of the Chicago *Tribune*, though he gets scant credit for strength because he was conservative rather than liberal, was a bold and fearless crusader.

Neutralism more common than activism. These three are leading examples of an unknown number of exceptions to the rule of non-involvement, a number unknown because the newspapers are highly local in character and their reputations are for the most part locked up in the communities where they are published. The neutralist in a community controversy not only is certain to be criticized by one or all parties to an argument, but he will find it hard to get sympathy when he defends himself. This has been the lot of the press. The press is neutralist because its content grows out of prepossession with the market rather than concern for causes and goals.

100

Owners select the content of their media to achieve a position of profit and security in the market; in so doing, they use a system of personal values that guides them in evaluating the choices turned up by the market. In this book we have now established a reasonable understanding of the market conditions under which proprietors work; we must now achieve equal understanding of the interplay of the value systems of journalism, the trade customs and assumptions which affect content, and the conscience-linked norms and group and community-based influences that are manifest through personal or economic pressures.

In reaching this understanding we must be aware of the basic assumption of our society that the media should be privately owned and operated, that under this form of control they will mirror for society, in analytical and logical clarity, the problems that cry out for attention. What follows describes society's complaints about public communication services. Since this criticism arises in opposition to the ruling standards of the subculture of journalism, some care is taken here to provide explanations from the internal frame of reference. A sort of dialog between the press and society ensues, one part of which reveals keen anxiety about the adequacy of our basic social control structure. It is from this anxiety that criticism of press performance arises. The author shares that anxiety and looks upon the press as the one social institution in a position to help renovate and perpetuate the system of personal values which, taken in the aggregate, make free society possible. If individuals will not voluntarily act in the long-run community interest, as well as in the short-run selfish interest, either coercion must be applied or the community declines in viability. For this reason, at the end of the dialog between the press, anxious about its freedom, and community leaders, concerned about weaknesses that have appeared in the voluntary control of interpersonal and social relationships, a program of institutional development for the mass media is suggested that will enlist the press directly in social responsibility under conditions consistent with its rejection of official controls.

⸗ CRITICISM OF PRESS CONTENT

Let us turn now to consideration of the content of today's mass media, first hearing two well-known publishers explain what happened inside their firms as advertising became increasingly important, and then turning to critics who are primarily concerned about the effect of the content of the media on society.

101

The Social Responsibility of the Press

The development of the business pattern. Henry J. Allen, editor and publisher of the Wichita *Beacon*, told in 1931 how his newspaper slipped increasingly into a business pattern while he was away serving as governor of Kansas. Trying to evaluate the changes, he named a few great editors of the past and observed that hardly anyone knew their successors. The papers with which their personalities had been intimately identified had become great institutions; they no longer provided the kind of personal career which had made the editors famous. Press associations and syndicates had sharply reduced the amount of locally prepared material. There was less opportunity for the "old-fashioned editor and old-fashioned local contributor to exercise their function, and the American newspapers became so similar to each other that the main distinguishing feature is the date line identifying the place in which they are printed."

Governor Allen said that after World War I and four years in the state capitol he returned to find the editor no longer the most important member of his newspaper staff. He had been superseded by the circulation manager, who was an ally of the advertising manager; these allies talked a great deal about advertising and its new power in the world. The circulation manager had crowded it from the second page to the last with syndicated material, fiction, humor, comic strips, and the kind of photographs known in the trade as cheesecake. "He said, 'Why, Governor, we have done this for reader interest.' I said, 'Well, weren't the readers already interested in the paper? They paid their subscriptions regularly.' 'Oh, yes,' he said, 'but we have added 25 per cent to the volume of our circulation.'"

When Governor Allen still seemed in doubt, his circulation manager said he thought the business manager of the paper was happy with the result and that the paper's banker was well pleased. He and the advertising manager talked much about the growing importance of national advertising.

I wouldn't go so far as to intimate that . . . advertising has affected our courage or our editorial emotions. It has simply absorbed all the spirit of the modern newspaper, changing the emphasis on the enterprise, and bringing us to a point where we contemplate circulation and advertising linage as the most sensational goals which test the success of the newspaper.[1]

At the same meeting at which Governor Allen spoke, Sevellon Brown, managing editor and later publisher of the Providence *Journal*, the founder and first underwriter of the American Press Institute at Columbia Uni-

102

versity, discussed the same trends. After reviewing the tenets of news selection, he anticipated by three decades some of the concern about the press as a symbol of mass society. When an editor attempts to conduct his paper on the democratic basis that it is really owned by the people who pay for it, he said, the "danger of demagoguery is inherent. . . . It is, therefore, a reasonable presumption that every popular publication like a newspaper will to a degree, truckle to the public as well as legitimately cater to it." The owners of newspapers are much affected by what happens to other newspapers and the death of such ideal newspapers as the New York *World* could not be forgotten. The newspapers were drifting toward "that undistinguished and standardized pattern of existence which is characteristic of mass culture," and he wondered if mass education and the consequences of industrialism were not being reflected in media content. He was concerned lest the newspapers seek a sterile neutrality as the most profitable basis of operation.[2]

The views of the social critics. In 1945, Robert M. Hutchins, then chancellor of the University of Chicago, crystallized and formalized much of the post-war criticism, and returned it to its cradle of political idealism, by organizing a private commission that reported on the state of freedom of the press. Six books by competent scholars resulted from the work of the commission: A general report entitled *A Free and Responsible Press*; a thorough legal analysis by Professor Zechariah Chafee, Jr., the leading writer in the field, *Government and Mass Communications*; a study and restatement of press theory by Professor William E. Hocking, *Freedom of Press, A Framework of Principle*; a study of international communication by two staff members, *Peoples Speaking to Peoples; Freedom of the Movies* by Ruth A. Inglis and *The American Radio* by Llewellyn White. The first three books have a timeless quality and remain today the outstanding works that discuss the subject of this present book.

Standards for press performance. The general report laid down a definition of the services the press should perform for the community, as follows:

Today our society needs, first, a truthful, comprehensive, and intelligent account of the day's events in a context which gives them meaning;
Second, a forum for the exchange of comment and criticism;
Third, a means of projecting the opinions and attitudes of the groups in society to one another;
Fourth, a method of presenting and clarifying the goals and values of society; and

Fifth, a way of reaching every member of the society by the currents of information, thought, and feeling which the press supplies.[3]

As may be seen, this set of standards is pure rationalism from the same stream as the *Areopagitica* and Jefferson's ideal of government. As was the case with Milton's presentment to Parliament, these sentences hint not at all of the war of ideas implied by the model of a tournament of reason, but the commission is not unaware of the ugly struggle for dominance of opinion. It takes note of the mechanical and electronic revolution which has reduced to small consequence the time/space separation of peoples and states, and it notes the impact on Miltonic theory of the consolidation of print media and the ownership of print and electronic media by the same persons. It appears to conclude that the machinery of diversity still exists, but that the media lack the will to provide the variety of information and debate that the people need for self-government. It says that motion-picture producers and the owners of most newspapers, magazines, and broadcasting stations are preoccupied with the business aspects of their property, that they are interested in getting the widest possible circulation and apparently ready to settle for standards of content required to reach the masses. In such media, entertainment takes precedence over matters of importance to social understanding and self-government. The urgencies of conciliation between nations and between racial and religious groups at home are minimized or overlooked by media with such a distributive goal. Salestalk through advertising and propaganda in the news constitutes a hazard to clear description and understanding of human problems. Concentration in the media is matched by concentration in business as a whole.

In the midst of the leveling down of communication to reach the masses, the quality of media content has suffered and the understanding of human problems has been overlooked. Ways are needed to bring back to the forefront moral values in human behavior, whether of individuals or governments. The self-regulation of journalists is suggested as a leading possibility, and a warning given that if performance is not improved society will find the media inadequate to its needs and changes will be forced by indignation, disapproval, or rejection of the press — if, indeed, government is not persuaded to step in and perform a monitor-like role. Government, in the meantime, was asked actively to make information available, to speak out and clarify its own programs, and to promote by traditional means increased competition among the units of the media so as to maintain a true market place of thought. The commission urged the removal of legal restraints on individual and group communication and the avoidance of governmental and private threats and intimidation that would discourage self-expression; it suggested that there should be no legal interference with communication important to self-government short of the clear and present danger of violent behavior by participants in the process of communication.

The press was asked to open its services wide enough that in effect it would become a common carrier of information, to experiment with possibilities for improving and increasing the flow of information to the people, and to become sufficiently self-critical that it could recognize and remedy the defects of its own system.

As for the public, the commission asked it to abandon its apparently obtuse lack of interest in the important affairs of the world; to accept the responsibilities implied by self-government; to encourage, through non-profit institutions, universities, centers of advanced study, councils, and foundations, constant analysis of mass communication so as to replace with scrutiny and zeal of this kind the portions of the self-righting mechanism lost through economic and political change. The commission said:

The outside forces of law and public opinion can in various ways check bad aspects of press performance, but good press performance can come only from the human beings who operate the instrumentalities of communication. . . . the preservation of democracy and perhaps of civilization may now depend upon a free and responsible press. Such a press we must have if we would have progress and peace.[4]

Though written before the advent of mass-scale television, the commission's analysis seems now to apply equally to electronic and print media; in fact, one suggestion current for improvement of television programing is the appointment of a national council that would stand between the advertiser and the broadcaster and work to reconcile differences of opinion.

Opinion leaders evaluate the media. Edward L. Bernays, a public relations counsel, made a study for the National Newspaper Promotion Association in 1952 which states the ideals of the press in the language of noted editors and then asks a selected group of contemporary leaders whether the press lives up to those ideals today. Representatives of 213 newspapers out of 1,773 invited and 171 opinion leaders selected from *Who's Who in America* responded to the survey.

Mr. Bernays chose the following statements of Joseph Pulitzer, owner of the St. Louis *Post-Dispatch* and the old New York *World*, Adolph S. Ochs of the New York *Times*, and Thomas Gibson of the old *Rocky Mountain Herald* to send to his survey panel:

Pulitzer (from his message to his staff on April 10, 1907): [The *Post-Dispatch* is] an institution that should always fight for progress and reform, never tolerate injustice and corruption, always fight demagogues of all parties, never belong to any party, always oppose privileged classes and public plunderers, never lack sympathy with the poor, always remain devoted to the public welfare, never be satisfied with merely printing news, always be drastically independent, never be afraid to attack wrong, whether by predatory plutocracy or predatory poverty.

Ochs (from his statement in the *Times* of August 18, 1896, upon assuming control): It will be my earnest aim that the New York *Times* give the news, all the news, in concise and attractive form, in language that is permissible in good society, and give it early, if not earlier, than it can be learned through any other medium. To give the news impartially, without fear or favor, regardless of party, sect, or interest involved; to make the columns of the New York *Times* a forum for the consideration of all public questions of public importance, and to that end, to invite intelligent discussion for all shades of opinion.

Gibson (from his salutatory of the *Rocky Mountain Herald*, Denver, May 1, 1860): A newspaper untrammeled by sinister influence from any quarter — the advocate of the right and the denouncer of the wrong — an independent vehicle for the free expression of opinions of all candid, honest and intelligent minds — a medium of free discussion, moral, religious, social and scientific.[5]

Mr. Bernays asked the leaders and newspaper publishers whether the goals set by Pulitzer, Ochs, and Gibson still were valid, and the overwhelming response (94 and 95 per cent) said they were. He then asked if the newspapers today, by and large, meet the ideals set forth. The replies were distributed as shown in the accompanying tabulation.

	Group Leaders	Newspaper Proprietors
Yes	47%	68%
No	44	25
In part	9	7

Bernays asked which American newspapers most nearly live up to the ideals stated. The newspaper proprietors listed 261 different publications and the group leaders named 129. When the top ten publications mentioned by each group are given a percentile rank calculated from the combined mentions of the two groups the result is as shown in Table 5. When

Table 5. Ten Modern Newspapers Which Best
Meet Pulitzer-Ochs-Gibson Ideals, as Named by
Newspaper Proprietors and Group Leaders

Paper	Percentage in Both Groups Mentioning This Paper
New York *Times*	93.0
St. Louis *Post-Dispatch*	64.0
New York *Herald-Tribune*	50.0
Christian Science Monitor	49.5
Washington *Post*	35.0
Louisville *Courier-Journal*	30.5
Kansas City *Star*	29.5
Baltimore *Sun*	23.5

the group leaders and newspaper proprietors were asked to list the ways in which modern papers deviate from the ideals of Pulitzer, Ochs, and Gibson and to rank the deviations in the order of their frequency, the replies were distributed as shown in Table 6.

The Bernays survey has obvious imperfections in sampling but when allowance is made for its probable bias it remains as a sincere response of editors and group leaders to questions about the ideal performance of the press. A survey of the literature validates the Bernays report as representative of contemporary criticism of the mass media even if not representative of the public at large.

Claims of political bias. Since political bias heads the list of deviations from the stated ideals, let James A. Wechsler, editor of the New York *Post*, speak for the minority through the *Bulletin* of the American Society of Newspaper Editors, February 1, 1957, page 5.

Table 6. Modern Newspapers' Deviations from Pulitzer-Ochs-Gibson Ideal, as Named by Newspaper Proprietors and Group Leaders

Deviation	Newspaper Proprietors	Group Leaders
Political bias	22%	18%
Failure to perform public service	20	8
Slanting the news	20	33
Response to economic pressures	17	8
Bias and self-interest of publisher	7	6
Pressure groups (not otherwise defined)	4	2
Sensationalism	0	12
Miscellaneous (chiefly details of news treatment and use of syndicated material)	10	13

The Social Responsibility of the Press

Wechsler said his complaint is simple:

The American press is overwhelmingly owned and operated by Republicans who fix the rules of U.S. political debate. And I use the word "fix" advisedly.

I know it is a freer press than any prevailing in Communist or fascist countries; but that is nothing to be complacent about. It is a press that has generally grown comfortable, fat and self-righteous; and which with some noteworthy exceptions voices the prejudices and preconceptions of entrenched wealth rather than those qualities of critical inquiry and rebellious spirit we associate with our noblest journalistic traditions.

It is a press that is generally more concerned with the tax privileges of any fat cat than with the care and feeding of any underdog.

It is a press that sanctimoniously boasts of its independence and means by that its right to do what its Republican owners damn please. The press used to be regarded as a public trust, not a private playground.

It is a press that is far more forthright and resolute in combatting Communist tyranny in Hungary than in waging the fight for freedom in the United States.

. . . Frankly, I am weary of listening to lectures about the virtues of our newspapers or magazines. They manipulate news; they select their big stories and bury others; they pontificate about the purity of their news columns and yet few of them are willing to risk real debate about the great issues of our time. . . .

I speak with some passion on this matter. I value my profession. It is the only one I know. But this I also know — that there are only a handful of newspapers in America on which liberal newspapermen could hold a policy-making position without selling their souls.

However we look at the anxiety about the content of the media, as educators, businessmen, ministers of religion, labor leaders, writers on economics, liberal editors of newspapers, specialists in foreign policy, it is much the same. If we divide the criticism into historical periods — 1900 to 1930, 1930 to 1945, 1945 to the present — we find little difference in pattern, though changing national problems give a different turn or twist. It becomes clear, after reading and listening, that the press occupies a position in which group and individual frustrations of all kinds are readily referred or transferred to it. If the Democrats lose, the fault is the bias of the publishers; if the Republicans lose, it is the bias of the underling journalists who warp the news.

Other professions view the press. Men of religion, who have one of the most serious and important social assignments of all, feel that the press is "basically ignorant of the true meaning and contemporary usefulness of

108

religious news." The press fails to recognize the significance of ecclesiastical affairs apart from denominational conflict.[6] Educators, through their journals, express fears of advertising's influence on the media and they try to teach their pupils to analyze propaganda. They are much puzzled when students turn the techniques on teacher.[7] Businessmen are dissatisfied that the media are not more zealous in explaining, advocating, and even crusading for business in its battle with government.[8] Citizens close to foreign relations problems want the press to take the lead in stirring interest, understanding, and discussion of foreign policy, even though they admit the government fails to release much information needed for logical consideration. The chauvinistic attitude of the press keeps the public from learning about possible alternatives in our national policy. We rearm the Germans without discussing the consequences. We do not consider on their merits the proposals from the other side.[9] The people have been assured so often that the Soviet Union is about to collapse, and that the Russian people do not support their government, that none of us can now understand why the opposite appears to be true. We hold ideological prejudices, taught to us by the press, and are blind to the facts.[10]

The journalists who report great and complex events are not particularly qualified by training or experience to do so. They seem to feel that a strong pair of legs and a sharp pencil qualify them for any informational task, be it writing about sports, atomic energy, or economic theory. Lacking a fund of information upon which they can rely in such diverse situations, some become captives of bland spokesmen for special interests who can supply words and phrases to fill the gap.[11] When Khrushchev comes to America, the people and the media are not prepared emotionally for the experience and they both mess it up. So many reporters and cameramen try to cover the story, without advance preparation, that all they can do is to interview each other while Khrushchev's Iowa-farmer host throws fodder at the journalistic mob.[12] When the work of contemporary journalism is viewed in the context of the concept of Milton's market place of thought, it is asserted that the most prized yardstick of journalism, objectivity, is just a means of avoiding the responsibility of finding and printing the truth, routing out and revealing biases and selfish interests. As an institution, the press is big, fat, happy, and satisfied. It no longer digs for news but takes publicity handouts and passes them off as its own work. At a time when the society is changing from top to bottom, the press is not helping the people understand what is happening. To get at the heart of the news takes too much trouble and costs too much. To help the people find centers of power and make themselves felt on matters of policy seems no longer a journalistic duty.[13] Journalists print wire news and syndicated material and don't even realize their neglect of important problems. Some observers say that there is no security for this kind of newspaper, but the prevailing trade theory apparently assumes that newspapers with aggressive news and editorial policies are the least secure of all. Not so, say those who publish such newspapers; Elmer Davis was right, the nation was not built by cowards and will not be preserved by them.[14] The newspapers are sensitive and can't take criticism. Some men with executive power, particularly in absentee-run publications and broadcasting operations, ruthlessly chase out editors and writers who call for improvement of the media and of society.[15]

What the people want. Survey experts like Elmo Roper, who study what the people want, think the news media are giving the people just about what they like. If any more hard news were supplied, it wouldn't really be appreciated. The lower section of the public, as classified by educational preparation, wants a newspaper that is easy to read, that has a good sports page, and that over all is lively and interesting. The middle group wants to be kept well informed through a "good family paper" and likes the sports page. The top group wants information and sports and a good editorial page. Women find that advertising is the thing they miss most when they can't have a newspaper. The public isn't really concerned about monopoly and bigness in communications, but it is wary of the misuse of bigness, and perhaps that is just as well, because the monopoly papers are better all around than those that have to scream for attention and scramble for street sales. No one likes monopoly, but radio and television do serve as real competitors of newspapers and help prod editors into doing their job well.[16]

⟨ COMPARISON OF LEADING PAPERS

Does the foregoing tell only one side of the story? Is the press, or any part of it, meeting these constructive challenges? Do some parts of the mass media system come to grips intellectually with the problems of the modern world?

The answer is yes, but we really do not know as much about the press as a positive and authoritative answer would require. The newspapers and broadcasting stations are hidden away in the nooks and crannies of our industrial towns and cities, isolated in their own corn and wheat fields and cattle ranches, so difficult to get at in any meaningful way that most have not been studied at all, none of them particularly well. Some of the critics argue that the defects reviewed here can be seen without expert measurement. But is the press so easy to analyze and to judge? Let's take a sample of such analysis, a classification of the content of forty daily newspapers in the March 1960 issue of *Social Progress*, a publication of the United Presbyterian Church in the U.S.A. The study intended to show how the reading matter was divided among such categories as accidents and crime; business, economics, finance; community education, housing, health; human relations, civil liberties; international relations; state and national politics; and sports. The staff members doing the work reported ruefully that it took three to five hours to read and measure only one edition of one newspaper, and they started out to deal with forty newspapers for a period of two weeks!

Bias in the surveys. We shall not go into difficulties here that experts report in training workers so that each one classifies items more or less alike; we shall assume that the work was well done. What does the survey show? The authors say it shows that readers of papers in the Atlantic coastal area and around the Great Lakes are "served considerably better" with international news than residents in other areas. The papers with a high count of sensational items were rebuked, the New York *Times* and the *Christian Science Monitor*, using very little of this material, were praised. Other newspapers singled out for praise were the Baltimore *Sun*, the Washington *Post and Times Herald*, the Milwaukee *Journal*, the Minneapolis *Tribune*, the Salt Lake City *Tribune* and the Spokane *Spokesman-Review*.

Let us arrange the data so that we can make value judgments of our own:

How much news of crime and violence do the papers print? The lowest quartile gave .2 to 5.9 per cent of space to news of this category; the second quartile gave 6.4 to 9 per cent; the third quartile 9.6 to 13.6 per cent, and the top quartile, 13.8 to 51.6 per cent. The median percentage of space was 9.3, the minimum .2 (*Christian Science Monitor*) and the maximum 51.6 per cent (New York *Post*).

We can move on through the categories: community education, housing, and health — minimum, 1.1 (New York *Herald-Tribune*), maximum 26.2 per cent (Jacksonville *Journal*), median for this category, 7.15 per cent;

111

international relations — minimum, 2.0 (Detroit *Times*), maximum, 36.2 (*Christian Science Monitor*), median, 7.15; sports — minimum, 8.1 (New York *Times*), maximum, 37.2 (San Francisco *Chronicle*), median, 23.5.

New definitions, new values. Now let us use our average scores to rank the papers from 1 to 40. In so doing, shall we give the paper with the most sports news the rank of No. 1 in that category, or the rank of No. 40? It makes a great deal of difference and here's why: if we decide that the more sports the better, as millions of readers apparently do, the first ten papers, averaging all categories, are Baltimore *Sun*, Cleveland *Press*, Jacksonville *Journal*, Dallas *News*,* Milwaukee *Journal*,* Minneapolis *Tribune*,* Nashville *Tennessean*, New Orleans *Times-Picayune*, St. Petersburg (Florida) *Times*, Washington *Post and Times Herald.**

If we decide that heavy use of sports news deprives the reader of other information of great importance, the best ten papers on the list of forty are Dallas *News*,* Louisville *Times*, New York *Times*, Washington *Post and Times Herald*, *Christian Science Monitor*, Milwaukee *Journal*,* Minneapolis *Tribune*,* Des Moines *Register*, Great Falls *Tribune*, Los Angeles *Times*.

The papers marked with an asterisk appear in both lists. The rank in all categories other than sports is maintained. When sports is given the first or premium value, the papers on the bottom of the list of forty, when all categories are averaged, included some of the world's best known: Detroit *News*, New York *Herald-Tribune*, Philadelphia *Bulletin*, Atlanta *Constitution*, Chicago *Daily News*, Kansas City *Times*, Kansas City *Star*.

Judgments are imprecise. Similar weightings affect the judgment of every person, lay or expert, who attempts to study the press. The resulting distortion does not mean that ventures in evaluation are hopeless; it means that the units of value differ for every individual and for every newspaper and that judgment of the press's performance must be understood to be based on this kind of imperfect measurement. Let us remind ourselves that the press is not an institution separable from society, from the business community, or from the millions who love amateur and professional sports, and that it may not be separately judged.

⟩ THE PUBLISHER AS CITIZEN

Erwin D. Canham, editor of the *Christian Science Monitor*, long before he served a term as president of the Chamber of Commerce of the United

States, praised the service contribution of businessmen to the community, a service in which newspapermen certainly share.

Each kind of organization [social or special interest] has an important bearing on free society, and each kind has expanded and progressed enormously in the last few decades. If citizens in American communities had not accepted the obligation of meeting social needs voluntarily, through community funds and service organizations, government inevitably would have stepped in. The amount of time the typical good citizen gives to community service is often impressive and astonishing. There is many a business leader who donates just about as much time and energy to non-official, unremunerated, voluntary activities as he does to his job. And more often than not, this extracurricular work has a deeper influence than his job on the community and on society as a whole.

Such a typical business man is a director of the chamber of commerce, a trustee of one or more colleges, a member of the community fund board, a director of one or more national philanthropies, a member of a fraternal order. He may be a man who is active in a church, a member of a service club, a man vigorous in some political work, a supporter of a boys' club, an active patron of the arts. This formidable list is probably a modest statement of the public-service activities of an average American business or professional man. All of us could name individuals who carry an even larger load.[17]

Canham says the modern businessman is eager to confront and solve community problems, for he realizes that if these problems had been faced in the past the nation would not be in such difficulty today. He is aware that his decisions affect the people of the community and he judges their welfare along with his own. He realizes his interdependence with others and accepts the relationship as his incentive to social responsibility. The result is "a deeply spiritual doctrine stemming straight from religious traditions and conventions of mankind."

Newspaper publishers and editors are participators in their communities in the way that Canham describes. Occupying a central position in the community, they feel first and strongly the impact of dislocations, rivalries, neglects, and needs, and it is up to them and the business community of which they are a part to come forward with a constructive program if one is devised.

John Cowles interprets changes in the press. Publishers have analyzed the argument that the condition of monopoly in most of our cities threatens the free exchange of information. One of them, Barry Bingham, already has been quoted. Another, whose newspapers have appeared twice on lists

113

herein of publications doing a superior job of news handling, is John Cowles of the Minneapolis *Star* and *Tribune*. While serving as honorary president of Sigma Delta Chi, national professional journalistic fraternity, Mr. Cowles spoke about the record of monopoly papers.

Newspapers have enormously improved in the last three or four decades, he said, and there are few traces of the bad conditions at the turn of the century. There is no longer a kept press of any significance, and marginal newspapers have almost disappeared. Today, Cowles said, the social problem is to manage for the public good something (in this case newspapers) which is by nature monopolistic. With few exceptions the best newspapers do not have competition in the same field, and the publishers have deeper feelings of responsibility because they are alone in their fields. He defined "best newspapers" as "the most responsibly edited, the fairest, the most complete, the most accurate, the best written and the most objective." "The paper that is alone in the field can present the news in better perspective, and resist pressure for immediacy which makes for incomplete, shoddy, or premature reporting . . . and are less inhibited about correcting their own errors fully and fairly."

Quality and breadth of material. Cowles observes that there is considerable competition from television, radio, news magazines, labor papers, community papers, daily papers from outside the community, that minimizes the danger of suppression of new ideas and points of view. Besides, he says, a really bad monopoly paper will soon have newspaper competition.

The public is aware of intrinsic quality in today's newspapers, and the good papers have been gaining circulation while those in the same markets that feature partisanship or sensational news have been losing. In part this trend may be due to television, which specializes in entertainment, but the trend is very clear.

On another occasion, Cowles told how he wanted his staff to handle the news:

"We are trying to report the news, all of it, in our news columns as honestly and fairly and intelligently as we can." The goal is "to appeal to people of both sexes, of all ages, of all vocations and all educational levels . . . We are trying to serve the highest common denominator of our readers' interest, not the lowest, and we are constantly trying to raise the common denominator."

Cowles said his staff was a trailblazer in exploring such "neglected areas of news as education, and science, and religion, and of government as contrasted with news of politics."

The ideal journalist. A newspaper, he said, is an educational institution. Most Americans are out of school by age eighteen and thereafter what they learn comes from the press.

"A good newspaper reporter, whether in the field of science, government, industrial relations, education, politics, religion or crime news, ought to know as much in his field as a good college instructor knows in his . . . A good reporter should be as objective and as untiring in his pursuit of truth as a scientist doing research work at a university." This, at least, was the goal toward which he and his associates were striving. He felt the men of this description would be entitled to somewhat more latitude to plan and do their own work than has been customary in the past. "If a newspaper is staffed by men of high professional competence whose basic journalistic philosophy is similar the newspaper is better off if the team is driven with loose reins." [18]

The publisher fears misunderstanding. Very few publishers have taken occasion, as Cowles has done, to explain their goals and motivations. The reason most others fail to acknowledge criticism and deal with it systematically is that they feel they are doing a reasonably good job for the community and if they take time out to defend themselves there is no one else to do their daily work. The writing man — as typified by the members of the Commission on Freedom of the Press, who individually and collectively achieved the highest positions open to such men — is fortunately able to combine business and social criticism in the day's work. Such men are dedicated to building a new Jerusalem, one free of many of the defects of the old community. To them this activity is freedom, the unfettered cooperative activity of hearts voluntarily engaged in a common enterprise of great value.

For the newspaper proprietor and journalist, freedom is achieved through the daily operation of an independent profit-making firm. The freedom they desire is to ask individual citizens and government officials to reply to pertinent questions, to print the answers honestly, and afterward to receive the protection of the community against reprisal. Their job is to describe the city; it is up to the community to alter or rebuild it.

A few editors and publishers are striving to persuade others to cooperate in systematic study and evaluation of content and performance, looking upon truth as the greatest defense, but the great majority is still gun-

115

shy. Sigma Delta Chi, national professional journalistic fraternity, tried in 1956 to launch a study of national election-news coverage under the direction of scholarly content analysts. The proposal was presented to a "jury" of seventy-five editors and publishers for approval in advance of soliciting financial support for the work. The result was an overwhelming rejection of the study, with thirty-five editors opposed, nineteen favorable, eight favorable with significant reservations, two noncommittal, twelve not voting. The replies of opponents showed that they based their judgment largely on a misunderstanding of systematic methods and distrust of social scientists in general. Partly open and partly concealed is the feeling that nobody, not even social scientists, has any business holding the press up to any non-journalistic system of artificial judgment; the real judges are presumed to be the readers and they alone should make decisions of this sort.[19]

Here are two views representative of the cooperators and the opponents among the jury of seventy-six journalists:

Turner Catledge, managing editor of the New York *Times*, said:

While we are not too hopeful about the results that can be obtained . . . we are willing to assume that a useful job could be done and for that purpose to co-operate with those carrying it out . . . Because of the broad scope of the proposal and the danger that the complexities of its research techniques will cause it to lose touch with reality, we feel that it is most important that the entire project be put under the direction of an executive committee which will include not only experts in research but also practical newspaper men and individuals with experience in public affairs.

Norman Chandler, president of the Los Angeles *Times*, said:

This is in effect an invitation to join an organization of thought police for newspapers. [The part] which proposes that editors explain . . . why they did thus and thus . . . would put almost any editor on defense, impair his judgment and destroy intuition . . . In consenting to such an analysis . . . a newspaper would acknowledge, at least by implication, that certain obligations can be imposed on it from outside. And this should not be . . . A newspaper is a public service but not a public utility.[20]

A critique of the critics. The builder of a new Jerusalem is obliged by the rules of his intellectual craft to plan for all of the people and to seek wider opportunity for growth and self-expression. This obligation would practically guarantee, even without other considerations, that no new Jerusalem popular with the liberal community could be more or less the same as the old one. Criticism, rejection of the status quo, is strongly indicated, though not required. As for journalists, they, too, have biases built into their way of doing things: service to both the community and to selfish interests means compromises to minimize public interference with newspaper publishing. Selfish interest can be, and often is, interpreted as being close to the general interest of the community; nevertheless, self-preservation is an immutable urge and it is not prevailingly altruistic.

Scholars work with words; businessmen and other activists work with people. The difference between the two procedures is not commonly respected — certainly it is too little recognized in the literature of social criticism. Reason is supposed to space out the scholar's words and to determine their meaning; his concepts are to be judged in terms of logic and closeness to reality. Yet the scholar rarely meets in breadth and depth the full range of meaning that the practical leader finds in his efforts to relate people and to adjust institutions.

Critics Write, Publishers Act. The owner of a newspaper or other mass medium works with people as well as with words. He must start and end each day in conference with persons — employees, businessmen, government officials, professional men, community leaders. Each person has a different definition of reality and of freedom — that is, a different set of personal needs and values. From each of them the publisher or his agent must win consent to a proposal that requires a balancing of interests. From the government official he must get not only news, but news that may damage the personal interests of the official; from the department-store owner he must win purchase of large advertising space on a promise that it will bring customers to the store; from the subscribing reader or voluntary viewer he must each day win renewed attention.

The scholar and the activist are useful to each other because they can discuss alternatives to decisions taken during the daily person-to-person negotiations in active life. It is easier to transpose or erase words, to rewrite sentences, to edit paragraphs, even when the writing represents a faithful effort to capture reality, than it is to stand face to face with other persons, to interest and persuade them. Moving or shifting people from a conviction is far more expensive in time and energy. The owner of a large-scale newspaper and his employees must make such face-to-face persuasions hundreds of times each day. It is no wonder that the new Jerusalem, as a rule, has less appeal to them than continued work on improvement of the present city. The scope of their concern for the welfare of the community is limited by interests of the firm; even though broadly interpreted, this condition practically guarantees the cross-interest, multi-group approach of the scholar against obsolescence.

All Papers Are Different. When standards of criticism are applied to the mass media, they can deal properly with only one unit at a time — one newspaper, one magazine, one radio or television station. There are fragmentary studies of reading, listening, or viewing, inventories of content or of reading; but systematic evaluation of a publication or broadcasting station with a visible scale of values is very rare.[21]

Expert opinion is reliable and useful, even though presented in subjective rather than systematic form, and constitutes our best guide at this time to press performance. The difficulty with the present situation is that there are several kinds of expert in this case who use highly specialized information in one field to judge a complex institution lying largely outside the scope of their experience. The Hutchins commission was quite frank about this; it excluded technically trained and professionally qualified journalists from the commission. Apparently the assumption is that the press system cannot be criticized in terms of professional insight, but only by individuals who, though they have not come to understand it, wish to impose upon it the standards and values of their own personal frame of reference.

A Dispute over Values. This is tantamount to adopting the position of Norman Chandler in reverse, and makes clear that proprietors and Mr. Hutchins have differences which are irreconcilable. Mr. Hutchins' point of view, as a moralist, evidently is that lawyers, philosophers, poets, statisticians, political scientists, and ministers of religion cannot undertake critical evaluation of the press within the frame of reference of professional journalism, and to attempt to do so would destroy their intuition as to what ought to be done and what it is possible to do. Thus the pro-press and anti-press groups are at loggerheads and a fission seems to be called for — the development of social scientists who can bring the best of moral ideals to the task of measuring a press system which they understand because they, too, have experienced the limitations of dealing face to face with members of the public in the context of the free-enterprise economic and political system. The reader who looks through these pages will find that the beginnings of such study already is visible, for among the critics of press performance are editors, publishers, and journalists whose conclusions are derived from successful careers as professional men as well as from the ideals of the community.

118

↑ THE INFLUENCE OF RADIO AND TELEVISION NETWORKS

Radio and television from the beginning have been visible to the general community as national and international media in contrast to the localism of the newspapers. The higher visibility arises perhaps in the early development of the network broadcasting system which relegates individual stations to the status of subordinate personalities. National advertising support has been intrinsic to the development of the chains. Uniting programing and advertising in one system of control means in the case of television that the features which built station prestige and account for more than half of all revenue come from one customer. It will be recalled that a quarter of a typical newspaper's advertising revenue came from eight or ten large advertisers and that eighty to a hundred firms may provide virtually all of the income a daily with 100,000 circulation receives from display advertising. Yet the papers derive a third of their revenue from readers, and 10 to 15 per cent from a host of small classified accounts. Radio network revenues have been cut to 10 per cent of the total by television competition, forcing the medium to build a diversified local clientele like that of display advertising in newspapers.

The newspapers have had telegraph news networks since 1854, when the New York publishers became associated in gathering outside news. From the start, however, the newspapers have controlled the press association networks through the cooperative ownership form of the Associated Press or through stock ownership such as that of Scripps-Howard in United Press Associations and its successor, United Press International.

Network control of station policy. The decisions affecting Associated Press service have been made on a national, regional, and state basis by representatives of the members who own it and pay for the service. The Associated Press has never had anything to do with the sale and service of advertising, although performance of this function would have seemed natural enough and has been associated with news distribution from time to time in Europe. This difference in ownership and the separation from advertising has prevented the press association from playing the same role in newspapers that the networks have had in radio and television. The availability of Associated Press news alone, however, is a great economic and prestige asset, as the evidence in the anti-trust case shows.[22]

Diversity of station ownership. Federal regulation of radio and television has brought about national consideration of network practices and reporting of industry problems, adding still further to the appearance of

119

a unified communications business in contrast to the parochialism of the newspapers. However, the history of business and public utility regulation indicates that the administrative boards tend to become industry-minded rather than user-oriented. The natural effects of propinquity are strengthened by pressures exerted through the Congress, many of which represent minority views defeated when regulatory laws originally were enacted. Thus the FCC's tortured efforts to promote diversity in the ownership of the various agencies of mass communication have been checked by the influence of committees in Congress and strong political pressures against the agency.[23] The courts have on occasion gone as far in inviting FCC to make more of the public policy of diversity as they could under their authority to review administrative decisions. At present, however, as FCC rulings, upheld by the courts, make clear diversity is only one of many factors considered in granting licenses.[24] Rules of the commission prevent one licensee from holding more than one radio and one television license in each community. Ownership, operation, or control directly of more than seven AM, seven FM, or seven television (no more than five of which may be in the ultra-high frequency band) broadcasting stations by any party constitutes, in the language of the rule, "concentration of control contrary to the public interest," and even minor stock interest holdings or official links to more than fourteen AM, twelve FM, or ten television broadcasting stations are prohibited.

Political pressure affects the FCC. Former Chairman James Lawrence Fly of FCC says that pressure on the commission from newspapers and owners of stations is very intense — right down to the grass roots — when proposals to encourage diversity, that is to limit concentration and cross-channel ownership, are under active consideration. The newspapers and stations are generators of discussion and influential in the formation of public opinion; they are of importance to members of the Congress when they run for office and when difficult issues arise that need to be talked out by the public.

The FCC has not released figures on that part of broadcast revenues currently going to capital invested in both multi-station and cross-channel properties, but it does show that television chains and stations they own and operate had 49 per cent of the revenues in 1957 and 50.2 per cent in 1958. The FCC rule limits the amount of time in a broadcast day that the networks may put under option and has several times considered elimination of option time altogether.[25] FCC figures show that in 1955–56 networks occupied 51.4 per cent of the time of all stations, both affiliated and non-affiliated, and during prime evening hours CBS and NBC took 91 per cent of the time of affiliated stations, or 80 per cent of all broadcast time.[26] Fly says FCC controls are so loosely held that the networks and stations feel it is their air.[27] Only three stations have lost their licenses under government regulation and there has been, until now, no serious attempt to hold licensees to the promises of public service made at the time of original application. Under Chairman Newton N. Minow, however, the FCC has begun a program of audits of the actual programing against the promises made upon application and says it will consider the answers filed when renewing licenses. Minow, who achieved great publicity shortly after appointment by terming television programing a "vast wasteland," says that censorship is not contemplated. The commission is just asking the stations to set forth their programing proposals when asking for a license and then is comparing the performance with the promises, he says.[28] He adds that if the stations want a permanent lease, rather than one renewable on a showing of merit, they should ask the Congress for it.

Minow said he thinks Ibsen, Shakespeare, or Shaw would not have been acceptable to advertisers if they had been writing for television. "At the same time, the amount of violence, murder, mayhem and sadism on television shows increases because, in somebody's opinion — the sponsor's, or the agency's or the network's — the ratings demand a jolt." This, he reiterated, is not in the public interest.[29] The FCC chairman said that a comparison of promises and performance was in the interest of the responsible broadcasters as well as the public, and he said the broadcasters would also be asked how many public service programs offered by the networks were refused in order to take commercial bookings with a higher rating.

The high cost of obtaining permits. Fly makes a number of other significant complaints about conditions within the broadcast industry. Advertising agencies that are large users of time on networks apply their bargaining power, he says, to get the time spots they want for other advertising on local stations. Selling prices of stations, based in large part on network affiliation, have become so high that only well-financed applicants now dare compete for licenses. Sometimes as much as $100,000 is spent even by unsuccessful applicants for television permits. Fly finds evidence that the networks are reluctant to buy programs from independent producers.

Advertising influence on programs. David Susskind, one of these producers, explains these difficulties as getting access to good time slots for material above the level of westerns and stereotyped drama. However, he believes the situation is improving. "Broadcasting is a dynamic business and the two years (1960–1962) have brought significant changes in television." [30] Fly thinks that local stations should have more freedom to do their own programing and a correlative responsibility for doing it well. They use too much film under the guise of network operations. Together with the networks, they show a preference for program talent that is under network control. Dominant advertisers have far too much influence, even control, and occupy too much of the broadcast day. Discussion and opinion shows are too greatly influenced by sponsors, and the prevailing hope seems to be to get an audience without touching on problems that are controversial.

The Behavior of Broadcasters. In short, the patrons of the television industry and the managers of chains and stations alike lack courage to deal with ugly and difficult public issues. This has led to the use of weather-vane tests as a substitute for criteria derived from talent and intrinsic content value, and slant and bias in public affairs discussion. Clifford Durr, former member of the FCC, says the guiding considerations are (1) how do you get the most people interested and (2) how do you avoid making anybody sore? [31] Durr says that questions as to what people want are generally answered in terms of what they are getting. Local stations don't employ creative talent. The average for the country as a whole is half a musician and a third of an actor. It is some such condition as this which prompts the International Typographical Union to require resetting in local shops of some materials, but neither the unions nor public preference are sufficiently strong to force the use of local writers in place of those working for syndicates. Newspapers don't sell the whole paper to advertisers, but the stations sell everything, Durr says. Could stations be required to sell only the time needed for reading of the commercial and come to be responsible for the quality of the material in between, he asks? Durr regards this as an appropriate question since the press has only an ethical responsibility for content while stations have a legal responsibility as occupants of public property. Somewhere down the line, Durr says the FCC has to inflict the death penalty on unworthy stations to show that public regulation is based on standards and means something.

Response to Public Criticism. Broadcasting had a great season of soul-searching after a congressional investigation showed widespread fraud in quiz programs, the payment of money and the giving of favors to secure special privileges for makers of records and businesses of several other kinds. The National Association of Broadcasters and the networks amended their rules to forbid the practices discovered and there was virtually a clean sweep of quiz shows from the air. Several producers of such shows, and numerous disc jockeys, were discharged for culpability in the several kinds of unethical conduct found. The only criterion of right and wrong used by the guilty persons, said Edward P. Morgan, American Broadcasting Company commentator, was last night's audience rating. Ethics, morality, honor, truth, were equally sacrificed to popularity.[32] Morgan feels that the headlong rush to bigness of audience and of the business organizations that control the medium has condoned program appeal that makes no contribution to our culture and perhaps even degrades it. "Each news, advertising and entertainment medium is an exponent of big business because it is big business itself." Maybe the media need government competition, Morgan says, adding that he rejects the idea. The wire services that supply both print and electronic media are an "assembly line operation with a curse on it, too — the curse of superficiality, sensation and mediocrity." The general cast of foreign news coverage is chauvinistic and reporters see only those events churned up by conflict.[33]

The Views of Edward R. Murrow. As Morgan's comments show, television, like the newspapers, has among its leaders men and women who are dedicated to improvement of their medium as part of their personal commitment to democratic society and their patriotic concern for the country's leadership in world affairs. Edward R. Murrow analyzes his profession with the same earnestness that he gives to other social institutions. A homogenized gruel of entertainment, flecked with the desiccated parsley of the news, is evidence of decadence, escapism, and insulation from realities of the world in which we live, he thinks. Murrow regarded the Russian military, economic and propaganda threat as a mortal danger to America, and he wanted the great mass television audience between seven and ten P.M. to learn the facts he thought they needed for survival. As it is, these people are being shielded from anything unpleasant. Murrow says:

I have reason to know that when the evidence on a controversial subject is fairly and calmly presented, the public recognizes it for what it is — an effort to illuminate rather than to agitate. If radio news has to be regarded as a commodity, only acceptable when saleable, and only when packaged

123

to fit the advertising appropriation of a sponsor, then I don't care what you call it, I say it isn't news.

Stations and networks cut back on staff for news and public affairs at the first signs of business decline even though profits are at a peak, he says. The newspapers and magazines are the only uncriticized instruments of mass communication and radio and television could supply that criticism. Those who control national radio and television do not stand up against criticism and as a consequence traditions which support full, free, and fair reporting of public problems are eroding and may be permanently lost. News, entertainment, and advertising are each demanding and bizarre professions. "And when you get all three under one roof the dust never settles." Men trained in advertising, sales, research, and show business also make the critical decisions about news and public affairs. "Frequently they have neither the time nor the competence to do this."

Murrow recalls that station licensees promise specific programs and services in return for use of public property. "Many recipients of licenses have, in blunt language, welshed on those promises. The money-making machine somehow blunts their memories." Murrow thinks that even the giant advertisers might consider the wisdom of putting some information into the time now given to sale of goods and services. He doubts that such an idea can ever get to them through the several layers of their own employees and advertising men who find it easier to carry on as they are. The competitors of these businessmen, he says, are not only fellow Americans who sell goods but vast rival foreign populations being taught to outreach and outdistance them in competition for world leadership.

If we go on as we are, we are protecting the minds of the American public from any real contact with the menacing world that squeezes in upon us. We are engaged in a great experiment to discover whether a free public opinion can devise and direct methods of managing the affairs of the nation. We may fail but we are handicapping ourselves needlessly. . . . The trouble with television is that as a sword for enlightenment it is rusting in the scabbard.[34]

More Time for Public Affairs. After the television quiz show and payola scandals, the networks and the stations they control collectively added a minimum of two and a half hours a week of public-affairs programing in prime evening time. Frank Stanton, president of CBS, said that this additional time for cultural and information programs would quicken knowledge and serve to develop the mass taste for serious material.[35]

124

The sponsor and the television writer. Marya Mannes and a group of television writers agree that the pressure to package and shape material for a broad mass audience are more strongly felt by writers who produce drama and other entertainment. As a consequence, they say, many if not most of the talented writers no longer work for this medium. The sponsor holds such power over the creative act of writing that it is often impossible to come close to life in dealing with the emotions and conflicts in society. Advertising agencies, as representatives of the client, are interested only in selling goods, not in the creative arts. One of them, supervising a show for a tobacco account, eliminated the word "American" from a Rod Serling script because it was part of the name of a rival manufacturer. Moreover, all drama for television, regardless of creative problems and traditional forms, must be fitted into neatly timed units between the commercials. No matter how carefully the writers put them together, the stories are torn apart by the advertisers to space out their sales messages evenly. The status of writers in television may be suggested by the fact that FCC has never asked them for their views on how the medium is being operated.[36]

Frank Stanton compares television and the press. These comments are in the constructively critical tradition and only brief rebuttal is required to put them into perspective. Eric Sevareid, who attained professional success in the print media before moving to broadcasting, says that the camera can show things a reporter cannot describe. For example, it was through television that the public came to know Senator Joseph J. McCarthy, his voice, his sarcasm, the caustic way he dealt with witnesses. Television, face to face with persons in an important or critical situation, can convey the quality of fact and feeling that leads — far more deeply than print — to understanding. The fact and feeling are not always available together, far less frequently in the print media now than when journalism benefited by a strong literary tradition.[37]

Stanton gave back to the American Society of Newspaper Editors some of the criticism the journalists had handed to him. Some of the most righteous indignation about violence on television has come from sex-and-crime-chasing newspapers who do not themselves deal meaningfully with serious news, he said. Newspapers, as well as television, concentrate book reviews, art and music news, and other cultural features in "Sunday ghettos." The television entertainers who get the most publicity in newspapers are those also criticized, perhaps by editorial writers, as light. The print

125

media rarely are outdistanced by television in a race for a pretty figure or a piquant bosom for they, too, must entertain as well as inform. Advertising crowds on the content of the print media as well as on television, he says, although he did not claim that it presses as hard.

Both Fear Government Regulation. The electronic and print media have in common the basic difficulties of keeping free of the forces that would enslave them, particularly the agencies of government that seek to manipulate them as tools of policy. Thus the press has been kept out of China, the most populous and potentially the most powerful of the oriental nations, leaving the American people in a dark and perhaps vulnerable corner with reference to the most important revolution of our time. "A press that is reduced to being a mere agent of the government seems to me not only to fall short of fulfilling its catalytic role in a self-governing society but actually to contradict that role," Stanton said.

A Defense of Programing. On other occasions, Stanton has stoutly defended programing on the networks as designed for the people rather than for the critics. He rejected suggestions that the networks should be used to elevate taste and foster culture because these proposals indicate a passive society, "a huddling image of the public, which does not do the public justice." Instead, he wishes to put quality into everything done. "Each program should be as good as we possibly can make it," he says. Television's way is to broadcast, "for example, a Shakespeare play and not only please those who already know and love Shakespeare, but through the broadcast attract those whose taste in drama has previously been limited to situation comedy and westerns and who, in their turning of the dial, stopped and discovered Shakespeare for the first time and enjoyed the new adventure." [38] Stanton told the FCC that from January through March 1960 CBS network time was divided as follows: entertainment, 82.1 per cent (adventure, cartoons, general drama, serious music, mystery, panel, quiz, serial, situation comedy, talk, variety (comedy), western) and 17.9 per cent news, public affairs, sports (1.7 per cent discussion, 2.2 per cent documentary, .6 per cent education, 5.1 per cent news, 1.3 per cent religion, 7 per cent sports). If sports were moved into entertainment the proportions would be 89.1 per cent entertainment and 10.9 per cent the other items listed.

Public confidence still high. Elmo Roper surveyed public opinion about television after the quiz scandals and found interest and confidence still high: only 41 per cent of the respondents regarded rigged quizzes as a moral problem, and if allowed to keep only one and required to give up all other media, the public choice was television 42 per cent, newspapers 32 per cent, radio 19 per cent, magazines 4 per cent. Evidently the public was as tolerant of errant television as of the newspapers in the days when so many hoaxes were being perpetrated that Dr. Curtis D. McDougall could compile a book about them in 1940. Among the most ingenious was the New York *Sun*'s fabrication, in 1835, of the discoveries of a fictitious Sir John Herschel, with a marvelous telescope that enabled him to view the moon "as from a distance of 100 yards." Even the professors of astronomy at Yale came down to consult the original unedited text of Sir John's articles and the world was agog until the journalist who conceived the fraud spilled it to another reporter while in his cups.[39] An around-the-world travelog, one of the early distinctions of Mark Hellinger, according to Emile Gauvreau, was ghost written by associates in the Hearst organization when Hellinger, the highly advertised original traveler, was last heard from in gay Vienna.[40]

High culture widely available. Donald Gillmor argues that much of the comment on the influence of the mass media on cultural standards is based on inadequate recognition of the variety and depth of contemporary listening, viewing, and reading opportunities. The undoubted rise in circulation of inferior materials has not been at the expense of high culture, necessarily, he says. Gillmor selected at random the week of May 2, 1960, to inventory the cultural offerings in Minneapolis, Minnesota. Here is what he found:

Commercial television included dramatizations of G. B. Shaw's *Captain Brassbound's Conversion*, Horton Foote's *Life of Mark Twain*, Wolcott Gibbs's comedy, *Full Moon Over Brooklyn*; two documentaries, one by John Gunther on Viet Nam and a full-hour CBS presentation of the political and military development of the post-war West German state; a conversation among the playwrights Tennessee Williams and Yukio Mishima and the English critic Dilys Powell. The highlight of the commercial radio week was an hour of music by the New York Philharmonic under the direction of Leonard Bernstein.

Educational radio and television presented discussions of Einstein's theory of relativity, religions of the world, and the United States–Japanese security pact; the Conant Report on high school education; highlights of two centuries of the symphony; interviews with Reinhold Niebuhr on the question of American morality and Eleanor Roosevelt on world peace; an

127

address by the Reverend Martin Luther King; performances of Wagner's *Die Meistersinger* by the Vienna State Opera, Mahler's Fourth Symphony, Stravinsky's *Petroushka*; plus instruction in foreign languages, art and the dance.

The evening newspapers offered the condensation of an article by Arnold Toynbee on the American electorate; a continuing series of articles on South America by two journalists who had made a twenty-three-thousand-mile tour of eight Latin American republics; an article, reprinted from the *Progressive*, by Karl E. Meyer, Latin American correspondent for the Washington *Post*; and excerpts from a letter by the undersecretary of state, Douglas Dillon, to Senator Fulbright, concerning an amendment to the foreign-aid bill offered by Senator Douglas of Illinois.

Meanwhile, a Shakespeare festival was in progress at a neighborhood cinema, presenting *Romeo and Juliet, Othello, Henry V*, and *Richard III*. A number of other theaters were showing highly acclaimed French and Swedish films, while a brilliant documentary of the Ruanda-Urindi area of the Belgian Congo, produced by French and Belgian photographers for King Leopold, continued in a number of local theaters.

The aesthete might have supplemented the content of the mass media by attending such live performances as a violin concert, a theological drama, the Twin City Philharmonic Orchestra playing in a shopping-center courtyard, Haydn's *The Creation*, an organ recital, a Beethoven-Bach flute concert, a poetry forum, an interpretative reading of Yeats's plays, or a modern art exhibit. A University of California sociologist discussed the world population crisis, an astrophysicist the physical nature of the universe, a rabbi the moral order, and a social psychologist the problems of social welfare. One might have added to the week's fare any number of analytical periodicals and serious books.

"The fact remains that the foregoing material constituted a small proportion of the total mass media content, yet it was available to the seeker of aesthetic experience and required little more than a glance at program schedules or a flick of the wrist." [41]

The effect on magazine content. Television's specializing in entertainment has put pressure on newspapers and magazines that cater to the same mass tastes. The general magazines, in a strong or stronger position in the field under the full impact of television, have turned their content toward a more serious and informative cast. The magazine industry as a whole continues its infinite variety of specialized appeals where, in the words of

Ford Stewart, publisher of the *Christian Herald* — while serving as chairman of the board of the Magazine Publishers Association — the individual "can partake of knockwurst or caviar," as he chooses. The failure of *Collier's*, however, and the decline in the sale of mass-appeal newspapers already noted, is generally attributed to television's competition for the same class of customers. The circulation of general magazines increased 92 per cent between 1939 and 1955 while movies were losing 46 per cent of their paying customers and while newspapers were gaining only half as fast. The increase in advertising income has been even greater: 363 per cent for the period. Stewart, drawing on the content analysis service of Lloyd A. Hall Company for 1938 through 1955, said that fiction in magazines declined 30 per cent between 1938 and 1955. Material dealing with food, health, home furnishings, and house-building and modernization, advice on child care and training, increased 58 per cent by volume.[42] John Fischer, editor of *Harper's*, says that magazines have had circulation on a national basis and influence to go with it. By contrast, newspapers have had local or regional readerships, he says. In both entertainment and public affairs reporting, then, network television has more the character of the popular magazines than of the newspapers.

Books and the mass market. Book publishing has met the same general sales or acceptance problems of the other media without any support from advertising. It also has two problems peculiarly its own — vigorous competition and a dearth of retail outlets for general books. Because publishing costs have trebled, the book with a sale under six thousand copies has become unprofitable. Working for sales in a market slow to respond to quality books, the publishers have resorted to selling tactics in which they compete with booksellers through mail-order sales and through the premium and cut-price offers of the book clubs. Volume has been secured in this way for a few of the books published each year. The publishers apparently have no other way out, because the bookstores are few and their combined volume small. Thousands of racks have been placed in drug and other retail stores, but this kind of outlet is limited to paperbacks selling for a dollar or less — small-profit items requiring a large volume of sale. Many publishers count on secondary income, such as the sale of motion picture rights, to make their operations profitable. Fiction has possibilities of wide subsidiary sale and is the staple item in trade-book publishing. Others classified as trade books include history; biography; poetry; popular science and psychology; stories of family life, travel, and war; and per-

129

sonal books on public or private affairs. As is true elsewhere in mass communication, sex in many guises is a dependable commodity for marketing through trade books. The formula needed to attract attention calls for famous writers to produce detective stories, westerns, light romances, novels with sex appeal, books for family consumption with a religious or sentimental motif, or historical tales in which romantic adventure has some link with reality.

William Miller says that book publishing is concerned with units sold rather than with quality, but even so remains at least as open to ideas of all sorts and to the work of young and mature artists who for a time may set themselves against the main trend as any other big American opinion forum, and more open than most. Despite the age of panicky fear, he says, the industry remains "remarkably liberal and free" but still unfree enough to postpone publishing some great controversial books for a long time.[43]

Summary. The main points that emerge from this discussion of the content and focus of the mass media can be summarized in this way:

1. The press in the United States is not an institution separable from society and cannot be separately judged. At the moment it is allied with the business community, and it is clear that this is a satisfactory base of operations only to the extent that business believes in representative and popular government, the bill of rights, an independent judiciary, and traditions under which government is authorized to define and give effect to a balance of the duties and obligations of the citizenry.

2. The press in the United States — if we base our judgment on the few leading newspapers and magazines and the best of our television — is second to none in the world. These are not weasel words designed to mask an unpatriotic judgment; rather they show the general feeling in the western world. Aside from the best of our output, the data adequate for a closer judgment are not available. The press anywhere is the creature of environment; to decide which nation has the best press we must also consider the question of which nation has the best culture, the best life for the common man, the best hope of survival and progress in the modern world.

The question of the adequacy or inadequacy of the American press at the present time can only be dealt with from the point of view of one of the groups concerned. To most of these groups the press appears quite satisfactory. To other groups — in which must be included many intellectuals whose frame of reference is idealism in the pattern of Jefferson and Milton — the press as a basic institution responsible for the moral integrity

130

and cultural development of the civilization is improving too slowly to cope with society's problems. The penalty for such slowness may be extinction by bombs or the ignominy of becoming second or third best in a race which stouter hearts could easily have won.

There is a real question whether the press could pursue the objectives of its principal critics and remain free and independent; it is equally unproved that the critics could agree upon a social program to be adopted and propagated by the mass media, given the opportunity. The critics are, unfortunately, saved from such inquiry because the press is largely indifferent to them. The question of the adequacy of the press, however, cannot be evaded by doubts of the competence of the critics.

3. Whatever the virtues and values of the press system, it is of great importance to democracy that the media exist and that they are constantly available to the public for the purposes of self-government. They do not have to be established for a crisis, as is the case with armies, or organized by a committee, as is the case with government services. They accept the burdens that go with earning their own livings. They have thousands of experienced and reasonably skilled observers at work ready to report the government's plans and its need for cooperation, as well as to reveal the misconduct of officials and conspiracies against the public interest. The journalistic observers vary as to zeal in pursuit of malfeasance in office and malfunction in social institutions, but they do not have a reputation for corruption. At the same time, there are no reliable data about the extent to which they passively accept the status quo in society and are myopic in examining of the needs of the people. Neither is there systematic information about their understanding of the general ideals of American society or their wisdom in suggesting choices among the various alternatives that confront the people from day to day.

The media are within reach of the whole population. They are self-energizing, self-sustaining, and available at a cost everyone can afford. They function on days of low political interest as well as on days when the news is so important that it helps to sell papers or to increase the traffic of viewers and listeners. They absorb in their own financial operations the results of the fluctuations of public interest and lack of interest in the merchandise of public information.

4. When the claims are balanced and a course of future action sought, it should be remembered that the freedom given to business and the press is solely for accomplishing the ideals of the open society and the commu-

nity's concern for man as man. The society needs to keep its institutions in repair; it cannot become subservient to them and still preserve liberty. So long as the unit of ultimate value is the individual, the focus of critical judgment should be upon individual performance. If individuals cannot make their social institutions do the work assigned to them, then those institutions must and will be revised unless individuals are to become imprisoned within them.

This conclusion means that continuous work must be done to make and keep the press system adequate to the needs of the community and that we should turn to that work now with a sense of urgency impelled by understanding of its importance.

, VI

FREEDOM'S NEW COMMUNITY

OUR society takes it for granted that men make their own history. This is implicit both in the assumption that the open society is workable and that it will provide the general run of men an opportunity for self-realization and in the view that the elite must take control for their own safety and for realization of their view of the common good. It is also implicit in the belief that we must keep the way open for the self-righting process of the market place of thought, and that if we eschew violence and coercion truth will sooner or later win out.

But obviously the architects of the rational system of thought conceived of freedom as arising within an already established system of moral values which defined the limits of competition and rivalry. It is widely assumed that our present-day society is caught up in a slow-moving reaction against a remote overly centralized and overly severe moral authoritarianism which, at one stage, was close to a theocratic state. The questions for us are: To what extent is moral consensus necessary for the existence of a viable social and political structure? Has the reaction gone far enough to endanger us? Has the time now come, or will it soon come, when we must start tightening up our individual and group discipline, with some elements of new moderate moral authority, if need be, in order to preserve the practicability and the success of the present system? These questions take a hundred directions, from outlawing nuclear weapons to providing more competition to students in schools and colleges. Every time a thoughtful person confronts the basic questions he must turn to examine the strength of the moral web of the community to see if the voluntary internalized con-

133

trols are adequate to provide motivation for community development and to keep violence and intimidation in leash so that democracy can continue.

The press and the community's moral web. Is the press important in the maintenance of a strong and cohesive moral web? Does mass communication affect individual political and moral decisions and, in the long run, decide the shape of group attitudes and institutions? If so, the press is then entitled to the attention intellectuals have lavished upon it on the assumption that it is essential to democracy, and we might be justified in asking the owners of the mass media, the majority of whom are neutralists with respect to maintaining the moral web, to take stock of their attitudes. If not, then we should find and give attention to social institutions more influential than the mass media of communication.

⟡ EFFECTS OF COMMUNICATION *

Wilbur Schramm is one of those who think the mass communications media worth the attention given to them. He says they make themselves felt in somewhat the same way that a stream or creek influences the soil in its drainage of fields and slopes, feeding "the ground it touches, following the lines of existing contours but preparing the way for change over a long period of time." [1] The stream, representing the flow of communication, would bring about changes dependent on the soil, the weather, and the quantity of water. It can be seen at once that all of these conditions cannot be precisely weighed. To a certain extent we have to accept what appears to be obvious, to make use of the assumption stated early in this book that, while each individual brings his peculiar nature to the environment, the mind is built up by countless impressions and its rate of growth varies according to circumstances.

The mass media accomplish their influence by selecting and disseminating materials which enter into the mind of the masses of the people. For example, it is well known that the press selects and makes the public heroes in the fields of sports and adventure, in business and in military life, in education and in government, and of course in Hollywood and on Broadway. The names of Ty Cobb, Babe Ruth, Sir Edmund Hillary and Tensing Norkay, Alfred P. Sloan, Sewell Avery, Admirals Byrd and Rickover,

* The section on effects of communication is adapted in part, by permission, from "The Role of the Press," by J. Edward Gerald and Raymond B. Nixon, in *Controlling Human Behavior*, Minneapolis: Social Science Research Center of the Graduate School, University of Minnesota, 1959.

Generals Eisenhower and DeGaulle, Robert M. Hutchins and James B. Conant, J. Edgar Hoover and Nelson Rockefeller, Gary Cooper and Tallulah Bankhead are examples. As with men and women, so with cities like Paris, London, New York, and with states like Texas. According to the reputation established by the mass media, the brightest young men and women migrate to New York. Youth and talent cannot establish itself except in the great metropolis. Not quite all Texans are rich, but some are bigger and richer than anyone else. It is always springtime in Paris. California is the promised land. No southerner can be elected president. City people make more money than farmers. Natural scientists are more glamorous than social scientists.

In these matters we already have been controlled by the mass media and its pictures are fixed in our heads. These particular pictures were easy to establish because they were not the object of determined opposition or controversy. Those adversely affected by them could not, or did not, organize in opposition. When organized dissent is present, it forces a form of mental conflict that blurs the image being formed. When the images of the mass media are sharp, we begin to feel that its statements are proper or that they are precisely true.

The effect of the mass media might be seen in another example. If a man undertakes to add to his diet half a dozen bananas each day indefinitely he will, alas, not come to look like a banana, but he may come to have pretty definite ideas about bananas. Let us assume that he likes them and that he can persuade others in the community to eat them. If he can get a photogenic actor or two, persons with fine gray hair, high forehead, and sparse iron-gray mustache who will pose as dietary experts for his advertising, and if he can find a publicist as eccentric in his skill as Albert D. Lasker, the sale of bananas may greatly increase. Economic and social adjustments may be necessary in order to meet the growing demand. A significant part of the population may become, let us say, anti-potato and pro-banana, and shifts will occur in population as the potato-growing areas of Maine, Minnesota, and Idaho decline. All of these effects stem not alone from one man's appetite for bananas, but from the skill of other men in using the mass media to control human behavior. The consumption of coffee and the sad state of tea-drinking in North America, the heavy use of vitamins and our new fear of fats in our diets, are traceable to mass communication. What can happen to our attitudes toward bananas or vitamins or tea can happen to us in political and economic aspects of our personal

135

and group existence. Clearly, it is sometimes worth the time and effort required to control public attitudes through communication.

Rival disseminators criticize the press. The existence of the press as a force in the formation of opinion shows why it is often criticized, for disseminators at times become rivals for its facilities in order to obtain special advantages in dealing with the public. Since the press system was designed to facilitate controversy, the individual units have met the problem of public criticism in three ways. Some units or firms have adopted a biased position and have processed most of the information they receive according to the preconceived pattern. Both liberal and conservative units sometimes perform in this way. Other units, as we have seen, have developed an objective approach that undertakes to render a reasonably fair, accurate, and unbiased account of news events, and to segregate opinion from the news and identify both clearly. This requires vigorous effort at reporting and verifying information. The third group is neutralist. It covers the news of a few key units of government and takes and prints what comes in from syndicates, news services, local people and organizations. It is unruffled and unperturbed by — even uninterested in — the flow of news and what it means.

Walter Lippmann said that as a consequence of their nature, the newspapers necessarily and inevitably reflect, and therefore, in greater or lesser measure, intensify, the defective organization of public opinion. "My conclusion," he said, "is that public opinions must be organized for the press, if they are to be sound, not by the press as is the case today. This organization I conceive to be . . . the task of a political science that has won its own proper place as formulator, in advance of a real decision, instead of apologist, critic or reporter after the decision has been made."

The large-influence theory. Views of the influence of the mass media diverge widely. Louis Wirth, a leading exponent of the large-influence theory, applied about the same preconditions as Lippmann: someone had to plan out in advance a program for the press to advocate; it could not work out such a program for itself. Wirth saw the individuals composing the mass as unattached, discrete entities. We express ourselves through groups, but no group can speak for us in all of the roles we play. And no group can keep us in close touch with the whole area of human affairs. From the regions outside individual and group experience come important and influential ideas which are subject to manipulation and about which we can talk to no one who has had first-hand experience with them. "It

136

is this area of life that furnishes the opportunity for others to entrap us or lead us toward goals with the formulation of which we had little or nothing to do. Hence, all of us are in some respects characterized in our conduct by mass behavior."

The media do provide an opportunity for appeals over the heads of the leaders and manipulators but great resources of men and money are required to make an appeal effective. Perhaps it is for this reason that Wirth looks upon control of the media as the "most important source of power in the social universe."

Communication and the shape of society. The press is utilized unconsciously or undeliberately by those who organize patterns of action. Harold A. Innis, an economist and historian, explains that historians distort events by giving emphasis to sensational episodes and to fear, and newspapers learned to present news in the same way. When foreign affairs became important, he says, the press used the "sensations and orgies" technique of the sensationalist historians, and such news added to the unsettling effect of other illusions created by journalism. Innis said these illusions included the ideas of democracy, freedom of speech, and individualism; their propagation served, through mediated or mechanical communication, to divide reason and emotion and to emphasize the latter. Thus the mass media influence us in another dimension, for the risk of emotional instability tends to be greater in the crowd, which is highly suggestible, and can be manipulated, through the media, by propagandists, public-relations men, and professional organizers of the sort who learned their trade during World War I.

Innis adds one more observation: at the time of World War I, public opinion in England was dominated by powerful newspapers; but in Germany the book was more influential. These two media carry their own intrinsic biases, derived from frequency of issue and ability to represent groups within the population, into public opinion structure. The newspapers appeared frequently and regularly and were thus able to establish a monopoly of news, but this very fact, combined with the language barrier, limited their influence across national frontiers. They reached the excitable masses and evoked from them reactions that served to limit the initiative of elite groups. Books, on the other hand, dealt more inflexibly with problems, had no geographical limitations and met an insignificant language barrier among elite groups; but circulation among the masses was limited. So the First World War was described as a clash between

137

book-oriented and newspaper-oriented publics; but the Second World War found the dominance of books in Germany being replaced by radio, which could easily reach the masses and cross national frontiers; in the hands of skillful propagandists it met no language barrier. Thus the second great war saw newspapers and radio pitted against each other as the control media in England and Germany.[2]

Sceptical attitudes toward press influence. Finally, back in the context of the social psychologist, Lazarsfeld and Merton, reasoning from the scanty laboratory data so far available, doubt that the influence of the mass media of communication is anything like as great as popularly supposed. The misconception comes, they say, because persons who feel duped by events turn on the newspapers and blame them for their troubles. However, these writers do not regard the media as wholly without influence. The control aspects of the media are exercised in the building and maintenance of the moral web of the community, and when a deviant person is challenged publicly he must take a stand for or against the social norm, they say. "The moral framework closes the gap between 'private attitudes' and 'public morality.'" This alone provides a substantial element of control, in the sociological sense, and the direction of this control is indicated by other characteristics found in the press. The people who read, view, or listen come to mistake this action for participation in public affairs. The press itself confirms the status quo. It fails to raise substantial and critical questions and cannot be relied upon to work for changes, even minor ones, in the social structure. For all its show of diversity and independence, these writers say, it is doubtful if the press provides more meaningful discussion in democratic than in totalitarian societies.[3] Innis had an explanation for that. He said the press, in either society, had to stay rather close to the government line in order to win authority; the range of variation from the government line was deliberately held to narrow limits so that the press could adjust itself to government action, when it came, without too great a loss of face.

It is understandable that in a systematic search for the crystallization of opinion the effect of the press would turn up second in importance to personal influence. The leading characteristics of the press — objectivity, neutralism, preoccupation with advertising and circulation — guarantee priority to information over leadership of opinion. Individuals are conditioned from infancy to make decisions in consultation with others, first with parents and later with authority figures who are substitutes for parents. The role of the authority figure is to interpret information which is held in common, and the press is the source of information for all parties in the personal influence role. The prime influence in such a situation is also subject to personal influence up the line in the informal communication system. The burden of proof is on those influential persons who recommend action; but they avoid responsibility by finding scapegoats, directing attention to the future and away from present errors, or attributing some form of satanic power to the opposition.

ꜰ SOCIETY AND COMMON VALUES

It is at this point that the importance of organizing society around a commonly recognized set of values becomes apparent. Robert Cooley Angell, a sociologist, gives systematic treatment to the ethical factors in social control and thus puts into a context of political order matters which in contemporary times have been mainly confined to didactic if not dogmatic frames of reference.[4] Angell shows that the hope for order in society is based on the effectiveness of the institutions that inculcate behavior norms, particularly the family, other intimate groups, and the mass media. The most important norms have to be internalized as conscience. The individual who acts against his conscience feels guilty; it is guilt and the fear of guilt which are the major guides to unity in contemporary society. Shame results when one is revealed to be acting differently than the group. When action in conflict with conscience is suggested, the individual has to choose between conforming or the consequences of guilt and shame.

The integrated community. Angell pictures the integrated society as one where the individuals are caught up in the fabric of common values, institutions, and law — a moral web binding and guiding them, furnishing a basis for trust and cooperation, and an ecological web composed of established activity, exchange of labor, and association in work groups.

The society in trouble finds that instead of one moral web, good for the whole community, there are several and these are not congruent. The norms of persons in cross-group relations tend to be confused or in conflict, leading to conditions hazardous for the community. Angell joins Bertrand Russell in saying that "social cohesion demands a creed, or a code of behavior, or a prevailing sentiment, or best, some combination of all three." A community without cohesion "disintegrates and becomes subject to tyrant or foreign conqueror." This is as true of the complex society and its evolution as for simple or primitive ones. "All the various

The Social Responsibility of the Press

segments must be woven together into a firm moral web through society-wide norms." [5]

Illegitimate power and the social order. Angell says nucleation — the concentration of population in large centers — makes it particularly difficult to control four kinds of individual: (1) persons with military or political power who act selfishly; (2) ordinary persons with financial power who may act against the spirit of common values; (3) unscrupulous individuals who flout well-established norms and law through coercion; (4) little men of the lower socio-economic class who have been left exposed to insecurity and rejection by the sliding apart of social classes in large cities, and totally without resources, must still work out their own destiny.

The safeguard against abuses by these groups is to have anti-social action called to the attention of the community, but information is useless if moral integration is low; in that case those who seek to bring non-moral power under control would not find the necessary political support. "Widespread illegitimate power pulverizes the moral order." [6] The remedy is decentralization or diffusion of power, and "not only must the controls be there in theory, but must be exercised. . . . When leaders are corrupt, the assertion of power by those below in order to restore the institutional pattern is necessary and proper." [7]

✓ COMMUNICATION AND SOCIAL ACTION

The course of events within society is marked out by efforts of the leadership groups to establish patterns of value and to persuade the whole society to accept them. There are periods of high and low effectiveness in the effort to propagate values, periods in which society seems in equilibrium or consensus, and periods of imbalance in which for one reason or another values are changing rapidly and there is, as a result, an uneasy tension and distress in the community accompanying the search for a new consensus. We are engaged at the present time in a wide search for a new equilibrium in a number of problem areas. As our society is seen by some students of social institutions, we are emerging from a period during which internalized ethical values, such as those expressed by the great religions, dominated individual attitudes toward others.

It is said that this was a time when individuals acted according to norms embedded in conscience and in common ethical values. In such a society, when the individual and group attitude toward common values was positive, activity and ethic were well integrated and there was a sustained re-

140

lease of energy to accomplish objectives in keeping with the ethic. When the individual and group attitudes were prevailingly negative, as the result of inability to achieve internalized goals, frustration arose from failure to integrate values and action. The system of personal reference that is taking the place of the internalized ethic comes from emphasis on group activity; the value-giving function of the family has been markedly diluted by re-action of acquaintances and associates to the family values. In part, the new value system is a function of mass communication that deals with problems of self and of social relationships. The person with strongly internalized values was enabled to maintain his defenses because he was less often and less intensely under attack from the outside.

The influence of mass communication might be seen in this example: The effort to outlaw the use of intoxicating liquor in the United States proceeded successfully because for a time prohibitionists dominated mass communication. Their use of high-ranking common values disorganized opponents; anti-prohibitionists had to speak for values that seemed less important to society than the ones advanced by the prohibitionists. But soon after the Eighteenth Amendment was passed, the imbalance in mass communication began to favor the anti-prohibitionists. Instead of the values of the prohibitionists, the mass media came to emphasize news of criminal activity in opposition to the prohibition law. As the weight of communication shifted more and more to the activities of the deviants and non-conformists, the anti-prohibitionists achieved a sense of unity and community in their opposition to a law which was based on a divided loyalty to common values. Eventually, they were able to express their goal in terms of reform — that is, a positive value — and to repeal the law.

Another instance in which deviants may have derived a sense of community from publicity is found in the published work of Professor Alfred Kinsey, who said his research revealed large deviations in sexual behavior from the ideals of the community. The mass media provided society-wide communication of this assertion, supported by the prestige of science, and in so doing gave the deviants about the same sense of community as the adherents to the ethic had possessed. Behind the communication lies community practice, however, and this may arise from the fact that in the family verbalized ethical taboos were substituted for the psychic and social experience which gave rise to the taboos in the first place.

Which set of values gains and loses most in this shift of the image presented in the mass communications? Which society do individuals most desire, the one aware of its actual nature or the one caught up in ethical myths? Which society has the best chance of curing its own defects, the one in which defectors live quietly under the protective cover of myth-maintaining mass communication or the one which understands the degree of integration of the moral web?

Children under the authority of their parents grow in conditions favorable to discipline and inner-direction, and the social consensus supports the structure of such discipline. Then psychologists, psychiatrists, schools, and the mass media in unison tell children and parents that emotional frustration arises from parental domination and that much delinquency can be explained by conflict between parent and child. Not enough information is provided to make it possible for even a sophisticated parent to recognize and evaluate frustration that might lead to deviant behavior. As a consequence, overly sentimental parents try to spare their children any frustration and soon the authority enjoyed by parents for millennia begins to crumble. The mass media switch from emphasis upon parental authority to emphasis upon juvenile delinquency. No one knows whether there is a causal relation, but there is soon clearly visible in the mass media a struggle between the inner-directed and the other-directed parents over control of their children.

⚹ THE STATE OF THE MODERN COMMUNITY

Angell has caught the flavor of our time:

Man today seems at odds with himself. Security is a vanishing quality of life. The world presses in upon us, insistent, confusing, often tragic. Although there is basic social order in most places and most of the time, it is an order continually strained, frequently violated, occasionally disrupted. Some men form aggressive groups to fight for what they conceive to be their rights. Others, uprooted and drifting on a sea of social change, are buffeted by moral storms, often sinking into crime or vice or trying to save themselves by clutching at flotsam in the form of exotic social movements.[8]

The sociologist may see modern man's social ailments as a by-product of urbanism. The economist may see them stemming from industrialization and the necessity of establishing control over an ever-widening economic jurisdiction. The psychiatrist may find them arising from the conflicts between the conventions of civilization and the personal drives of a primitive nature. The political scientist may see them in terms of bigness or the welfare state, overlapping jurisdictions, outmoded concepts of taxation, or the shallowness of political party loyalties. The natural scientist gets his satisfactions out of triggering the actions and reactions of natural phenomena and may come to wonder why human beings cannot be treated as nature treats some other orders of organic and inorganic matter. The journalist may see conditions and events as unrelated phenomena a record of which can be sold to the mass public through electronic or printed media. All of these groups find it easier to keep records and to deal with diagnoses of past difficulties than to predict the future, for in dealing with the past one needs only to manipulate words, whereas in dealing with the future, or even with the present, one must manipulate individuals, groups, and institutions through persuasive devices that bring co-operation.

The amorphous society. Social upset, too, is a by-product of communication — mass communication — which puts man at last in touch with the confusions and perplexities that are associated with control of forces not heard of a few generations ago and incomprehensible even now to most individuals who read, view, or listen to the mass media. Out of the confusion and upset arises the concept of the amorphous society in which the members are linked by the thread of communication in a network of apprehension and confusion but are impotent to direct themselves in such a manner as to cope with the problems of achieving and maintaining social order.

A characteristic of the amorphous dynamic or democratic state is that power seems remote from the individual, both power to organize and get things done and power to veto movements. When the individual wishes to influence his group he often finds that the authority to make the desired changes lies not within reach in his community but at some remote point. When he seeks out the remote point he finds that the power sought there is a mirage; authority is not in one place but is scattered in fragments. To reach and influence persons in several centers of authority the individual discovers that some kind of communications group and pressure organization dealing with people as well as with officials is needed. When he forms an organization, he must then try to persuade the people who compose it to accept his views. Even if they should do so, the elements of control of the organization are not secure in his hands; this human apparatus of access to the seats of power must be specially directed each time it is used. There may be somewhat less difficulty in constructing a negative organization, a veto group, for psychologically it is easier to arouse fears than it is to promote confidence; but in the long run the problems are the same. The man who seeks power must construct with his own hands the apparatus of control itself.

Riesman describes an aspect of this phenomenon: The veto groups occupy the ground between the thinned out ranks of those who were once leaders and those who were once led. The distance between them gives some "moralizers a sense of vacuum in American political life." [9]

Who really runs the community? Science has not helped the moralizers; in fact, it has merely confirmed for them the plastic nature of human personality and human institutions and made clearer the difficulty they confront: if society is to have any particular design and if individuals are to have any particular values, those who wish it so shall have to construct both men and institutions with their own hands and sustain the structure with continuous effort. Science has made clear that when the individual comes into the world his personality is plastic and the mold in which it is cast is shaped by society.[10]

If power is so widely spread as to leave uncomfortably large spaces between the people and those whom they appoint as governors, who, then, really runs things? The answer to that seems to be "Nobody special," and this answer holds good until problems arise which force specially affected groups to put forward leadership and a program. In a decentralized system, there are so many administrators, so many legislators in thousands of units of local government, so many managers in hundreds of thousands of business firms, that no special unification is required most of the time.[11] What Warren G. Harding called "normalcy" and what Calvin Coolidge practiced was genuinely inert government and more or less illustrates the point. Further evidence is found in the long experience the country has had with political bossism in cities and states, and with various pressure groups formed to achieve specific objectives. Those who organize can go a long way before counter-organization can stop them.

Explosive growth, inadequate control. Into a society for which no one in particular feels responsible has been loosed the genuinely revolutionary industrial growth of the nineteenth and twentieth centuries. Cities were put compactly together around industrial establishments and then torn apart by the automobile and the movement to the suburbs. In the wake of migration, blight moved in. The lower classes became tenants of run-down areas and are worse off than when they had less political liberty and greater economic claims on the classes above them. To get relief from neglect they not only must construct their own network of political communication but do so through a miasma of apathy that makes their task appear beyond their powers. "The decline of the neighborhood as a vital social unit has reduced the reliability of information that comes from informal channels. The instability and anonymity of the city make for uncritical acceptance of rumors and distortions" that further afflict group relations and morale.[12]

Rapid changes in business have bewildered the independent merchant; though he remains the traditional symbol of private enterprise, he has chosen to turn his back on free enterprise and sue for fair trade rather than free trade. Big units of business operation have become subcultures in their own right, processing the careers and personal lives of their employees as casually as they process the goods they put up for sale. Retail merchants feel less and less obligation to the customer, regarding themselves as mere representatives of the manufacturer whose product-design and advertising create the market. This attitude heightens the amorphous nature of responsibility in the business world, just as similar dispersals of power in politics confuse the citizen. There is uproar and tension when the country is considering policy alternatives, such as whether to accelerate or go slow on desegregation, whether to force the Supreme Court to read the law according to the political gales that blow through the Congress or to allow it to pursue its constitutional function, whether to fashion inflation curbs so as to favor borrowers of big money or borrowers of small sums, wage earners or property owners.

Confusion of goals leads to conflict. Goals in America have come into conflict and confusion of purpose results. Economic stability sometimes must be sought at the cost of economic progress, and personal security often is possible only at the sacrifice of personal freedom.[13] The uproar over McCarthyism even made it difficult for a man to know when his inner motivations are patriotic, and millions apparently left the resolution of this important matter to political demagogues; at the same time, even members of Congress found their patriotism questioned if they followed an independent course of judgment on such matters as the budget for armaments. The Russians have done their semantic best to purloin the word *democracy* and to use the new definition as a weapon against capitalist countries.

It might seem that conflict is dominant and that consensus does not exist in our national community, but we are assured that while consensus changes its superficial appearance from time to time the fundamental ingredients are still present.[14] However, the self-righting process of political action and mass communication upon which the consensus depends is widely suspect as being out of kilter, afflicted with bias, restraints, and propaganda traps to an extent that it is hardly reliable for the consensus needed in forming opinion, let alone periods of real emergency. Large sections of the public business dealing with military and diplomatic strategy have been closed to the general public, and some of them even to the Congress and the courts.

Childs and Cater say that the impersonal forces inherent in modern large-scale business dim the conscience of individual managers and employees, and as a result there is utter inhumanity of man toward man when the interests of a giant corporation are involved. Noting the contradiction between ethics and personal corporate action, they say the sense of community with which in former times individuals could together face social discipline, integration, and maturity has vanished.[15]

The requirements of social order. It is just such uproar and confusion that any society finds difficult to handle. People cannot work together unless standards of conduct correspond to their common values. Even the family must have some moral integration. Moral integration is low when there is a low degree of correspondence between institutional and moral norms, and there are many signs that while the Golden Rule continues to receive widespread lip-service, not much is done to enforce it through disapproval of violations.[16] J. W. Bunting writes that only the most successful business, or one allied with a dominant group, can afford the economic luxury of ethical practice.[17]

Erich Fromm states the requirement: In order that any society may function well, its members must acquire the kind of character which makes them want to act in a way they have to act as members of the society or of a special class within it. They have to desire to do what is objectively necessary for them to do. Outer force is replaced by inner compulsion and by the particular kind of human energy which is channeled into character traits.[18]

New values chosen randomly. The conclusion that emerges from examination of these aspects of society is that the system by which values are selected and inculcated is increasingly random and haphazard in operation. The argument that changes in social norms have the approval of large masses of people, that other-direction is a genuine revolt against inner-direction, is valid only up to a point. Insofar as the changes repre-

146

sent reaction against an older system, they in their own time have to be evaluated for direction, purpose, and result and corrected where found to be erratic. The agencies of mass communication, through selection of content by trial and error and by the economic yardstick of market demand, have been at once the vehicle by which new ideas were transported to the community and the beneficiaries of the new habits of reading, listening, and viewing. Economically and culturally, they have grown clearly in the image of the new society. Their importance in the old as well as in the new scheme of things is everywhere acknowledged, although there is dispute as to the precise nature of their cultural influence. The media are regarded as indispensable to the social process of moral readjustment and consensus, but they are also viewed somewhat nervously by social scientists for fear that they will introduce bias into communication and thus prejudice the result. Moreover, they do not always provide information in a form understandable to those who need it and in this respect they err as often by being incomprehensible as by being commonplace.[19] They serve to help administer the sanctions against deviant individuals which are necessary to keep cohesion in the social order. They can, if they wish, keep alive in the society a consciousness of moral norms and help each person to compare his own conscience, the norms, and the common values in society and thus facilitate a strengthening of the moral web. "No society can maintain itself if the consciences of most of its citizens are out of tune with the norms. The everyday operation of the system requires that there be a high degree of moral consensus," Angell says.[20] The mass media in their normal day-to-day functioning have the capacity to help maintain that degree of consensus. But they can do so only if organized for that purpose as well as for the random reporting of news.

Moral norms vs. institutional controls. The press is an institution that reinforces, or fails to reinforce, specific controls embedded in the social structure through it and other communicative processes. Angell reminds us that the efficacy of institutions as reinforcers of moral norms is in dispute. Kenneth Boulding prefers to entrust the individual's responsiveness to moral norms, fearing that institutions become complex and bureaucratic, and thus morally obtuse. Reinhold Niebuhr, on the other hand, thinks institutions can keep their moral freshness, and he likes the possibilities of influence on societal regeneration which he sees in their "solidity and their incorporation of persons."[21]

Conflicts arising out of differing interpretations of moral norms are

147

particularly unsettling because rules promulgated by an institution and moral norms internalized in conscience both appeal to the individual as being right.[22] When the mass media are properly conversant with common values, they can help considerably in resolving such conflicts. Common values are implemented and inculcated by institutions, particularly by the family.

Professional training and social control. There are two main inculcating processes of a society, the moral indoctrination of children and professionalization of key institutions. Children are influenced largely through groups like family, school, and church. Professionalization intends to give ethical training to those "who are going to fill roles in the society that are both powerful and difficult to monitor." As a social device for monitoring the behavior of important institutions, professionalization uses a code of ethics — a set of professional norms which must be internalized to be effective.[23]

The old-style apprenticeship has been replaced in large part by educational institutions. The acceptance of norms of craft and professional behavior is in significant part a function of youth and receptivity to authority. Angell observes that the moral standards of professional men already are set today by the time they finish college. Moreover, the inculcation of ethics in the classroom is not an adequate substitute for primary-group experience. The strength of the family's ability to influence children is missing in the professions. "It is probable that the code of ethics is transmitted in situations of mainly a master-apprentice kind." The behavior of professional men has great influence on society and their lapses "impair the moral health of the system." The only alternative to self-control, he adds, is control by political means, and the only direction the sociologist can give is to contrive intimacy of contact and stability of personal relationships. Such a relationship might be achieved only by complete restructuring of professional training.[24]

Institutional groups contribute to maintenance of a steady state by providing a flow of professional men adequately trained for a customary role. The assumption is, Angell says, that when any unusual strain occurs, the professionals will "rise to the occasion and keep the group functioning in accordance with the institutional pattern." They will provide a monitor-like watchfulness over the policies of the institutions and the state.

The work of the institutions of mass communication is difficult to monitor. Government can deal only with the worst abuses; for the rest, it must keep its hands off in deference to the central position occupied by the press in the democratic community. The press, then, must monitor itself or deny any responsibility for or loyalty to social norms. The big problem in persuading the press to abandon its neutralist position and make a serious effort to understand and influence society is to convince its owners that its influence is as important as the systematic and inferential evidence shows it to be, to assure it a reasonable set of rules by which to operate, and to provide community support when, at work under the rules, it begins to be isolated and to feel insecure.

Two steps are necessary to protect the press. One is to provide the press with personnel able to understand the intricate problems of the day and competent to make an adequate appraisal; the other is to rehabilitate in the community the principles that were in the minds of the founders of the free-enterprise community, those ethical assumptions that lead them to believe that a self-righting process exists and that it assures the correction of errors.

Is this an assignment that can be given to a professional organization? What is the condition of the professional spirit in journalism? What hope is there that journalists can grow toward professional status and provide the monitoring of their important institution that the society appears to require? These questions will be confronted in the remaining portion of the book.

⨍ THE INSTRUCTION OF NEOPHYTES: FAIRNESS, ACCURACY, OBJECTIVITY

What are the conventions journalists are taught to respect? What are the rules of their trade? What skills in communication entitle a journalist to the acclaim of his fellows? What errors bring loss of face?

Textbooks published for schools of journalism during the last fifty years show that all of them closely agree on the duty of journalists and that the teaching has not changed appreciably in that time. Charles G. Ross, pioneer teacher of journalism who made his career with the St. Louis *Post-Dispatch* Washington bureau, expresses the principles simply in *The Writing of News.*

The news writer is the agent of the paper that employs him. As such, in a wider sense, he is the agent of the public, which relies on the newspaper to keep it informed of the day's happenings. The story is the all-important thing; the reader as a rule cares nothing about who wrote it or what the writer thinks of it. The viewpoint of the news writer must be that of the unprejudiced, but alert observer. He must approach his story with a mind open to the facts and he must record the facts unvarnished by his own preferences and opinion. Comment on the news of the day is the function of the editorial columns. It has no place in the news story. The writer who willfully injects his own likes and dislikes into the story breaks faith with his employer, whose space he is using, and with the public that buys the paper.[25]

The whole of journalism's dependability and usefulness rests in adequate conformance to the articles of faith upon which communication is based and upon rewards and punishments for behavior. The reporter, like the doctor or lawyer, does his work under conditions which fix direct responsibility on him. The only way he can be corrected is through subsequent review and criticism of his work. This fact makes him a professional man and puts upon society the choice of being served by quacks or by men who submit their work to the critical judgment of their fellows, judgments based on expert comparison of acts performed with articles of faith.

Crawford's review of professional ethics. Toward the end of the period of prosperity that followed World War I, while businessmen still talked of governing conduct by codes as well as by competition, Nelson Antrim Crawford reviewed the many professional versions of creeds and sought to record pertinent attitudes of leaders in journalism. Crawford, a professional journalist turned teacher-idealist, did his work before two major social and economic upheavals, the great depression and World War II, and those events require updating of his study.[26]

Code-writing, it must be made clear, was the work of an elite group within journalism. Codes were presented to and endorsed by associations but there was hardly any thought of stern enforcement measures. For persons like Crawford of Kansas, and Walter Williams and Casper Yost of Missouri, the codes were devices for implementing a view of life. Williams was an example of the gifted writer and speaker who used his creed as a theme in countless appearances before industrial groups and as a set of principles to be taught to his classes in the first school of journalism. Yost, as editorial-page editor of the St. Louis *Globe-Democrat*, took the same general philosophy with him to meetings of the American Society of Newspaper Editors, which had been organized under his leadership. The canons, adopted at the second annual meeting, represented his ethical views although the chief author was H. J. Wright, founder of the New York *Globe*.

The sponsors of the press association codes were divided in their atti-

150

tudes toward enforcement. ASNE tried on one occasion to expel a member adjudged guilty of violating its canons, but found that its bylaws did not confer the necessary authority. The bylaws were amended, but the attendant discussions appear to have deprived the members of any desire to use them. It was conventional to express professional ideals in a code, but the sort of tradition that gives strength of will was lacking when sanctions affected individual careers.

Crawford's summary of ethics places great emphasis upon editorial independence and integrity, defined as rejection of influence in reporting and resistance to interference with objective policy by any individual motivated by private interest as opposed to the public interest. This is what Ochs meant when he instructed his editors to handle the news without fear or favor. A serious and subtle task of discrimination is placed on the writer by this command, because — as John Stuart Mill said — the tyranny of established ideas "tends to a dread uniformity of taste and opinion and method of life that will finally lead to a more than Chinese stagnation." Fear is worse than corruption for it involves no clear-cut issue of any sort and "undermines every intellectual, ethical, and emotional resistance." The bias of apathy and neutralism found in newspapers is due to fear, and persists in staff members even when editors issue instructions to be fair and honest. The reporters cannot believe the editor so foolish as to issue orders against his best interest.

⌁ THE CANONS OF THE AMERICAN SOCIETY OF NEWSPAPER EDITORS

The American Society of Newspaper Editors adopted ethical canons at the time enthusiasm for codes and creeds was higher than at the present, but, despite a more cautious attitude, they represent then and now the ideals of the journalistic community. Their canons state that the primary function of newspapers is to set up a web of communication between all individuals in society on a level of broad knowledge, experience, and intelligence. This puts the news department into the accepted system of logic and reason and renders it accountable for illogical or biased acts. This fact is emphasized by the confession of obligation in the canons not only to convey information but to teach and to interpret its values and meanings in a context of the general welfare.

Editors are responsible only to public opinion. Editors are not to be praised or blamed in any court except that of public opinion, but the public

151

is invited to judge the use a publication makes of the community time absorbed in its reading, and each member of the staff is told of his individual responsibility for the judgment rendered. If the power of a journal is used for any unworthy purpose its lack of responsibility is said to be shared by the individual journalists. The root word by which responsibility is to be defined is faith — faithfulness to a high trust.

The canons charge the journalist to defend freedom of press as a vital right of mankind, and they assert that freedom of press is linked to corresponding duty of intelligent fidelity to our Constitution.

The canons assert that freedom from all obligations except those to the public interest are essential; they reject private interests that are in conflict with that principle as "dishonest." In fidelity to the public interest, the journalist is charged with revealing the source of all private information, or with a duty to substantiate it "both in form and substance."

Knowing departures from the truth. Knowing departures from the truth are said to be of two kinds: willful error in the news, which is termed subversive of fundamental principle, and in editorial opinion, which is branded as violating professional spirit. It is possible for journalists to know the difference between news reports and expressions of opinion and to develop sound procedures for keeping the two separated. "News reports [except those signed by an author who clearly confesses his breach of the rule] should be free from opinion or bias of any kind." Good faith with the reader is equated with sincerity, truthfulness, and accuracy in text and headline, and a journal is warned not to seek excuse for weakness or lack of industry in rendering a truthful report. Again the key word is faith.

Fair play is said to require that unofficial charges not be published unless the accused is given a chance to be heard in his own defense, but official actions are exempted from this stipulation. Newspapers are told not to "invade rights of private feelings without sure warrant of public right as distinguished from public curiosity." Correction of erroneous report is described as a privilege and duty.

Offensive content. If a newspaper publishes details of crime and vice it must demonstrate to critics that they are appropriate to the general good or else be clearly insincere in any expression of high moral purpose. Lacking any means of enforcing the canon against offenders, the code expresses the hope "that deliberate pandering to vicious instincts will encounter effective public disapproval or yield to the influence" of a preponderant professional disapproval.[27]

Walter Williams' creed. The "Journalist's Creed" of Walter Williams contains much that is set forth in the ASNE canons but is addressed more personally to the individual. The journalist is asked to write only what he holds in his heart to be true, to suppress the news only for the welfare of society, to avoid bribery by his own pocketbook or the pocketbook of anyone else. He is told that he may not escape responsibility for his acts by pleading instruction from his superiors, and he is assigned a spiritual orientation in the conventions of gentlemanly behavior and the ideals of human brotherhood.

The ASNE canons were written after journalism already had become big business and at a time when it was clear that many newspapers did not and would not meet the conditions set down. There is a phrase in the canons limiting them to "the journalism here represented," and an effort to extend coverage of the code by invoking public disapproval of undesirable actions. Writing a few years earlier, Williams and Martin observed the wide disparity in performance by saying that when the journalist

buys and sells news he is in business, when he merely records, he is a clerk and bookkeeper for the day's doings, when he interprets, whether as contributor, writer, editor, journalism is akin to literature, if it is not literature. In its highest sense journalism is not trade nor business, but profession, the profession of the interpreter.[28]

⚹ ETHICS AND OBJECTIVITY

Ethical principles are closely related to the concept of objectivity in news-writing, a concept that has arisen to prominence as the older ethical affirmations tend to receive less emphasis. But there is great confusion as to what it does and should mean and how the journalist should deal with it.

Ronald Shilen, who wrote a doctoral dissertation about objectivity, shows how the term originated outside journalism. The definitions he quotes have in common a theme less concerned with textual accuracy than with a keen sense of social responsibility in reporting, and with an attitude of personal detachment.

Shilen says that in achieving objectivity the writer must keep neutral his wants, tastes, and moral or religious beliefs; moreover, he must curb wishful thinking and concern himself with proof based on first-hand comparison of reports by credible witnesses.[29]

This apparently means that the journalist is asked to enter frames of reference not his own and to report actions or attitudes found there so that

153

persons who hold those opinions will accept the report as their own. The test of objectivity most suitable for modern news reporting is whether those persons quoted will say, when they read the news story, "Yes, that's what I said," or, when shown descriptions of conditions will say, "Yes, that's the way it is." The journalist long ago made himself responsible for this kind of fidelity by accepting the obligation to be accurate. In a controversy, all frames of reference important to society must be represented in the news reports. Until the advent of interpretative reporting, the obligation of the journalist was merely to make himself available, space permitting, to those who wanted to say something. It was up to the contending forces to establish predominance in public opinion and the hope of the community rested upon them and not upon journalists. The addition of the obligation of interpretative reporting requires the journalist to fill in, through investigation and truthful report, facts overlooked or not stated in the public discussion — that is, to supply the "truth about the facts." This is what Williams and Martin meant by interpretation.

Newsmen themselves tend to take two positions toward objectivity. One is that it is impossible of achievement and should frankly be discarded as a concept for journalistic operations. The other is that a diligent reporter interested only in getting and printing the facts will be able to realize a reasonable level of objectivity and truth in reporting.

Attitudes toward objectivity. The scientists who doubt their ability to eliminate personal temperament from observation do not as a consequence advise the abandonment of efforts at precision. Some journalists do, and assertions that objective reporting is impossible often screen deliberate rejection of the obligation to dig up and relate all the important facts. The personal style of writing offers greater leeway for individual idiosyncrasy in news-writing, releases the inhibitions of the requirement of objectivity, gives the individual reporter, particularly the specialist or the foreign correspondent, an opportunity to develop his own personal line of prediction or analysis. The reporter tends to come before the reader as vividly as the news event itself, and it is difficult, if not impossible, to tell which is fact and which is reporter. This type of reporting would be acceptable under the ethical codes set out above if the articles were signed and if it were clear that the reporter was expressing his personal opinion rather than making an effort at presenting the facts without bias; but unless such material were balanced by a factual account in the same publication, the reader would be treated unethically.

154

The veteran English journalist Robert Sinclair provides evidence that objectivity is an ideal that, to a certain extent, conflicts with the staff spirit of some newspapers. Sinclair says that loyalty to one's paper, in the same sense that the actor is loyal to the stage, is "one of the strongest of the springs that animate journalists of any age or any rank." [30] It is this spirit that puts general ethical standards into conflict with shop goals and makes ideal conduct difficult. "Tell the truth," "Be fair," Sinclair says, are injunctions that "reflect only general principles. . . . The principal perplexity in life lies in deciding how to be fair [and] it is impossible to learn the whole truth about anything." Moreover, he says, in news reporting one often is given seventy-five minutes, more or less, because of edition times, to find out the truth about very complex and weighty problems. The problems of journalists are not easy—"they are on the level of other men's problems of conscience," the kind the doctor faces when he considers sustaining the life of a doomed and suffering patient.[31]

The very word "fact" is a snare. . . . Nothing in writing can be a fact. . . . To ask for "the facts" is to ask someone to tell you about an event. How much his narrative is related to the event depends on his memory, his vocabulary, his sincerity. . . . A fact is as much mixed up with [a journalist's] personality as a baby is mixed up with its mother at the moment of birth. . . . News is an entirely subjective and personal thing which arises in and issues from the human mind; as read by the reader it is a manufactured article of highly complex character, and unless we make an effort of imagination and share in the journalist's personal problems, our pontifications about the ethics of the press will merit dismissal on the score of ignorance.[32]

Forces that override objectivity. Sinclair pictures the reporters and editors in the news room of a paper which has stiff competition, observes that pressures to keep abreast of the other papers sweep physically through them edition by edition so that some journalists wobble "like a nervous cyclist on a wet day." As a result,

The commonest operational phrase on the lips of Fleet Street men in my time has been, "What exactly is wanted?" . . . It is in that atmosphere of confusion that silly articles and silly headlines are written, the blame for which falls on the journalists who have penned them and not on the fruit-barrow manager whose clumsy hand has brought coarseness and indecision to a difficult and delicate pursuit — the disinterested pursuit of truth.[33]

As to the political bias of the men themselves, Sinclair says that "except for the *Daily Worker*, the staffs will include conservatives, socialists, liberals, communists, ignoramuses and weathercocks. This gives the reader great protection against indoctrination by one school." This diversity is traceable to the hiring policies of the proprietors who, in the main, try to select men for journalistic ability rather than for political opinion.[34]

There are striking parallels in Sinclair's personal account and the survey of American conditions twenty years earlier by Crawford.[35] The parallels suggest that the problems growing up in two freely competitive press systems fall into a pattern that does not change rapidly. One of the problems of this study is to obtain material abreast of conditions. Tests for change over the decades help get the desired perspective. Such tests are substitutes for comprehensive surveys of actual conditions which ought to be made and would be made if money were available. The reputation of the press probably is distorted because under present conditions studies of it cannot be undertaken which mainly utilize contemporary data. Even if all recent and appropriate source material is used, it is difficult, even impossible, to tell how much that is old and perhaps now inapplicable has been brought forward and applied to today's conditions. A majority of the leaders in the American press are, in large part, responsible for the makeshifts to which students, writers, lecturers, research workers, and social critics must resort. Members of the majority appear to be on the defensive against outside studies of the press and to express this attitude in several ways: They largely reject social analysis of the press, asserting that competence for such analysis does not exist, and that published material is academic and not worth the time of busy men. The majority declines to provide financial support or to encourage others to provide financial support for studies making use of sound and tested methods that would analyze press content and performance. Foundations with a deep interest in the press, because of its relationship to domestic progress, to public and private morality, and to foreign policy, are reluctant to provide support and risk political criticism based on severely myopic and demagogic versions of the facts. When a team of editors and experienced research workers in academic institutions undertook to study the objectivity of newspapers during the 1956 presidential election, the basic decision appears to have been left not to the directors of the foundations who were asked for support but to a jury of the individuals whose work would have been reviewed had the study been made. Before this jury could be assembled, *Editor & Publisher*, in a quite orthodox pursuit of the news, released a skeletonized and unofficial version of the proposal. It then polled the directors of the Associated

Press, the American Society of Newspaper Editors, the American Newspaper Publishers Association, and a few other persons on whether they favored the study. As it turned out, the men polled by *Editor & Publisher* constituted a substantial segment of the group who were to be consulted later by the study committee representing Sigma Delta Chi, the professional journalistic society. This meant that the proposal was prejudged. Norman Isaacs, managing editor of the Louisville *Times* and chairman of the Sigma Delta Chi committee, commented: "If we can't even get the facts straight about our own business, I can hardly be blamed for getting the shivers about our reporting of other people's affairs." [36]

New depths to reporting. The fear and distaste for controversy of which Crawford wrote operate in periods of tension so as to give a narrow and constricted range to the principle of objectivity. When it is not feasible to print some of the news, the balance of points of view is lost. Objectivity as a concept in journalism is keyed to breadth and depth of inquiry. The ideal — to get at the truth, the whole truth, and nothing but the truth — is not looked upon as an impractical goal. Its benefits to the trained journalist and to the public are wholly in the certainty that uninhibited effort to get the facts will be made. Under this concept, information can be gathered and validated without any fear except of the consequences of factual error. The rules of objectivity push aside considerations based on the reaction of private interest and make possible a closer approach to the truth. No advocate of objectivity ever expects to get the whole truth in a complicated situation, but journalists regard their profession as more adequate and satisfying if they are free to try.

Arthur Hays Sulzberger said something like this in a talk to the Association for Education in Journalism in 1952. The Association was meeting in the Pulitzer-endowed school of journalism at Columbia University, and this fact moved Sulzberger to contrast Ochs and Pulitzer. In so doing, he revealed his attitude toward objectivity. Pulitzer's emotional fervor and crusading zeal indicated that he was not concerned with objectivity, Sulzberger said. Ochs reserved his feelings for the editorial page, but even here he feared too much intensity might affect the reporter's objectivity and that, before long, editorial-page biases would color the news. "I shared this opinion," Sulzberger said, but he believed it impossible to give news without fear or favor, without regard to any party, sect or interest involved . . . I do not think it possible to be strictly objective or to present the news without any bias.

The Social Responsibility of the Press

I do believe, however, that one can aspire to these ideals . . . I believe further that only those who are aware that these ideals are, in fact, beyond their reach can ever truly approach them.

During the World War II crisis, Sulzberger's anxiety overcame his fear of editorial-page influence on reporting.

I was comforted by the thought that the subtle influence I had feared was no longer a threat because the *Times* long since had become firmly established as an objective purveyor of the news and the men who made the *Times* fully understood and adhered to the guiding principles of the paper.

And then slowly, bit by bit, something new emerged, a new form of journalism shaped to fit the period . . . The time had come when news had to be explained, when interpretation had to go hand in hand with the statement of the fact itself, when the meaning of things that occurred had to be made clear if they were indeed to have meaning. And out of it all came this new approach, something which in effect was the development of a new craft.

Objectivity and journalistic duty. What Mr. Sulzberger described was a wider fulfillment of the principle of objective news report. The reporter had simply extended the range of his inquiry as events in the news became more complex. He was giving the public notice of other factors in the situation than those visible in today's one small segment of news. He was giving perspective and meaning, bringing into focus more of the longer-run conditions in which the day's news events were embedded. If his motive was to give the reader greater insight and a more balanced factual report, the objective principle was better served. If his motive was to mislead and to control, to persuade by giving a partial view of the facts, or to use a signed story as a substitute for digging out facts he could gloss over in a clever statement of opinion, then he was as guilty of perjury in the court of public opinion now as he was when the problems of the country were simpler and when, because the people had a better chance to observe significant events for themselves, the coloring of news was less deceptive.

There are other points of view about objectivity that deserve description because of the position in journalism of the men who hold them. Shilen, in his study, said that newspapers, in separating opinion and fact in the news, left the way open for the development of the so-called news magazines. These publications differ among themselves in method and policy, but *Time* magazine is the oldest. Catering to the college-educated professional and business classes with a weekly summary of news and with opinion that has the form and typographical style of news, it advertises itself as a magazine of news, not of opinion. On its thirtieth anniversary, *Time* published a five-thousand word essay setting forth its philosophy; speeches by its top-level executives on other occasions have rounded out the image. James A. Linen, speaking as the publisher, told the Poor Richard Club in Philadelphia on February 25, 1958, that during the 1930's *Time*'s staff believed it "*was* possible to be utterly objective and impersonal in reporting the news." At that particular moment, the magazine relied upon a highly stylized writing technique to differentiate its product from the daily newspapers and other magazines in its field. Linen said that Wolcott Gibbs described this style well in a *New Yorker* article: "Backward ran sentences until reeled the mind," and "Where it all will end, knows God."

After weathering the economic difficulties of the depression period, *Time* hit upon a new device for product differentiation — a greatly expanded reporting staff and its own particular kind of interpretation, frankly abandoning objectivity. *Time*'s contemporary attitude toward objectivity was described by Linen in this way:

As for utter objectivity, this is, in our opinion and in the opinion of an ever-increasing number of journalists, as impossible as it is undesirable. But we are often told that the function of journalism is simply to tell what happened, what the man said or did. No opinion, no judgments, just the facts. But if a newspaper or newsmagazine simply stacks up all the facts it can print on a story, is it fulfilling its responsibilities to its readers? I think not. This obsession with mere factuality, it seems to me, can lead to absurdity. . . . Primarily, I believe, we at *Time* should be concerned with values, with the meaning of the world about us. I would say that we are committed to the proposition that a journalist must, to the best of his ability, tell the news fairly, and tell also what the news means. We recognize, of course, that not all our readers will agree with our findings, with our judgments; and we know that we might be, and often have been, wrong. But the responsibility is there.

A similar account of the magazine's purpose was presented orally by Max Ways, one of the senior editors, to the Association for Education in Journalism when some of its members visited *Time*'s offices in August 1952. On this occasion, the author suggested to Mr. Ways that, as described, *Time*'s pursuit of information upon which to base its value judgments was quite like the pattern of specialization in the modern university. A university, however, was so set up that each scholar had to run a gantlet of critical evaluation of his work by equally well-trained scholars in his own and other institutions. Did *Time* have such an internal system of criticism of its own judgments? Mr. Ways did not answer at the time. The information sought was provided a few months later however, in the thirtieth-anniversary essay.

Time *magazine's view of journalistic duty*. Because it represents a rare attempt in modern journalism by a major news publication to explain the scope and nature of its biases, and to defend them, the essay is summarized here. No other publication is on record as having so thoroughly considered its reporting problems and as being so ready to accept the consequences of its judgment.

Time explained in this essay that in its view modern intellectuals are confused. In the words of Eric Vogelin, whose thesis stated in *The New Science of Politics* (Chicago: University of Chicago Press, 1952) *Time* adopted as its own, the modern intellectuals are followers of Joachim of Flora, "the first Christian to pervert the hope of salvation into a systematic belief in an earthly society of purified and perfected men." Joachim is said to have found the intellectual support he needed for his ideas in Gnosticism, the philosophy of a sect that dreamed of an earthly paradise, a society without government, rather than of one in an after-life. Joachim substituted dreams for reality, with reality defined as the danger of getting one's head knocked off. *Time* affirmed a moral foundation for human life under God; it lamented the decline of logical positivism as the source of definition and clarification of the moral basis of life and it asserted that new forms of economic relationship, that is, new labor-management patterns of organizing work, would — if understood in terms of moral law — help to achieve stability and purpose in America.

Time criticized western leaders as Gnostic-oriented, having the ability to recognize dangers when they see them, but attempting to meet and control perils with slogans and other magic or manipulative operations in a dream world, such a disapproval, moral condemnation, declarations of intention, resolutions, appeals to the opinion of mankind, branding of enemies as aggressors, outlawing of war, propaganda for world peace and world government. *Time* said that such tactics brought on World War II because the western leaders complainingly watched the rise of National

Socialism in Germany but did nothing realistic about it until a major war was inevitable.

"Phenomena of this magnitude cannot be expressed by ignorance and stupidity: these policies were pursued as a matter of principle, on the basis of the Gnostic dream assumptions about the nature of man."

Time labels the western leadership Gnostic. It blames Gnostic principles for failure to push the Korean war to victory and for the policies that allowed the cold war stalemate; it labels as Gnostics those idealists who pushed beyond the concept of the United Nations to argue for an "extravagant one-worldism" and it asserts that educators neglect American values for the same reason. Moreover, *Time* fears that public distrust of "Gnostic" individuals could become distrust of all intellectuals: "The way to meet the threat to intellectuality is by a kind of intellectual guidance to the public that does not end in disappointment, frustration, suspicion and fear."

Time criticizes the western propagandists (but neglects to identify them as businessmen) who talk about America in terms of bathtubs, automobiles, and popular music. It laments that intellectuals disagree as to the fundamental American message and it notes that those who depend on morality as a guiding force in life apparently have not heard the news of the positivist decay. Mortimer Adler and Reinhold Niebuhr are praised for their understanding of the social situation and for the view of man they expound. *Time* looks to the day when those in authority will be able to apply what is known about man's nature to the facts of the world as they are — not in trying to fit imagined men into imagined facts.

Finally, the essay quotes A. N. Whitehead: "It is our duty . . . It is our business — . . . to recreate a vision of the world including the elements of reverence and order without which society lapses into riot." It then states *Time*'s credo for journalism.

To discharge his part of this responsibility, a journalist must conduct, first, "an avid, ceaseless, sweating pursuit of facts, not as an editor imagines them to be, but as they are. This is primarily the business of the reporter." Second, the reporter's facts and the relations between them must be considered in the light of other facts and of principles of experience. Without such consideration, the news makes no sense — to the journalist, to the intellectual, or to the public. This judgment or adding up is primarily the business of an editor.

161

The Social Responsibility of the Press

T. S. Matthews, former managing editor and editor of *Time* tells how the principle of responsibility just explained works inside the organization:

The fact I kept forgetting, or wouldn't admit, was that *Time* was not only Luce's invention but his property. I still won't agree that one follows from the other. Grover Cleveland had already said it for me: "A public property is a public trust." . . . *Time* in a sense was also a public trust, and therefore must not be subject to the whims or dictates of one man. And, in practice, *Time* wasn't. In practice, no newspaper or magazine ever is, altogether. It was Luce's theory I objected to, much more than to his practice. In my view the responsibility for *Time* was shared among the men who produced it and their responsibility must carry with it a corresponding share of authority (which, to a greater or less extent it had to); in Luce's view, the final authority was vested, more or less entirely, in him. Practice and theory on this question frequently clashed. I suppose they should have clashed more. For until the question was settled one way or the other, the theory of Luce's omnipotent authority tended to shackle our responsible practice.

. . . And as private citizens we had our own opinions: Two of the writers were passionate supporters of Roosevelt, the other two and I favored Willkie. But as journalists I think we all tried to play it straight. This must have been the last presidential campaign when that could be said about *Time*.[37]

. . . In 1952, when it sniffed victory in the air at long last, there was no holding *Time*. The distortions, suppositions and slanting of its political "news" seemed to me to pass the bounds of politics and to commit an offense against the ethics of journalism.[38]

A critique of Time'*s credo.* Time's credo appears at first glance to be quite like the objective ideal, but there are two important deviations. The reporter in the orthodox system not only gathers the facts but he writes the story; that is, he decides what the facts mean. The reader is expected to help organize the facts in terms of his own value system. Though the reporter is ordinarily subordinate in staff rank to the editor, he is not the editor's intellectual subordinate. In a dispute over fact, tradition supports the reporter — the man who gathered the facts — until he is proved wrong; in an argument over interpretation, he would be privileged to disassociate himself completely from any point of view. The first deviation in the interpretative system is that the reporter is a faceless hewer of wood and drawer of water; his material is passed along to an editor representing the authority of the central management and loses its individual integrity. The second deviation is that the editor produces the final story, mixing the institution's opinion with the facts provided by the reporter.

When the reader gets the final article the facts and opinion are indistinguishable. In the orthodox objective system, the factual account goes into the news columns and the opinions into a clearly separate opinion page. The materials of logical analysis, which the individual reader can use to arrive at his own conclusions, are set clearly apart from value judgments.

Time, in common with others who reject objectivity, defends its operation as intellectual and asserts that the intellectual worker must be free to think and must be encouraged to press his conclusions on the public. If the public follows him and he is wrong, he should not be held accountable criminally, but criticized, even bitterly. The intellectual or the journalist without the courage to accept the criticism should get out of the business.

The plea that journalists and intellectuals should be subjected to only limited responsibility is an old one, even in the democratic world. It was stated in the West in Milton's protest against an authoritarian government and restated in Jefferson's faith in the community's ability to arrive at unity through diversity. Immunity was claimed on the plea that the self-righting process, using rival versions of the facts, had a chance to work under the existing circumstances. However, resort by corporate mass-media enterprise in the industrial age to a claim heretofore valid only for individuals poses a legal and ethical question tentatively debated but not resolved. Should the powerful corporate voice, a voice that has the communication capability of tens of thousands of individual voices, and is often the only voice heard by large groups in the community, have the same immunity against reprisal claimed by the individual scholar and writer putting his thesis forward in a competitive market of thought?

The views of two press commissions. This question was answered by two groups of scholars: the Commission on Freedom of the Press (1943–45), organized and headed by Dr. Hutchins, and the British Royal Commission on the Press (1947–49) chaired by Sir William David Ross. Since these commissions and their published work represent the outstanding ventures in the field during this century, their findings might be expected to help us with our judgment of the press's performance.

The commissions agree that the democratic form of government demands of its members an active and intelligent participation in the affairs of their community, whether local or national. This activity should not be confined to political matters, but should extend to the adjustment of social problems of the community.

The Social Responsibility of the Press

The freedom of the press is essential to political activities of this sort. The American commission relied heavily upon one of its members, Professor William E. Hocking, and worked out a formal convention of freedom and responsibility. In this convention the individual is assumed to be under obligation to express his thoughts, but the object or goal of expression appears to be the rectification of the community's own thought or consensus. In democratic societies, the participant persons are assumed to be in control of the communal life and to give effect to a system of values that meets the needs and requirements held in the consensus rather than the requirements of any subgroup. This society has provided special constitutional safeguards against governmental interference in order to facilitate communication for the self-governing community. The safeguards can be modified or withdrawn by the electorate, by the courts, and by changes in folk practices; they will be modified or withdrawn, the American commission asserted, unless the persons perform the service needed by the society.

The two commissions use similar definitions of needs. Democratic society needs a clear and truthful account of events and their background and causes, a forum for discussion and informed criticism, and a means whereby individuals and groups can express a point of view or organize to promote a cause. The British commission asked editors and proprietors themselves how they viewed their obligation to society; the responses it obtained were more idealistic, in the main, than appear to be compatible with the industrial character of the press. The editors and the two commissions are in general agreement in their statement of the needs of the community.

The Right to Be in Error. The right of free public discussion includes the right to be in error, the American commission said. Liberty consists of opportunity to try many things in order to select the one best suited to the time and the circumstances. "Debate itself could not exist unless wrong opinions could be rightfully offered by those who suppose them to be right." But this privilege belongs only to the writer who is honestly in search of truth, not to those who have made up their minds and are "deliberately or irresponsibly in error." [39]

The commissions are in agreement as to how the press should handle its opinions. Said the British:

If a paper adheres to a political party it should be plain to the reader that it does so, but from the columns of opinion, not from the coloring given

164

the news. A paper's politics and those of its readers will inevitably and legitimately affect its judgment of the relative interest of certain items of news, but the news it reports it should report truthfully and without excessive bias.[40]

Said the American:

the press is not free if those who operate it behave as though their position conferred on them the privilege of being deaf to ideas which the processes of free speech have brought to public attention. In the absence of accepted moral duties there are no moral rights.

The need of the citizen for information useful to self-government is so great that he is "under a duty to get it." He has a right to it and it is this right of all citizens which journalists use when they claim freedom of the press. But "the press must know that its faults and errors have ceased to be private vagaries and have become public dangers." Among these vagaries is monopoly that deprives some voices of a hearing and keeps the public from knowing all the facts when it performs an act of self-government.[41] The American commission called on the giant units to "assume the duty of publishing significant ideas contrary to their own, as a matter of objective reporting, distinct from their proper function of advocacy." It said their claim to freedom was grounded on rendering a trustworthy report. "All of the important viewpoints and interests in the society should be represented."

The American commission said that identification of fact as fact and opinion as opinion —"and their separation"— was as important as accuracy. The whole journalistic establishment — the reporter, the copy editors, the editors who plan page layout and display, the editorial writers who, on their opinion pages, interpret the news — all are under equal obligation to identify fact and keep it clearly distinguishable from opinion.

Admittedly, said the American commission, all facts have contexts that need to be explained and explanations cannot be entirely uncolored by opinions of the reporters. "But modern conditions require greater effort than ever to make the distinction between fact and opinions."

The mass media were asked to assume a responsibility like that of educators in stating and clarifying the ideals toward which the community should strive.

By necessity or choice, large numbers of people voluntarily delegate analysis and decision to leaders whom they trust. Such leadership is freely chosen and constantly changing; it is informal, unofficial, and flexible.

. . . The leaders are not identified; we can inform them only by making information available to everybody. In terms of quality, the information provided must be provided in such a form and with so scrupulous a regard for the wholeness of truth and the fairness of its presentation, that the American people may make for themselves, by the exercise of reason and conscience, the fundamental decisions necessary to the direction of their government and of their lives.[42]

The defect which the system cannot countenance, then, is deceitful or hidden handling of opinion in the dress, or in the form, or under the label of "news." The commissions make clear that the right to be in error is individual and personal; the giant carriers of information are described as common carriers facilitating but not limiting public debate.

ʹ VII

PROFESSIONAL ORGANIZATION OF MASS COMMUNICATORS

T H E nature of the mass media has by now been established. Historically, it should be clear that through considerable economic growth the largest units are industrial-type businesses. As a result, although originally established for the intellectual task of purveying news and opinion, they have become factories geared for the mass production of advertising. They cater to public taste for information and entertainment primarily to get and hold a pool of regular readers, listeners, or viewers whose attention can be sold to advertisers. The news-gathering and reporting service, and the editorial or opinion pages, represent financially small parts of the whole. Yet it is this news-reporting and opinion function upon which society relies for self-government. The news-reporting function has caused the press and government to be regarded as of coordinate importance; constitutional protection of the press against interference by government is grounded on the same reasoning.

The reversal inside the firm in weight and scope of the information and the advertising roles brings about a confusion of the controls on accuracy and interpretation of the news. It is not the first instance of such confusion, but it is the first time that it has grown naturally out of a basic change in the economic structure of the media. It now appears that the self-righting process — that is, the provision for equal and open encounter between opposing points of view — is dependent upon the journalists' ability to assure a fair hearing for each of the important constituent groups in national and international society. The control structure, as it supports or impedes the individual journalist's honesty, integrity, and courage in gathering, writing, and editing the news, and in expressing opinion, is similar to that affecting lawyers, doctors, and clergymen. It is impossible for a public agency to supervise the work of such individuals and unwise for it to attempt to do so. Journalists must check and correct each other, if it is to be done, and this means that they must construct and use a system of self-government based on professional ethics. The fact that they may be employed in a business primarily devoted to selling goods and services does not alter the lines of their responsibility, or those of business managers of the media, directly to society.

Ethics as a limit on business goals. Can an ethical structure be provided within the individual business firm, and within the mass-communication industry, that will provide protection adequate to the needs of the community? To arrive at an answer to that question we must examine the control system already established and other contemporary ethical control structures in business and the professions, and venture a suggestion as to how the support needed by journalism could be constructed.

We do not have a great deal of reliable information about the extent to which the public agrees or disagrees with the policy and the performance of the news media. Franklin D. Roosevelt's success over heavy opposition made it appear that the print media lack influence, but the long-term swing of popular voting from 1932 to 1956 is contrary. Aside from their endorsement of political candidates, newspaper proprietors appear to hold few views or adhere to few policies in common. Efforts to study them have been frustrated by their somewhat canny reluctance to put their reputations in the hands of social-science research workers. However, we know from the Bernays surveys that some of the best of them, at least, believe the performance of the press varies from the ideals stated by respected figures in journalism.

⌁ STAFF TRAINING AND DISCIPLINE

It is clear that deviations from ideal journalism arise in the control structure of the self-sufficient, closely-disciplined news room. As a group, journalists lack an image of themselves as persons of importance able to negotiate with the community from the strength of a set of assumptions that guarantees their security. They are under the kind of discipline, from the time of entering upon work as young men until they retire, that sharply limits their initiative; they are concerned about their personal performance

168

and efficiency rather than the performance of the firm. In its simplest aspect, perhaps, this discipline has to do with the style of writing and the arbitrary choices that have to be made among words, word forms, abbreviations, kinds of sentence structure, and rigidly arbitrary headline forms. The journalist is accustomed to adjusting rapidly to the exigencies of available space and to the difficulties that the copyreader may confront in letter-counting a headline. But this authority over form, whether personalized or inherent in typographical limitations, is dogmatic and final; it engenders a frame of mind that makes it difficult to switch from obedience to dissent when discussion of policy takes place in the same context used to deal with grammar. In far too many offices this discipline is administered in schoolmasterish fashion by an editor who has arbitrary dismissal powers. As a result, the journalist develops a negative image of himself and his submissiveness increases. Whether such powers are used (in some offices they are conditioned by labor contracts, in others by a professional spirit) is relatively less important than the psychological effect created when the journalist is subjected to rebuke and nagging in the intimate group to which his prestige is entrusted.

The system of internal control is described by Warren Breed, a sociologist, who has studied non-metropolitan daily newspaper staffs.[1] He limited himself to newspapers with 100,000 circulation or less, and thus excluded the largest and best-known newspapers in the country. However, the internal control system appears to be a function of the personality of the owner rather than size or metropolitan location.

Formation of attitudes. Editors, as a class senior to the journeyman journalist, form their attitudes during a considerable apprenticeship; they have been schooled in the publisher's policy while rising through the ranks. They read their own paper and become familiar with its social orientation. They have more or less frequent contact with the publisher through news conferences, policy meetings, routine office meetings, informal conversations, and perhaps social engagements. It is in the editor's own interest, in position, in advancement, and in enjoyment of the publisher's esteem, to know the office policy well. The editors do not take orders lying down. There is discussion, interaction, debate. The editor fights for his views, but it is taken for granted that the publisher has the final word when he wants it. This convention of discussion enables most editors to maintain their self-respect; few quit in disagreements with the publisher, and those who do tend to be younger men whose standards and values were brought in

169

from the outside. All in all, Breed says, the characteristics of the news operation, despite its association with the dynamic rush of events, are those of the slow-moving sacred society in which great emphasis is placed on harmonious protocol and obedience to authority.[2]

Writing what you know the boss wants to read is one road to recognition. "Nobody goes out and digs up something that is opposed to known policy," Breed says. "Thus the norms governing advancement in most cases are institutionalized in line with conformity." If a man shows independence in policy matters he is spoken to and set straight.[3]

Policy, once formed, tends to perpetuate itself. It becomes part of the structure to be viewed as a value or norm. If it conflicts with reality, rationalizations are found to support policy rather than reality . . . News men retain various professional ideals but apparently the in-group norms and social relationships exert stronger pressure in the direction of policy.[4]

Behavioral patterns of journalists. Breed classifies the staff men who have a relationship to executives on policy matters as follows: (1) Those who follow policy. (2) Those obligated to the boss for favors who therefore feel obligated to support his policy. Some staffs have a family spirit that accomplishes this purpose. (3) Those afraid to do anything except what they are told. (4) Those who follow because they respect the boss in spite of differences. (5) Open-minded writers of the sort who have not been disciplined to seek or ask for answers. Many such persons never think of professional obligations in terms of policy obligations. There is also an attitude of "Things are all right. Why fight?" Staff members of this kind feel no responsibility to the public. They argue that it is hard to prove who is right, hard to find time to gather evidence to counter official opinion. In the absence of evidence, authority rules and staffers frequently exceed the policy demands of the office. (6) There are independent staff members who consistently write what they see and feel without regard to office policy, even though their copy is changed by an editor. Such reporters, Breed found, were fortunate in family background, have personal qualities preferred by the group, and are of high socio-economic status; often a tolerant publisher aids their independence; they have a clear picture of a newspaperman's professional obligations and a firm determination to live them. (7) Finally, there is the ethical reporter who quits his job in protest. Such a one usually is also disillusioned with the press as an institution. These are few, because even when a writer operates within policy restrictions he has some influence on what is printed and this salves his

170

ego. He sees his job fundamentally as reporting, not as policy-making. Moreover, some of the reporters, because of personality differences, get more freedom than others and as a result the less fortunate ones personalize their feelings of frustration. This diverts their attention from the boss.

Because he is satisfied with his work, the newsman is not alert to the shortcomings of his vocation. Stereotypes and traditional ways of doing things more readily perpetuate themselves when critical appraisal is lacking. Routine is his great enemy. Journalists are not rewarded for conceptualizing or analyzing social problems, but for being reporters and editors satisfactory to management.

News is a never-ending stream, a continuous challenge, and meeting the daily challenge is the newsman's job.

In this process news becomes a value to the newsman. It guides his activity in important ways. He defines situations in terms of news values, acts and reacts in terms of them. . . . The true professional man probes into his motives; he is fully acquainted with the elements of his work. . . . Until [the journalist's] awareness of societal inter-relationships is increased, probably by better training, his work will be hampered by standardization and tradition rather than fixed by a systematic professional group.[5]

⌁ PRINCIPLES OF PROFESSIONALISM

The system of discipline for newsgatherers or reporters is not professional because most of the journalists do not take part positively in creating the spirit of the establishment. Instead, they are persuaded by the same routine of training and indoctrination that could produce a truly professional spirit to accept the role and the discipline that goes with the status of hired man. The question that now arises is whether or not this role for the journalist is the one that serves the best interests of the community and, if not, what changes might be suggested in the public interest?

This question is cardinal and fundamental: it brings into examination long-standing concepts of the role of the proprietor, the manager, and the employee. There is no standardized role for management, however. The power to hire and fire confers, by itself, no particular insight or skill in the management of men, and business history records an infinite variety of experimentation. Professionalism is simply one of the ways of seeking out the best employees available and of using the following principles, among others, in working with them:

1. A man who is interested in his work will give better service than one who is not. He comes to identify himself with the firm and to feel he has

171

a stake in it; he will require less supervision, produce more work, of higher quality, and provide a better example for others, than an employee who lacks such identification.

2. Management is only as intelligent as its employees and co-workers; all things considered, the most intelligent employee requires direction only in the sense of utilizing his drive, giving it, along with the energy of co-workers, unified purpose and a sense of direction.

3. Orderly classification of jobs and personnel policies — pay, promotion, problem and policy consultation, grievances — is part of the minimum professional system. This system curbs and harnesses many of the critical aspects of rivalry between men and assures the firm a level of experience and education suitable to each position.

4. Staff direction is supported by a consultation system based on order and precedent and is relatively free of whim and caprice.

5. Opportunities are provided for employees to get further education and to develop special competence that carries prestige with readers and fellow workers.

6. Opportunities are provided for leading members of the staff to cover news events of first importance wherever they happen, to become regional or national as well as local authorities on special problems.

7. Salary schedules compare favorably with community and national averages for work of similar difficulty and, in any event, are high enough to keep the salary negotiations of the professional-class employees out of the trade-union pattern.

8. Pension rights are funded and accompany the man if he changes jobs.

9. All the news of importance is printed or broadcast without deferring to the selfish interests that may be affected.

10. Financial control is unaffected; management retains all initiative and veto rights, but it is committed to delegating as much as possible of staff direction and work processes to professional-class employees. If delegation is incomplete, the benefits are reduced or denied; if delegation goes too far, if the authority is no longer actively and firmly in the hands of participant owners, the incentives are diluted and the staff may lack competition and drive.

The system is not simple to install and maintain, but when carefully managed it produces an institution that will maximize return on capital over the long run. It gives the owners the pleasure of association with intellectual equals and true companions and saves both the loneliness and

172

frustration of running a business solely by giving orders to one or two associates.

Two concepts of professional organization. There are two general concepts of professional organization of the press. The one most widely explored assumes that the ethics of journalism and of business are in conflict and that journalists must organize to protect themselves against the spirit of the counting room. This concept dominated the testimony of working journalists presented to the Royal Commission on the Press in England. Witnesses complained that the editor had lost status and power and that the business manager had taken over his prerogative. It is also implicit in the Hutchins commission's report wherein the press is told to provide the improved service society needs or risk governmental interference.

The other concept is that the whole institution, business and communication combined, should undertake professionalization. Although less often found in scholarly consideration, this concept accepts the unity of communicators and their business partners, rather than seeking to make them opponents within the same firm. The whole-institution proposal offers the best opportunity for long-run success. It is the only kind of professionalism we have at this time. The omission of government from any part in the relationship is deliberate, and eliminates any possibility that professionalism would be considered an abridgement of freedom of the press.

The press is by now familiar with the ability of government to modify policies within a firm or an industry with reference to advertising, manufacturing, or distribution. In all respects except in the standards of writing and editing, the mass media have long been regulated in the public interest. Management, for example, is left free to fix wages above a certain minimum, subject to its ability to bring in revenues to meet the costs. The standards of advertising copy are regulated by law, by shop and community rules enforced by management, and by a large number of state and federal boards, including the Federal Trade Commission, the Food and Drug Administration, and the Post Office Department. All of the regulatory measures, private and official, have been adopted in response to sustained public criticism of business hardly different from the criticism of political bias in the news which is currently heard.

✓ EDITORS AND MANAGERS AS RIVALS

Is the counting room a place which by its very nature excludes ethics of the sort needed by journalism? Is it hopeless to think of professionalizing the business of journalism and should attention be given, therefore, only to reporters and editors? An answer might depend upon the extent to which the professional ideals stated above are supported by conventions existing in business.

Would journalists organized apart from businessmen in the same institution be competent to define and meet the responsibilities outlined for them herein? That would depend on whether they were willing to accept a goal much more limited than that of the whole-institution concept. Their control would be, in the main, negative, even though it might have a number of positive benefits to society. The creative leadership needed to expand the information report would remain in the businessmen who handle the purse.

A British experiment in newspaper control. This point is supported by the testimony of Francis Williams, former editor of the *Daily Herald*, before the British Royal Commission on the Press. The *Daily Herald* at the time Williams was editor was owned 51 per cent by Odhams Press, a large private business also publishing a mass-circulation Sunday paper and magazines, and 49 per cent by the Trades Union Congress. The tie-up on Odham's part was intended to provide it a natural economic market for a daily newspaper favorable to labor's point of view; it was supposed to provide for the trade unions the management skills of a large and successful publishing firm in developing a mass-circulation daily paper able to carry labor's case to a wider audience than they could reach by themselves.

The agreement between Odhams and the trade unions was designed to give labor editorial control of the publication. However, in the normal course of the day's work, Odhams controlled the expenditures of the *Daily Herald*. Williams said this control was particularly important in "large matters of the general policy that the newspaper should follow, in the kind of news it should regard as important and deal with, the kind of space it should devote to particular subjects, the kind of feature articles it should run, and so on." [6] It was the responsibility of the business managers to see that the *Daily Herald*'s circulation was maintained at a point competitive for advertising with other newspapers in the market. The principal differences that arose concerned the editorial policy on public questions and the choice between serious political material important to the labor movement and human-interest reading matter deemed important to circulation growth.

The editor's position had other weaknesses: his budget was not fixed for a definite term but was decided upon daily in conference with Odhams.

Thus the Odhams control extended to the number of pages carried each day, to the features purchased, and to the money available for the expenses of news coverage, including approval of expenses of correspondents abroad or on special assignment.[7]

The publisher's contribution. In presenting its case to the Royal Commission, the National Union of Journalists complained that the faults of the press were due largely to intrusions of this sort by the business side into the editor's domain. Its representatives asserted that in its golden age journalism had achieved prestige and influence because control was largely vested in an editor-in-chief. These arguments were rebutted by the management side. One of the rebuttals came from W. W. Hadley, eighty-two-year-old editor of Kemsley's (now Roy Thomson's) *Sunday Times* who, in his youth, had been an active political dissenter as an associate of Professor A. V. Dicey of Oxford. He said the extent of the proprietor's collaboration with the editor depended wholly on the proprietor's personality. If he was interested in public affairs he discussed and collaborated with the editor in policy decisions; if he was uninformed about events, he kept silent to hide his ignorance. The collaboration "varies according to temperament and personal interest. I do not think it varies according to anything else."[8]

John S. Knight, the Detroit, Akron, Miami, and Charlotte publisher, told a University of Missouri audience in 1949 how the editor-publisher of a large newspaper saw his role. He felt that he must stand responsible in his own conscience, and before the public, for the business and editorial policies of his firm. Such a man is likely to be a typical hard-working law-abiding citizen "with a passion for solvency," he said. He must decide whether to rely on flamboyant headlines and street sales or upon a quieter typography and home-delivered circulation.

He may be constructive, or destructive. He can color the news or insist upon accurate, factual and unbiased reporting from his staff. He can be an inveterate crusader for the right as he sees it or a Caspar Milquetoast who is never sure about anything.

A publisher can be a nasty, petty, mental pigmy who injects his personal prejudices into the columns of his newspaper, or he may stand for the best in constructive leadership and place his faith in the judgment of his readers to recognize integrity and purpose and honor it.

Theoretically the head of the news department should not be concerned with the problems of the business manager, Mr. Knight said, but "actually, co-operation between the two is essential and can be accomplished without making the editorial department an annex of the business office."

This view of the unity of the establishment confirms Francis Williams's experience. Journalists who want to make a radical break in the proprietor's control of communications media recognize that it can be accomplished only by legislation or by some other form of force.

⁊ A RADICAL PROGRAM OF REFORM

Haydn Davies, one of the journalist members of Parliament who testified before the Royal Commission, asked for legislation which would prevent owners from controlling their own businesses. He suggested outlawing monopolies, a statutory press commission treating the press as a public utility, fixed ratios of advertising and news, fixed prices, elimination of all sales promotion except that calling attention to intrinsic values of the publication, and tax relief for proprietors who, in effect, would turn their stock interest and dividends over to a foundation. Finally, he wanted the government to own all printing facilities and to lease them to those who wish to print periodicals. No newspaper could be sold or its doors closed without government consent.

Mr. Davies' ideas show the massive controls that would be necessary to separate the editorial and business departments of a communication medium. They did not find approval inside the Royal Commission or elsewhere in the non-socialist world. They are in part quite like the ideas used by the post–World War II Czechoslovak government in its "bright passage" phase from a syndicate-type democracy to Communism. Even so, ideas of this sort deserve examination of their origins and purposes. If the origin is in frustration, meaning that such proposals are the products of fruitless attempts by minority parties to get a hearing for political alternatives in an open society, they do not deserve to be ignored. Restraint of trade in political ideas, no matter how high-minded and patriotic the monopolists, means — in the parlance of the market — bankruptcy for democracy.

The newspaper proprietor, as the man who has the strongest motive to manage his own capital, is inseparable from the mass-communications establishment in capitalistic society, and there is more point in considering a code of professional behavior for the whole establishment than one solely for news personnel. A balance of ideas in the market place of thought requires concern with the whole establishment. A code limited to the editorial department would either be weakly effective or result in a shift of responsibility to men without training for the job.

✓ THE CASE FOR BUSINESS LEADERSHIP

Does the moral web of the community support business principles upon which a professional organization of the press may be built? Are the principles enunciated by Clarence Francis adequate? Are they able to get acceptance as building blocks in a professional structure?

Business provides a basis for an ethical system more representative of society than does the craft of the journalist. Businessmen are accustomed to think about and deal practically with community-wide problems. The leaders among them have come to accept responsibility for the economic progress of the community, as defined both by themselves and by governmental policy, and insofar as that progress may be realized by initiative, intelligence, and work. In spite of the number of narrow persons among them, a narrow view of community objectives does not prevail, and present goals are subject to enlargement by discussion.

Journalists, by occupation, are trained for a passive but intellectual role in the service of the community and its leadership groups. Not all journalists accept this role; many admire and would follow the example of Greeley in his effort to organize the community politically as well as to lead it intellectually; but when they move out of the editorial conference room into the theater of political action, they no longer are subject to the authoritative interaction of other journalists alone but to the authority of the political group which they have joined.

Responsibilities of business. Businessmen grow up in roughly the same ethical environment as journalists, but today the responsibilities of business include the progress of the community, higher standards of living, higher productivity and abundance, control of the swings of the business cycle, as well as keeping the community favorable to the market place. Businessmen may lead or at least support such large-scale adjustments as the flight to the suburbs, but some of them — particularly those still in the central city — will also be interested in clearing away the blighted areas left behind; when curative measures are taken, businessmen will do the work. They are interested in freedom, although they are not always aware of the reciprocal obligations that attach to it and some may not voluntarily accept the rights-and-duties convention, but in this they are by no means alone; they are selfishly interested in maintaining freedom of choice, to

177

avoid having their hands tied by regulations. They occupy the central position in the communications institutions and they, and only they, have at this time the capacity to evoke a professional spirit in their establishments and to dedicate it to the community. They have at their disposal the bulk of the imagination, leadership, and enterprise needed, and they have control of the resources available for the work.

Businessmen are increasingly aware, because of studies they accept, of the extent to which the individual, in J. M. Clark's words, is "molded in body, mind, and character by his economic activities and relations, stimuli and disabilities, freedoms and servitudes" so that he is the social product of the system he helps maintain.[9] In addition, a surprisingly large number of businessmen — surprising in view of the prevailingly unfavorable publicity business has received at the hands of historians and social scientists in general — have high standards of truthfulness in advertising and selling, fair competition, fair self-assessment and payment of taxes and what Bowen calls the "rules of the game" of business.[10]

Long-term behavior patterns. The concern that business has for the economic well-being of the community might be described as enlightened self-interest, the kind of practical ethics that businessmen were taught in the nineteenth century. A moral judgment in this setting was likely to be motivated by religious teaching, internalized in conscience. In its post-depression twentieth-century orientation, the Judeo-Christian import of ethics has shifted away from the individual conscience to a pragmatic evaluation of action in terms of the risk that it will trigger legislative restraints or other reprisals by the community.

Bowen says that the nineteenth-century ethical heritage of business influences men to (1) observe the rules of property; (2) honor contracts; (3) refrain from deception and fraud; (4) be efficient and promote economic progress; (5) protect life and limb and the health of workers and the general public; (6) compete vigorously and, in case of the failure of competition, to act with restraint; (7) accept and respect the economic freedom of consumers, workers, and owners; and (8) have regard for the human rights of workers. These rules were implicit in Adam Smith's economic theory as contained in *The Wealth of Nations*, because his concept united self-interest and the public interest.[11] That these goals were somewhat beyond the ordinary reach of men, as are some of those expressed by Clarence Francis, does not invalidate the claim that they influence conduct. When A. T. Stewart, the New York large-scale merchant, established a policy of one price for all, plainly marked, and granted reasonable return privileges to his customers, he was applying literally the moral code of the nineteenth as well as the twentieth century, and the fact that his policies received considerable publicity and were widely copied by others, including Wanamaker, shows that in them the practical blending of ethics and business policy had a certain evangelical character in its impact on the public.[12]

Problems arise in industry, not ethics. Bowen says it has been the lot of businessmen since the enormous growth of industry that they have been judged as ethically derelict when in reality their problems stemmed more from malfunctioning of the economic system than from the ethical system. Large-scale enterprise conferred a power on individual capitalists derived from monopoly or concentration; fluctuations in business activity beyond the control of businessmen in a free-enterprise system produced unemployment and dislocation of human beings; technological unemployment grew out of the need to conserve resources and increase productivity; society afforded inadequate protection against illness and old age; the disparities in income and opportunity made the lot of some men intolerable and the life of others bare and uninteresting; there was wasteful exploitation of natural resources when the community lacked the wisdom or legal apparatus to protect itself. Some men were degraded by materialistic, competitive, and invidious standards of consumption. And there was frequent disregard for the social costs of economic activity.[13] The present-day mixed economy, the blend of freedom and regulation, resulted from social legislation critical of business operations. This criticism tended to express the ethical norms of the community; business practices were emended and today reflect an entirely different relationship to stockholders and to the community than in the nineteenth century.

Observance of the reaction of business to public opinion since the great depression provides hope for the objectives implicit in this concept. Although the ultra-conservative elements, those obviously favoring a system of business tyranny, have become more clearly visible as a result of heavy taxation and controversial legislation meshing American economic interests with those of other countries, the liberal element has also become more visible and effective. The intensity of conflict within the community provides an index of the responsiveness of some businessmen to the demands of public opinion and the reluctance of others to accept a new interpretation of self-interest in terms of public interest. The reaction of business to public opinion also suggests that improvement of ethical attitudes will flow

179

from more clearly articulated public demand. The communications media, being at the center of and visible to the whole community, cannot escape the full impact of this demand.

Businessmen are members of society who have acquired many or most of the social expectations of what business should contribute to the community.[14] The wide diffusion of ownership has given greater influence to professional managers who sit as members of a council on policy and project today's problems into the future, correcting insofar as they can for trends that appear unfavorable. "Business is sensitive to changes in the market for its goods and equally sensitive to changes in the market for the business system itself. In both markets it will rise to what is expected of it — but not much higher than that," Bowen says.[15]

✦ THE GENESIS OF PROFESSIONAL ORGANIZATION

Definition of a profession. What is a profession? What are its characteristics? The criteria Abraham Flexner formulated during and after his pioneer work with medical education and professional organization are those commonly relied upon; they are supported by a detailed and respected study in England by A. M. Carr-Saunders and P. A. Wilson. Flexner's criteria: (1) The activity consists of intellectual operations coupled with large individual responsibilities. (2) Raw materials of the work are drawn from science and learning. (3) The learning is practically applied. (4) The technique is communicable by education. (5) A tendency toward self-organization exists. (6) Practitioners are increasingly altruistic.[16]

In medicine and law, Carr-Saunders and Wilson found these characteristics: A technique is acquired by prolonged and specialized intellectual training. The practitioners, as a result of the training, are enabled to render a specialized service to the community. A fixed remuneration by fee or salary is offered. A sense of responsibility develops among the practitioners for the technique which they manifest in concern for the competence and honor of the profession as a whole. The practitioners build up an association which erects tests of competence for entrance and for retaining the right to practice. Considerations of income are not neglected, but the distinguished and overruling characteristic is possession of a technique. It is the existence of the specialized intellectual technique, acquired as the result of prolonged training, which gives rise to professionalism and accounts for its peculiar features. This technique may be either scientific or institutional.[17]

180

Does journalism meet the criteria of the definition? When professionalization of journalism is considered, it is often said that journalism does not fully possess either the general or the legal-medical criteria and it is sometimes assumed that for it professionalization is therefore difficult if not impossible. Such a conclusion overlooks the infinite variety professionalism takes; moreover, the practice of law and medicine is undergoing changes which bring it constantly closer to the institutional forms of journalism. The Hutchins commission, observing that most journalists are employees and that their employers take ultimate responsibility, found little hope that journalism could reach professional status. It observed:

No public service is more important than the service of communications. But the element of personal responsibility, which is of the essence of the organization of such professions as law and medicine, is missing in communications. Here the writer works for an employer, and the employer, not the writer, takes the responsibility. In the mass media, except at the higher levels of writing, the identity of the individual writer's product tends to be merged in a joint result, as in newspapers, where it is divided among reporter, copy desk, and makeup desk. The effective organization of writers on professional lines is therefore almost impossible.[18]

Is the Responsibility Personal? To what extent is this pessimism justified by comparison of the various professional structures found in this country?

The techniques used by journalism are, indeed, the same techniques used by literate and scholarly men throughout the ages; to them have been added the facilities of printing and these expand the responsibility of the journalist through the community in somewhat the same way that the responsibilities of teachers and ministers are spread through the community. Edition deadlines require completion of work in a fixed time, seriously straining the ability of the journalist to go through the routine of verification and evaluation of material which scholars prize so highly. Ability to do reliable work under these conditions results from mastery of specialized techniques. Do these techniques, even assuming their special difficulty, deserve classification as of less than professional grade merely because many men are literate and could do the work of journalists if they had extra training in work at high speed and under pressure? The answer appears to be affirmative unless the techniques and adaptation result from and are accompanied by a long period of systematic training that clearly makes the journalist a specialist, possessing not only the general arts of literacy but specific understanding that non-journalists do not have.

Compensation and Discipline. The method by which newsmen are paid

181

differs little from the way many doctors and lawyers in corporate or group practice are paid, but the range of earnings finds journalists in an inferior position and this fact causes many of them, at the peak of their abilities, to leave journalism for public relations or some other work. At the same time, others equally competent stay on all their lives.

Though journalists have a sense of responsibility for the competence and honor of the profession as a whole, they are frustrated in making this concern felt because there is no public or private forum in which they are free to express themselves. The lawyer and doctor are put under obligation to identify and to adopt the best available techniques. There is a large and complex system of professional publications serving, through reports of research, to criticize and rectify imperfect procedures and practices that do not meet professional standards. The journalist who wishes to identify the best techniques and to assert leadership must create his own forum, provide his own publication, and distribute it. If he has charges to bring against an unethical colleague, he must act in a situation where the values are more those of supervised schoolboys than of a mature profession.

Responsibility for the Joint Product. As to the assertion that the journalist's product tends to be merged in a joint result by the overlapping authority of the writer, the copy editor, and the makeup desk, there is hardly an essential difference in the organization of responsibility here than in the operating room of a hospital. If anything goes wrong with the way a story is handled it is fairly easy to pinpoint the blame; the law holds both author and publisher responsible. The task of the original writer is very complex: he deals with a living system in which his powers of observation are subject to several kinds of error. He is judged and criticized according to his ability to present a clear, concise, meaningful, and objective account of a significant event or phenomenon. After the story is written it has the stability of inert matter; it is not very hard to tell who did what in the editing and printing processes. It is more difficult to decide whose judgment was correct, but this is also true of a surgical team operating with a complex, living subject capable of several kinds of spontaneous reaction.

The group practice of law is also a fixture of the complex society. The lawyer is often as much responsible to the other lawyers for his performance as is the journalist to others of his staff, and while somebody in the firm is ultimately responsible to the client, the lawyer has at stake his public reputation — normally of greater value to him than an individual

182

fee. The journalist is less firmly rooted in one community only because his relationship to other journalists is governed by the rules of business rather than by the conventions of a profession. This impairment of journalistic status is not difficult to remedy, for it can be corrected by a more intense educational experience and by conventions inside the firm which confer commensurate status and dignity on the journalists.

How Professionalism Comes About. The impetus for a professional movement can develop either within or without the vocation concerned. If it arises within, the motive may be partly to create a shelter of monopoly under which practitioners can pursue their self-interest and partly to improve services to the community. If it arises without, it comes usually when society is in an ugly mood of reaction against abuses inside the vocation. Such an ominous and emotional mood is likely to result in blunderbuss efforts at correcting abuses through legislation; the only countermeasure open to practitioners is to correct or prevent abuses themselves.

When there is no professional organization, when as a consequence the practitioners are apathetic toward community needs, the way is open for non-moral behavior, for corruption and abuse of the institution. In the media, apathy forces the best elements to provide a shield behind which the incompetent elements can work their will in their communities. Freedom of the press, they say, protects them in their apathy, and it does.

When professional controls exist in a democratic society they tend to be highly decentralized. This makes them more difficult to use, and if they are not used a condition of disgust even worse than apathy develops as practitioners react against the pseudo-professionalism from which they had expected so much. A professional system without significant standards of excellence and discipline is worse than unorganized status, for society is likely to relax its vigilance, at least for a time, when professional controls are established. Professional organization is not effective without high-quality leadership, but it does provide rewards and recognition for leaders; in fact, professional organization is useless unless it is clearly an expression of an already existing professional spirit. Although this spirit may be shared by a minority of the persons affected, when it exists in a valid setting it can be taught to others.

⁊ JOURNALISM—A VEHICLE FOR LEADERSHIP

The importance of journalism is that it is a communications vehicle for leadership of all sorts in the community, a vehicle provided either by its practitioners in their own right or by them in their capacity as transmission agents for other leaders. Mass communication has a virtual monopoly on the attention of the mass public. If society is to be efficiently organized it would seem that the press will have to take part either as a principal or as an agent of principals. Apathy of individuals with respect to the whole society under these circumstances entails assignment of the leadership role on the basis of random or accidental factors and each crisis arising in the community makes necessary the selection of new leaders and the building of a new organization to deal with it.

Feedback from the community. Professional organization and communication provide the feedback of signals which enables individuals and firms to monitor their behavior. In the long run, the use of such feedback by an elite inside the professional group appears to be the only substitute for control from the outside by untrained members of the general public. It is feedback that provides an opportunity for a firm or practitioner to relate activities to social norms. Otherwise, events in the outside world appear to have no relevance; one can do as he pleases. For the firm, this feedback may have implications for news or editorial policy, for attitudes of employees toward the public, or for some aspect of service relationships with the public. For the individual, it may have to do with adequate training for the role of journalist, performance in an instance important to the community, conflicts or agreement between personal or professional behavior and the social norm.[19] At any rate, it is clear that instilling moral norms in the individual is not sufficient guarantee of professional behavior in the social interest; the situation of society is so complex that a set of institutional principles is needed to which the individual practitioner can refer when he is confronted with circumstances for which there is no norm, or at least none known to him. Professionalism provides these principles and specific rules as interpreted in the long stream of interaction with the community: it helps reject apathy and drift as directing forces in the organization of society.

Tests for entering a profession. Professional men give expression to their sense of responsibility by providing tests for the entrance of neophytes. Professional organizations in law and medicine, working with schools to which they can give or withhold accreditation — that is, the right to operate inside the profession — prescribe a minimum course of study for all trainees and cap this with formal examination and the issuance of a revocable license to practice. Many other professional organizations, including those of public-school teaching, social welfare, accounting, public administration, engineering, and architecture, also establish effective minimum standards in one way or another. At present, the only generally applied tests for entrance to the practice of journalism are the ability to read and write, and some critics of journalism doubt that this test is administered so as to catch all illiterates.

↗ NEWS AND ADVERTISING AS COMMODITIES

The joint interests and responsibilities of the firm with respect to advertisers and readers must be acknowledged, but they are clearly separable. Insofar as the entrepreneur in mass communication employs his capital for the sale and distribution of advertising services, the courts have held that he has no special privileges in business or in society. But in his semi-industrial role as a collector and disseminator of information, he has considerable protection against interference, because it is assumed that the political system cannot survive without this service. If adversaries conspire to use personal or political power to threaten his income from advertising in order to weaken his independence as a carrier of information and opinion, government will protect his establishment if called upon to do so. But if he chooses to give in to pressure rather than ask for protection, and if he surrenders quietly without the public's knowledge, the information he purveys is biased and works to accomplish a distortion of the political system. The protection society affords the press against official intimidation is considerable: it includes habeas corpus, trial by jury, sharp limitations upon the contempt powers of the courts, protection against special and punitive legislation, and a flat ban on the censorship of political material. But the private pressures on the management of mass-communication enterprises work against no countervailing force except that which is capable of ethical description. Only the personal character and intelligence of the individual entrepreneur, as expressed in his own actions and in instructions to his staff, protects the public against pollution of its information sources. And if the contaminants are carefully apportioned so as not to cause widespread loss of confidence, the mixture can be continued indefinitely. Typically, it is the work of ethical organization to monitor institutional performance in reporting news and to implement counterpressures to apathy and corruption. To say that advertising is in a position to dominate the mass media of communication is by no means correct, for, if in the mind of the controlling entrepreneur, his role in providing public information is of greater value than the service he performs for advertisers, regardless of the relative size of his income from readers and from merchants, then advertising merely contributes to support of the economic facility by which the news is carried to the masses in a manner and on a scale befitting the industrial age. It does not exert a damaging influence on contents of a medium whose staff is determined to put the news value first.

✓ COLLEGIATE INSTRUCTION IN JOURNALISM

Journalism is taught as an academic subject in scores of colleges and universities. In 1958, enrollment of 11,263 students, 23.7 per cent of them in graduate schools, was reported by one hundred institutions.[20] The standard educational plan sets up required work in journalism on about the same basis as the work in any of the major subjects in the curriculum leading to the bachelor's degree. In practice, students are allowed to take more than the minimum required. Master's degree plans are widely available. One or two schools emphasize the M.A. as the terminal degree rather than the B.A., thus allowing the student to choose his own mixture of a major, minor, and elective courses for the B.A. degree as well as taking work in journalism. This mixture is more limited when journalism is used as the major in a four-year program.

Education for journalism occupies the same position in the collegiate organization as education for business, for engineering, and for teaching in primary and secondary schools. Each of these areas is under criticism by those factions in education which insist that professional and vocational training be excluded from the bachelor's curriculum.

It is with education – and support for it in the mass communications industries – that professionalization in journalism could begin if it is to follow the general line of development in law and medicine. Two clear-cut goals of acknowledged value are involved, the general and the specialized education. The general, or liberal, education is intended to qualify the student for an active and participant role in the community, in economics, politics, sociology, and aesthetics. From these studies, it is assumed, the student derives a skill in understanding the aims and ends of life so that his inner vision of the cultured self will persist in whatever vocation he undertakes. Actually, the liberal education of tradition no longer exists in compact or accessible form. In its place have grown up several departments in the natural and social sciences and the humanities, each with a series of courses of length and variety sufficient to take most of the stu-

186

dent's time; material taught in courses in these departments overlaps to an important extent with knowledge available to students in the courses of sister departments.

The specialized or vocational curriculums based on the liberal arts are intended to provide the skill and the training needed to get a job. In law and medicine the special course of study is worked out by a professional-education council in conference with a similar group representing teachers. The aim, to provide broad training to deal with the many problems and contingencies that arise in practice, leads to a conflict for time between the general and the special curriculums. In this conflict, the general educational interest loses to the special interest. In medicine and law three years are spent in general education and work taken later in professional courses is then allowed to count toward both professional and arts degrees. The preparatory work in medicine is heavily concentrated in the science and mathematics needed to support specialized courses. The subject matter of law more closely relates to the social science aspects of general education, particularly history, economics, business administration, government, and sociology; but in the professional courses it is organized primarily to support performance in the practice of law. The overview of the community the student traditionally was expected to get from a liberal education is not usually provided, and is not predominant even in postgraduate work.

The natural pattern. The natural pattern of education for journalism is more like law than medicine, for while journalism's special province of concern is political and economic, the problems with which its writers and editors must deal are basically as broad as art and science themselves. For this reason, the basic professional curriculum must in large part be interchangeable with the curriculum of general education. The question that professional schools of journalism still debate is to what extent the curriculum, as it is extended after the pattern of other professional curriculums to five and, in some cases, seven years, should be specialized in one or more of the general education fields, and to what extent in the practice of communication.

The journalist who takes a bachelor's degree and goes to work on a print or electronic medium is like the accountant in the sense that he adds to his basic education a highly specialized and intimate knowledge of the problems of his firm and of his community. The knowledge obtained can be transferred only to a limited extent to another firm or community. The routine of work and the technique of analyzing problems can be transferred, but the operations data are different.

Crowded four-year curriculum. It is clear that journalism education already has taken as much time from the general pursuit of knowledge as have law and medicine; any addition to its professional curriculum, whether journalistic or drawn from the social or natural sciences, should be at the graduate level. The great majority of students entering schools of journalism at present do so to develop communication skills that have become important to them earlier in school. To accomplish this development, they are willing to submit to a regime of drill and practice in writing, editing, and presentation and to absorb the information about communication agencies as social institutions that is required by the journalism faculties. Some of them develop additional interests while still in school and carry these out by graduate study. The great majority of them go into professional work with special training only in writing and editing general material for the uncritical mass audience. That it is not adequate training for learned men is evidenced by two matters of common knowledge: most journalists regard themselves as inadequately informed in specialized areas and lean on specialists to make up the deficiency. The journalist is trained to lean on others and to pass along to others, through the convention of attribution, the responsibility for winnowing out truth in the windrows of error cast up in the day's news. To the extent that this creates a chronically dependent relationship, it lacks professional spirit of a tenacious and vigorous order. The network of professional journals in the social and natural sciences and the humanities shows that the specialist is unwilling to rely on general publications for his information and therefore provides his own literature for that purpose. This leads to his isolation from the general public, for only rarely does a subject-matter specialist have the gift of communication with the masses and with his fellow specialists at the same time. Sir James Jeans, the gifted writer and physicist, was a rare combination indeed. In part, this is because the vocabulary and the field theory that one learns in becoming a specialist is not readily translatable into the language of the layman; also involved is the fact that communication with laymen has few rewards for the specialist. The kind of recognition he wants is from his fellows, not from the general public.

Scholars require interpreters. It is this conflict between the general public's desire to know and the scholar's desire for relative privacy that puts the communicator between the scholar and the public. It is a role of importance and honor but it cannot be executed without considerable additions to the learning of the journalist. It is not a role forced upon the journalist by the mass public; rather, it is one assumed voluntarily to bring about an increase in public knowledge. The best units of the mass media are a long way ahead of their average reader.

The knowledge that journalists acquire by "virtue of prolonged and specialized intellectual training"— to refer again to the definition of a profession — can be selected from the sciences and social sciences. Such learning, by itself, is vocationally competitive with journalism. The learned man who stays with journalism must have something of the personal dedication that is found in the ministry, law, and medicine, and this spirit of service must be conveyed to the neophyte journalist while he is quite young. This can be done by recognizing that formal training must begin early; it should have about it the intimacy of the master-apprentice relationship. The use of journalistic employment supervised by educational institutions can help to provide the required internalization of precept, and will in substantial degree provide for commitment to a journalistic career. The students can then accomplish more quickly their simple training in reporting and editing. There remains much advanced work along that line to be done in school.

The subject matter of journalistic practice on the professional level and study of the arts and sciences will fill the undergraduate and graduate years. The neophyte will not have time, however, to develop a field of specialization as an undergraduate and, in most cases, he will not even become aware of the possibilities of growth in a particular direction until he has mastered, through work on the job, the ordinary communications skills and starts seeking a way in which to achieve a meaningful life. A system of graduate fellowships, probably requiring sums over the long run too large for private resources alone, will be required to make possible graduate education of journalists as specialists in fields such as physics or chemistry, law, economics, social welfare — fields important to civilization and to self-government. Students will differ as to the time of greatest readiness for graduate study and the system will have to be geared accordingly. Many journalists — the majority, perhaps — will not want this kind of training, preferring to make a career out of technical competence. While the First Amendment prevents government interference with editorial conduct of the press, freedom would be enhanced by academic fellowship grants to established journalists, administered by professional educators, designed to improve the quality of the American electorate through the broad graduate education of journalists. The precedent for such grants has been well established in the help given to medical and public-health education and the training of foreign-service personnel, social welfare workers, farmers, and teachers. Specialized graduate training for some journalists won't make the quality newspapers any more effective than the schools in imparting knowledge and improving the national character. But the method is the most promising avenue of journalistic preparation and is in the highest scholarly tradition our civilization affords.

Pattern of employment. Education for a profession cannot depart radically from the pattern approved by the profession itself. A characteristic facility for giving such approval is the council in which educators and practitioners join to decide upon standards of instruction. Manifestly, journalism is practiced in a very wide variety of establishments, ranging from the man-and-wife newspaper to very large organizations. A professional basis for journalistic practice exists wherever the medium is purchased directly by the public. The plan of specialized education advanced is not radical; many successful journalists today have followed it substantially. The media could finance it simply by paying the bill and charging the cost to the public; but this is unlikely and philanthropic and educational institutions already are leading the way. In these early stages of professionalism, only the largest concerns can afford professionally trained people; already the pioneers have demonstrated the profit of employing the best persons to be had.

The ideal educational pattern. The pattern of professional education will be changed both by society and by the employers. Employers can adopt standards that will reward those persons willing to spend a longer time in school. The ideal would be three levels of preparation, formalized as clearly attainable goals, corresponding to the professional opportunities that now exist. On the first level would be baccalaureate-degree holders who would be employed in simple writing and editing or advertising sales and service assignments. The second level would be reserved for holders of the master's degree or the equivalent, and the larger newspapers, magazines, and electronic units could draw the bulk of their beginning employees from this level. Workers on these two levels would be kept mobile by opportunities to win fellowships for specialized study. The third level, open to those with three years of graduate study or the equivalent, would be reserved for the fields where knowledge of theory and of basic specialized literature is necessary in order to write intelligibly of politics, economics, science, medicine, law, public welfare, and the host of other specialties important to self-government. It must be repeated, however, that criteria for employment can be established only by the employers. Not all journalists, far from a majority, could be expected to specialize on the third level. The general practitioner is needed; it is not at this time economic to hire a man of higher skill to perform his duties. He, as well as the specialist, is entitled to dignified and satisfying employment. But the opportunity of being promoted to the work of level two or three while having the intellectual and experience attainment of a level-one person should be restricted. Educational achievements on the three levels can become a basis for tests of competence and for promotion.[21] The scheme of preparation outlined is very similar to that maintained by the institutions of higher learning for their own faculties; it therefore is not particularly experimental. The needs of the media and of the institutions are similar, for their tasks are the same; but the schools affect only the few thousands who attend college and the media are in continuous touch with the masses. No good reasons appear why the media should not employ in their educational work men and women as well prepared as university teachers.

Under improved conditions of education, journalists can develop, as other men of professional attainment have done, suitable job tenure, higher compensation, wider freedom to gather and to write significant news, and dignified consultation procedures for the protection and development of the profession. The prime condition is unity of professional education and practice with the ownership and operation of the media. Uniformity of working conditions in all shops is not a desirable goal, though a statement of minimum conditions doubtless will someday be drawn up.

◆ THE PROFESSIONAL COUNCIL OF THE PRESS

The importance of a professional council has been mentioned. A council can give wide support to professional standards. The British, with a press system almost identical to ours, introduced a General Council of the Press for this purpose in 1953. It is an independent body of twenty-five members supported by organizations of editors, journalists, and newspaper proprietors; its jurisdiction is national in scope.

Fifteen members represent editors and journalists and ten represent owners. The participating groups are the British Guild of Newspaper Editors, somewhat like the American Society of Newspaper Editors; the National Union of Journalists, comparable to the American Newspaper Guild; the Institute of Journalists, an organization with some of the characteristics of Sigma Delta Chi, the ASNE and the Guild; the Newspaper Society, composed of proprietors of provincial dailies and London and provincial weeklies, a group somewhat like an amalgam of the regional daily groups, Inland Daily Press Association, Southern Newspaper Publishers Association, and the National Editorial Association; and two Scottish groups of proprietors. The members are elected by the groups they represent for three-year terms.

The purposes of the British council, as set out in its constitution, are to defend the established freedom of the press, to maintain the highest professional and commercial standards, to keep under review problems of access to information, to aid education for journalism, to "promote a proper functional relation among all sections of the profession," to promote research, to study concentration and monopoly, and to publish reports of its work and its investigations.

What the Council does. In practice, the Council sits to consider any problems it finds to be within its stated objects and it receives communications from the public and from government officials about the performance of the press. It has a general-purposes committee which meets on call and which investigates complaints about press performance. The full Council holds quarterly meetings, issuing statements of its findings after each meeting that are widely quoted in the press. It also publishes an annual report. Its sole method of influencing either the press or the public is through the medium of its public statements. These have the character, though not the force, of court opinions and are based on investigation and consideration of the facts in disputes brought to its attention. The Council has no privilege against libel suits or contempt action by the courts or Parliament; it is under the same obligation as any journalistic group to issue accurate reports.

Criticism of Journalistic Behavior. The largest part of the Council's business is dealing with complaints about the behavior of journalists in line of duty — complaints alleging violations of privacy; imposition on persons in the news or their families; sensationalism and even pornography in news, features, and photographs; breaches of professional ethics; and infringements of official privilege by publication of restricted documents. The Council has found itself speaking for the press in explaining how journalism does its work and what freedom of the press consists of. It has defended the popular mass-circulation newspapers except as to exploitation of sex crimes and sensation in the news and has been attacked, on this account, as a gang of journalists defending other journalists. To such complaints the Council has replied simply that it does not defend journalists, but the freedom of the press.

The problems dealt with are those which have long caused tension between the press and the public. Before the establishment of the Press Council complaints about press performance rarely were answered; the public tended to build up a general attitude of ire and indignation against the press. Prompt investigation by the Press Council has helped to clear away some of the indignation, but has not satisfied everyone. The Council says that some of the critics are "in need of the curbs they propose for others, since they themselves are guilty of the offenses they allege — wild exaggeration, distortion of the truth, and the unproved assumption that they speak for the nation." It has not hesitated to censure particular newspapers and particular journalists when they are found guilty of unprofessional practices. The Council's statements have been widely published, thus giving publicity to a wide variety of case studies of journalistic standards. They have made it more difficult for editors and journalists to engage in unethical and unfair competitive practices. When journalists have been unjustly accused, or have been imposed upon by persons selfishly interested in getting into print only their own version of an event, the Press Council has defended them with dignity and firmness.

Criticism of the Council. Thus the Council considers disputes according to the established ethical system of the community and lets its decision run accordingly. When criticized as ineffectual, it replies that it does not want the legal power to summon witnesses and take testimony under oath, nor the power to disqualify or punish journalists found guilty of unprofessional practices. Such powers would bring in the government and might interfere with freedom of the press, it says. Many critics find the Council unsatisfactory because it consists solely of journalists and is weakly financed by its sponsors. These critics describe reproof of erring journalists as mere slaps on calloused wrists. All such criticism runs either to the admitted immaturity of professional spirit or to the demand that the Council take on official status. The proponents of an official Council have yet to demonstrate that it is compatible with political freedom.

Representation of the lay public on press councils is much discussed.

The Social Responsibility of the Press

The British Royal Commission recommended that a lay chairman and members constitute a fifth of the council. The private commission headed by Dr. Hutchins contained no journalists and subsequent proposals for a press council influenced by Hutchins insists on lay representation.

Objection to lay councilmen. The press is not likely to accept a council strongly influenced or dominated by laymen; to do so would permit direct contradiction of the principle that a highly trained elite group can better serve society than laymen, no matter how well intentioned. But the public is in a more awkward position in dealing with the press than with professions not protected by the First Amendment. Law and medicine can be reached and influenced by legislation; education, insofar as it is supported by public funds and governed by public boards, is the creature of the state; but religion and journalism have constitutional protection and law reaches them indirectly if at all.

For this reason lay representation on a press council takes on greater importance. It appears to be more than a device by which frustrated minorities, crusaders, and bearers of grievances hope forcibly to urge their views upon the press. A council on which the press has four votes out of five, and in which legal sanctions are impossible, appears to provide adequate protection to journalistic interests; but if the chairman is a layman professional control is lost. Laymen seeking the power to influence the press cannot in any valid sense accept the responsibility that goes along with their power. The press, not they, pays the price for the council's errors of judgment. Journalists fear that a council with lay members would have to spend its energy explaining professional conditions to laymen and that lay members would encourage the public to make controversial demands upon the resources of the press.

A regional or national press council that arises naturally and spontaneously out of local professional units would consist wholly of journalists and their business associates and could have great influence on the practice of journalism. A council lacking this composition would not have the confidence of the press and would lack support and influence.

⌁ THE NUCLEUS OF PROFESSIONALISM

As we have seen, a large number of organizations already perform quasi-professional functions for journalism. Among them are Sigma Delta Chi, professional journalism society, the American Society of Newspaper Editors, the National Association of Broadcasters, the National Associa-

194

tion of Radio and Television News Editors, the American Newspaper Guild, the Association for Education in Journalism, and the American Council on Education for Journalism, the National Conference of Editorial Writers, and the American Newspaper Publishers Association. To achieve full professional status, these organizations would have to do the following things: (1) Unify that part of their effort concerned with professionalism. (2) Provide central facilities for hearing, analyzing, and answering public complaints about journalistic performance. (3) Represent most journalists concerned primarily with daily news reports important to self-government. (4) Provide a representative regional and national structure so that relations with the public could be dealt with uniformly in a local context. (5) Form a national council and provide it with financial support. (6) Accept responsibility, with the schools, for the implementation of a program of professional education. (7) Undertake comparative studies of professional employment standards.

The profession would then be in a position, for the first time, to deal with public misunderstanding of the media. Regional councils would be needed and could be organized by the many local professional and trade groups existing on that level. Blind public frustration could be ended by the adjudication of complaints against the press; public understanding of news-gathering problems could be enhanced by consultation.

It should be emphasized, however, that professionalism already exists, or can be established, in any local office where some or all of the conditions described have developed and are enforced. The council gives strength but it is a final, not a primary stage of organization.

⫸ THE PROSPECTS BEFORE US

What are the chances that the organizations listed above, and others that might join, will undertake formal professional organization?

There is hope that leaders who see the possibility of added contribution of the mass media to national energy and destiny will voluntarily bring about professionalism. They already have accomplished a professional spirit in their own offices. The evidence of this success is everywhere seen and admired, and the basic contribution of better status for journalists would be to raise many more publications and broadcasting stations to that level. The great newspapers today provide the nucleus around which professionalism is growing.

If one looks for a catalyzing influence in hastening professionalism, he

The Social Responsibility of the Press

finds it in the unfolding challenge of the world situation, the attendant development of a managed economy, and the compulsions that attend goals of full employment in the welfare state. The press is not able to stand aside from any of these influences; all of them compel a certain response to national requirements.

American society confronts the problems of world security with a government, and with supporting media of communication, based on relatively free private enterprise and initiative. Nuclear terror is the ultimate contradiction of such a value system; it is a force of such magnitude that it was subjected to national, rather than to private, control from the beginning. The control problem now is one of subjecting sovereign national governments to authority that will carry to terror-prone groups the assurance of peaceful relationships. Journalism and politics could hardly have a more difficult task in remaking the public mind so that it will accept the necessary limitations on traditional national prerogatives.

This difficult assignment has been evident since transportation and communication wiped out cultural isolation and threw into conflict functional, local, regional, national, and international groups seeking to insulate themselves against alien ways of carrying on accustomed roles. The interaction of these groups makes up the news of the hour, the problems of the decade, and the burdens of the century. Men become aware of needed adjustment in many ways, but the pattern and meaning of life are explained particularly by the mass media. In the way they present the news of the world and the community, media contribute positively or negatively to adjustment; they have the ability to define group values and to help apply sanctions with respect to "deviation," "heresy," and "treason," and to provide rewards for "patriotism" and "loyalty." These great words, and others like them, predominate in the struggle to widen the range of peaceful law and order.

The persuasive example of regulation. Radio and television, because they use electronic frequencies, must be licensed and regulated, and the anxieties the owners feel about government regulation are clearly visible. The printed media put too much reliance on the theory that there is no limit to the actual number of publications that may be printed and circulated. The number of publications is not calibrated according to the molecular structure of matter nor is it regulated by international convention, but it is a limited market just the same. Only a very few large general publications can enter it and survive. In all but sixty towns and cities there

196

appears to be only one "frequency" available for allocation in the newspaper market. When competition forces out of the market several hundred of the radio stations now existing, and limits television stations far below the number of available channels, the parallel may become clear.[22] Those media depending upon advertising for support are competing in the same market and the critics dissatisfied with the performance of the printed media can soon persuade themselves that if government regulates the electronic media in the public interest and necessity it ought also to regulate the printed media.

The experience of British journalism during World War II shows that economic stability can be achieved under private ownership by a cartel that allocates to each proprietor a share of the available readers and advertisers. Government sanctions are necessary to achieve this kind of economic balance, but in Britain the government delegated its power to a committee of proprietors and kept its distance. The effects came from a decision to budget for a total journalistic product only 21 per cent of normal demand and to force each firm to adjust its charges for advertising and its number of copies accordingly. When this arrangement ended, a deep swell of adjustment forced several important national papers out of business, brought about greater concentration of ownership, and left the country to puzzle over the paradox of competitive freedom that brings concentration and of cartel that achieves a diversity greater than the free market affords. The cartel produced frustration and bias in the market, too, as well as preserving direct representation for certain organized points of view, notably that of the Labour and Liberal parties. It was abandoned because the country wanted to maintain the traditional liberty of the press as long as possible, but the paradox remains.

Our preference for freedom. Our political theory assumes the media will be supported and governed by individual private enterprise; it compels a posture of optimism about the self-righting character of the opinion-forming process; it puts no particular premium on speedy rectification of conflict in the community. It provides no sure stimulus for consideration of problems now lost in areas of silence or inadequate communication and it leaves the community interest, in the late twentieth century, to be interpreted by private persons who must provide short-run protection for a business that, in association with national leadership, teaches the public long-run solutions to its problems. From this teaching or interpretation there is no effective appeal and, ordinarily, when inquiries are made about the nature of the private conscience of public communicators they are rejected as impertinent. Nevertheless, as these pages recount, such inquiries have been made and respected voices judge the general quality of our social institutions, including the mass media, to be largely inadequate to the needs of the society, under pressure as it is from cultural confusions and international competition. There is less confidence in Milton's calm assurance that, in the long run, all will be well; there is scant evidence that the people understand the problems of carrying on global competition with an ideology specifically designed to outmaneuver the private-enterprise system. There is, on the other hand, wide evidence that the content of the mass media is intended primarily to get large audiences for advertising; journalists by and large do not feel obliged to finance for the nation wider information and analysis of conditions in the interest of self-government.

The tradition of private enterprise is still strong, but so is the determination that nothing should stand in the way of giving the United States the institutions it needs for pre-eminence and security in the world. The constitutional protection of freedom of speech and press already gives way, in general, to war conditions. If the strains of international rivalry become more characteristic of the country than peace, the press has little protection; it cannot survive under severe material and labor shortages without accepting government economic control.

Would any American party dare modify the First Amendment by attempting to reform the press system? Hardly by frontal attack, but again the reference is to be found in conditions already much disturbed, not in traditional behavior. If the domestic or international situation lessens the people's confidence in their government, and if they blame journalists, as well as politicians, for failure to provide adequate notice of developments, reprisal is to be expected. The system of political liberty came about, in the first place, because no one faction could assert control of the government over the long run and protection for political rights had to be worked out that are good under any government. Only by such a convention — and by such a threat — can the First Amendment be preserved. When control of the press is unvaryingly in the hands of one party, or the dominant faction in a coalition government, the political truce represented by the First Amendment is in danger of collapse. There is no reason why the offended party or faction, in its day of power, should defer to an institution long and clearly biased against it. Unless a majority benefits from the guarantee of freedom of the press, the truce cannot endure.

Obstacles to press security. The conditions now developing do not yield readily to human negotiation or to law, for they represent basic alterations in the country's ecology. If the basic political transformation is from a condition where power is atomized to one where it is tellingly concentrated, the form of government, like the form of the press, is altered. President Kennedy and former President Eisenhower could hardly have been thinking of anything else when they separately asked military leaders to keep out of politics and foreign policy. Harrison Brown was thinking of similar problems when he spoke in 1961 to the American Association for the Advancement of Science: In the absence of nuclear war, fantastic growth in the population rate, accompanied by an advanced machine technology which leaves few jobs for workers, could force us to adopt more and more rules and regulations that can be enforced only by modern tools of coercion and persuasion in the hands of government. Once freedom is lost, he said, rulers can keep the people from regaining it by the use of modern technological power.

Timely provision of adequate information can give the people an opportunity to deliberate and to decide upon trends in the government and in society; serious communication is within the capability of the mass media. But the old agrarian world and its pleasant institutions, like the gentleman's tournament of reason, is no more; new institutions arise from conditions, from technology, and from the wills of determined, creative men. These institutions need not be democratic; only vigilance can make them so.

Professional spirit is a powerful defense against the acceptance of imbalanced government, against technological captivity, against coercion and disruption of political communication, because it attracts and trains persons able to cope with tasks of such magnitude. Pride in political liberty, internalized in the consciences of journalists and pre-eminent among the common values of the community, can release journalism from the thralldom of non-involvement and fear to work for the repair and maintenance of the self-governing community.

Jefferson said that when the people are free to read and understand, all will be well. He spoke with food in his fields and barns and a great moat of time and space around his homeland. Now there is room for doubt that the people are free, as he was, and that their reading and viewing bring understanding and control of the basic elements of political freedom.

Notes and Index

NOTES

I. *The Nature of Mass Communication*

¹ Carl I. Hovland, "Psychology of the Communications Process," in *Communications and Modern Society*. Urbana: University of Illinois Press, 1948, p. 62.

² Joyce O. Hertzler, *Social Institutions*. New York: McGraw-Hill, 1929, p. 29.

³ Sir Robert Hunter, "Commons," in *Encyclopaedia Britannica*, 11th edition, Vol. 6, p. 779.

⁴ Quoted by George H. Sabine, *History of Political Theory*. New York: Henry Holt and Company, 1937, pp. 451–454, from Coke's *Reports*, Part 12, p. 65.

⁵ T. W. Rhys Davids, *Encyclopaedia Britannica*, 11th edition, Vol. 14, p. 737; Celina LuZanne, *Heritage of Buddha*. New York: Philosophical Library, 1953, pp. 249–282.

⁶ Charles Warren, *Jacobin and Junto*. Cambridge: Harvard University Press, 1931, pp. 50–51.

⁷ Frank L. Mott, *Jefferson and the Press*. Baton Rouge: Louisiana State University Press, 1943, pp. 5–8.

⁸ Francis Samuel Philbrick, in *Encyclopaedia Britannica*, 11th edition, Vol. 15, p. 302.

⁹ See Croswell's case in Frank Thayer, *Legal Control of the Press*. Chicago: The Foundation Press, Inc., 4th edition, 1962, pp. 24–26.

¹⁰ Edwin Emery and Henry Ladd Smith, *The Press and America*. New York: Prentice-Hall, Inc., 1954, pp. 170–172.

¹¹ To Thomas Seymour, February 11, 1807. Andrew Adgate Lipscomb, *Writings of Jefferson*. Washington: Thomas Jefferson Memorial Association of the U.S. 1904–05, Vol. 11, p. 155; Warren, *op. cit.*, pp. 71–96.

¹² Mott, *op. cit.*, pp. 28–37; Emery and Smith, *op. cit.*, pp. 155–173.

¹³ This is the Peck-Lawless case; the 1941 Supreme Court decision is the case of *Bridges v. California*, 314 U.S. 252.

¹⁴ *Gitlow v. New York*, 268 U.S. 652 (1925).

¹⁵ Emery and Smith, *op. cit.*, p. 225.

¹⁶ "Getting on in Journalism," *Munsey's Magazine*, Vol. 19, No. 2, May 1898, p. 217.

¹⁷ Edith Merwin Barstow, *News and These United States*. New York: Funk & Wagnalls Company, 1952, pp. 251–253.

¹⁸ Helen MacGill Hughes, *News and the Human Interest Story*. Chicago: University of Chicago Press, 1940, pp. 12–15.

¹⁹ Emery and Smith, *op. cit.*, p. 416.

The Social Responsibility of the Press

[20] Emile Gauvreau, *My Last Million Readers*. New York: E. P. Dutton & Co., 1941, p. 112.

II. *Journalism as Big Business*

[1] Snyder and Tucker in *Historical Statistics of the United States*, 1789–1945. Washington: United States Department of Commerce, Bureau of the Census, 1949, pp. 231–232.

[2] Joseph H. Appel, *Business Biography of John Wanamaker*. New York: Macmillan Company, 1930, pp. 391–392.

[3] Frank A. Munsey, "Advertising in Some of Its Phases," *Munsey's Magazine*, Vol. 20, No. 3, December 1898, p. 476.

[4] *Encyclopaedia Britannica*, 11th edition, Vol. 24, p. 744.

[5] "The Quantitative Analysis Report of Newspaper Content" (1957), *Media Records*, March 14, 1958.

[6] *Statistical Abstract of the United States*, 1960, pp. 219, 858–862.

[7] Neil H. Borden, *The Economic Effects of Advertising*. Chicago: Richard D. Irwin, 1942, p. 923.

[8] *Ibid.*, p. 923.

[9] George A. Brandenburg, "Need of More Net Income Revealed in Cost Study," *Editor & Publisher*, May 19, 1956, p. 58.

[10] Alfred McClung Lee, *The Daily Newspaper in America*. New York: Macmillan Company, 1937, pp. 371–372.

[11] J. P. Wood, *The Story of Advertising*. New York: Ronald Press Company, 1958, p. 230. This book gives many details of advertising developments important to a social evaluation of the mass media.

[12] Victor O. Schwab, *How to Write a Good Advertisement*. New York: Schwab and Beatty, Inc., 1942, p. 17.

[13] *Ibid.*, pp. 25–26; James Davis Woolf, *Advertising to the Mass Market*. New York: Ronald Press Company, 1946, p. 57.

[14] Woolf, *op. cit.*, p. 46.

[15] Clarence Francis, "Businessmen's Responsibilities to the Public," in Harwood F. Merrill, editor, *The Responsibilities of Business Leadership*. Cambridge: Harvard University Press, 1948, pp. 5–12.

[16] For more detailed information about the early work of the Better Business Bureaus, see G. B. Hotchkiss, *An Outline of Advertising*. New York: Macmillan Company, 1933, pp. 452ff. Otis Pease, *The Responsibilities of American Advertising*. New Haven: Yale University Press, 1958, p. 70, reproduces the copy code of ANA and associated groups.

[17] Pease, *op. cit.*, pp. 98–105.

[18] *Ibid.*, pp. 149–150.

III. *The Natural Habitat of the Press*

[1] Based in part upon the annual statistical report prepared by Carl Webb, manager of the Oregon Press Association, covering 1956 operations of weekly newspapers.

[2] Poynter McEvoy, "Statistical Abstract of Newspaper Advertising in Indiana, 1959–60." Bloomington: Department of Journalism, Indiana University, April 1960, p. 9 (mimeographed).

[3] *Ibid.*, p. A-4.

IV. *The Proprietorship Role*

[1] The 1955 figures are from the FCC as reported by *Broadcasting* magazine; 1959 estimated by *Broadcasting*, February 15, 1960, p. 73.

[2] *Broadcasting Yearbook*, 1961–62, from A. C. Nielsen Co. reports, p. D-31; the

Sidlinger data were reported by *Broadcasting* magazine, February 15, 1960, pp. 126–129.

[3] "T.V. Finance: Eight Stations Exceed $3,000,000 Profit," *Advertising Age*, November 9, 1959, pp. 7, 73; Stanley E. Cohen, "Radio Stations Are Nifty Business — Don't Let FCC Data Fool You," *ibid.*, pp. 71, 84.

[4] "Radio Time Sales 1935–1959," *Broadcasting*, February 15, 1960, p. 73, from FCC reports and estimates.

[5] *An Economic Study of Standard Broadcasting.* Washington: Federal Communications Commission, 1947.

[6] *Ibid.*, pp. 1–48. *Advertising Age*, November 9, 1959, pp. 7, 73. An additional report on 1958 figures is in *Editor & Publisher*, October 10, 1959, p. 38.

[7] "T.V.'s Blow to Radio Detailed by Ad Agency," *Editor & Publisher*, March 23, 1957, p. 20.

[8] "Newspaper Circulation Dip Shows Effect of Price Rise," *Editor & Publisher*, International Yearbook, 1962, p. 15, for 1962 figure; see regular edition of July 5, 1958, p. 15, for the 1958 morning, evening, and Sunday figures.

[9] *Special Statistical Report*, Newspaper Audit and Research Bureau, M. S. Kuhns and Company, 11 South LaSalle Street, Chicago, 1958 and 1959 editions.

[10] As to the technical procedures in cost allocation, see *Cost Analysis Procedures for Newspaper Publishers.* New York: Institute of Newspaper Controllers and Finance Officers, 1954. The procedure here is briefly summarized in John B. Olson, "Is Newspaper Pricing Itself Out of the Market?" *Editor & Publisher*, December 4, 1954, p. 57.

[11] Olson, *loc. cit.*

[12] "Impartial Study Suggested to Correct 'Rate Inequity,'" *Editor & Publisher*, January 28, 1956, p. 10.

[13] Harold S. Barnes, "Why Papers Should Boost Dept. Store Ad. Rate 25 Per Cent," *Editor & Publisher*, May 25, 1957, p. 17.

[14] *Reports Presented to Annual Meetings.* New York: American Newspaper Publishers Association, 1954, p. 50.

[15] Max Ascoli, "No Time for Reflection," *The Reporter*, February 14, 1950, p. 4.

[16] *Editor & Publisher*, April 20, 1957, p. 75.

[17] New York *Times*, March 7, 1960, from National Industrial Conference Board: *Printer's Ink*, from McCann-Erickson.

[18] J. Edward Gerald, "The National Advertising Rate Differential," *Bulletin*, Institute of Newspaper Controllers and Finance Officers, No. 45, p. 7.

[19] Daniel Lionel, "Readership Falling? What Are the Causes?" *Editor & Publisher*, November 2, 1957, p. 50.

[20] "One-Pica Change in Column Widths Cut Demand by 312,000 Tons in 1959," *Newsprint Facts*, May 1960, p. 1.

[21] "Cost-Cutting Approach Raises Some Doubts," *Editor & Publisher*, March 17, 1956, p. 17.

[22] "Automation Boom Spreads TTS Operation on Papers," *Editor & Publisher*, June 18, 1960, p. 9.

[23] Poynter McEvoy, "Can Newspapers Reduce Costs by Decreasing News Content?" *The Newspaper Controller*, April 15, 1958, p. 4.

[24] "2 Yardsticks Measure Productivity Decline," *Editor & Publisher*, March 9, 1957, p. 16.

[25] Newspapers also have participated in the tests of the experimental machines and processes. Robert M. Choate of the Boston *Herald-Traveler*, one of the innovators, lists F. M. Flynn of the New York *Daily News*, Irwin Maier of the Milwaukee *Journal*, Prescott Low of the Quincy *Patriot-Ledger*, Samuel H. Kauffmann of the Washington *Star*, Franklin D. Schurtz of the South Bend *Tribune*, John D. Raridan of the Brush-Moore newspapers, Lisle H. Baker of the Louisville *Courier-Journal*, Samuel

W. and Donald P. Miller of the Allentown *Call-Chronicle*, John H. Perry, the Florida publisher, and Gaylord Donnelley of R. R. Donnelley & Sons Co., large-scale Chicago commercial printer.

[26] "Controllers' Studies Show Fringes Add 25 Per Cent to Payroll," *Editor & Publisher*, May 23, 1959, p. 11.

[27] Doris Willens, "Publishers Promote Pension Plans on Many Newspapers," *Editor & Publisher*, July 23, 1955, p. 11.

[28] *Statistical Abstract of Newspaper Advertising in Indiana, 1959–60.* Bloomington: Department of Journalism, Indiana University, 1960, pp. A-7–A-15 (mimeographed).

[29] "Flight to Suburbs," *The Bulletin*, American Society of Newspaper Editors, January 1, 1957, p. 7.

[30] See Robert Feit, "Ratings: TV's Own Numbers Game," *News Workshop*, New York University Department of Journalism, January 1959, p. 1. The Federal Trade Commission issued consent orders in early January 1963 affecting the methods and the claims of audience measurement by The Pulse, Inc., American Research Bureau division of C-E-I-R, Inc., and A. C. Nielsen Co. See "Broadcast Ratings, Inaccuracy Halted," *Editor & Publisher*, January 12, 1963, p. 18.

[31] *Ibid.*

[32] "14 Strikes Against Papers; Not Productive, Unpopular," *Editor & Publisher*, April 27, 1957, p. 27.

[33] George A. Brandenburg, "Chicago Dailies Round Out First Year of ITU Strike," *Editor & Publisher*, November 20, 1948, p. 7.

[34] "Randolph Asks Congress to End Closed Shop Ban," *Editor & Publisher*, May 24, 1958, p. 11.

[35] Jerry Walker, " 'Bogus' Demand Is Legal; Taft Asks Ideas for Ban," *Editor & Publisher*, March 14, 1953, p. 7.

[36] Charles T. Duncan, "Newspapers Slipping as No. 1 Outlet for Journalism Graduates," *Journalism Quarterly*, Fall 1959, p. 476.

[37] "Students Rank J-Work Low on Career Lists," *Editor & Publisher*, March 14, 1959, p. 67.

[38] *The Public Appraises the Newspaper.* Princeton, N.J.: American Institute of Public Opinion, undated (1957?), p. 15.

[39] I. W. Cole, "Reasons for Shortage of Press Personnel," *Editor & Publisher*, March 2, 1957, p. 12; Stanford Smith, "ANPA Offers to Prove Industry Advantages," *loc. cit.*

[40] Norman E. Isaacs, "A Newspaperman's Job Is Also a High Calling," *Quill*, June 1956, p. 7.

[41] "Austin Report Advocates Career Appeal to Youths," *Editor & Publisher*, December 13, 1958, p. 11.

[42] Robert M. Pockrass, "Typical Journalism Graduate Sticks to His Job, Is Optimistic of Future," *Quill*, July 1958, p. 13; 58 per cent of the Penn State graduates did not respond to the inquiry.

[43] "Austin Report Advocates Career Appeal to Youths," *Editor & Publisher*, December 13, 1958, p. 11.

[44] "APME Report Asks Personnel Program," *Editor & Publisher*, July 4, 1959, p. 12.

[45] "Knight Urges Inland Editors to Be More Individualistic," *Editor & Publisher*, February 27, 1960, p. 9.

v. Mass Communication Content

[1] Henry J. Allen, "Yesterday, Today and Tomorrow," in *Conference on the Press.* Princeton: School of Public and International Affairs, 1931, pp. 97–103.

[2] Sevellon Brown, "The Newspaper as a Commercial Enterprise and a Public Institution," in *Conference on the Press*. Princeton: School of Public and International Affairs, 1931, pp. 4–9.

[3] The Report of the Commission on Freedom of the Press, *A Free and Responsible Press* (Foreword by Robert M. Hutchins). Chicago: University of Chicago Press, 1947, pp. 20–21.

[4] *Ibid.*, p. 105.

[5] Edward L. Bernays, *Public Relations Problems of the American Press*. New York: National Newspaper Promotion Association, c/o Irvin S. Taubkin, New York *Times*, 229 West 43d Street, 1952. Two subsequent surveys were reported directly by Mr. Bernays from his office, 26 East 64th Street, New York 21, N.Y.

[6] A survey of religious publications was made by Mrs. Marjorie Allen for a seminar. Publications read from 1930 to 1950 were *Commonweal, Christian Century, Catholic World*, and *Social Action*. In them she found a large number of references to the press and 76 major articles that qualify as evaluative. She made checks of the tables of contents in the following: *Christendom, Humanist, Journal of Religion, Review of Religion, Commentary, Contemporary Jewish Record, Lutheran Church Quarterly*, the *Christian Science Journal* and the *Baptist Leader*.

[7] The author is indebted to his colleague, Professor Roy E. Carter, Jr., for access to his unpublished study of educational journals.

[8] Miss Kathryn Clark, one of the author's students, surveyed *Wall Street Journal, Business Week, Nation's Business*, the *Journal of Commerce, Manufacturer's Record*, and other publications.

[9] Clifton Daniel, James P. Warburg, Joseph P. Lyford, and Louis Lyons, "The Berlin Story," Numbers 10 and 11 in *The Press and the People*. New York: The Fund for the Republic, 1959. Pamphlets, undated.

[10] Adlai E. Stevenson, Barbara Ward, and Louis Lyons, "The Soviet Challenge," No. 13 in *The Press and the People, op. cit.*

[11] J. Kenneth Galbraith, Joseph A. Livingston, and Louis Lyons, "The Economic Facts of Life," No. 5 in *The Press and the People, op. cit.*

[12] Robert H. Estabrook, "What Is a Responsible Press?" in *Social Progress*, Vol. 50, No. 5, March 1960, p. 5.

[13] Louis B. Seltzer, "What's Happening to Our Newspapers?" *Saturday Review*, April 28, 1956, p. 7.

[14] Mark Ethridge, "The U.S. Press Is in Trouble: A Publisher's Diagnosis," *Saturday Review*, April 30, 1955, p. 10; Jonathan Daniels, "An Editor's Diagnosis," *ibid.*; also, Mark Ethridge and Donald McDonald in *The Press*. Santa Barbara: Center for Study of Democratic Institutions, 1961, *passim*.

[15] Carl L. Lindstrom, *The Fading American Newspaper*. Garden City: Doubleday and Company, Inc., 1960, pp. 99–102.

[16] Elmo Roper, Palmer Hoyt, and Louis Lyons, "The Public and the Publisher," in *The Press and the People*, No. 14, *op. cit.*

[17] Erwin D. Canham, *New Frontiers for Freedom*. New York: Longmans, Green and Co., 1954, p. 59.

[18] John Cowles, from an address to Sigma Delta Chi, Columbus, Ohio, November 11, 1954, and in a talk at the dedication of a new building for the Minneapolis *Star* and the Minneapolis *Tribune*, May 28, 1959.

[19] "Campaign Study Referred to 76 Editors, Publishers," *Editor & Publisher*, January 7, 1956, p. 14; "Proposed Study of Election Campaign Coverage Dropped," *Editor & Publisher*, January 28, 1956, p. 9.

[20] *Ibid.*

[21] Charles E. Swanson, "Mid-City Daily," *Journalism Quarterly*, Vol. 26, No. 1, March 1949, p. 20.

[22] *Associated Press v. United States*, 326 U.S. 1 (1945).

The Social Responsibility of the Press

[23] Jerome H. Heckman, "Diversification of Control of the Mass Media of Communication — Policy or Fallacy?" *Georgetown Law Journal*, March 1954, p. 378; J. Edward Gerald, "Governmental Efforts to Diversify Control of the Mass Media," a paper in honor of William Anderson on the occasion of his retirement as professor of political science at the University of Minnesota, 1957 (mimeographed).

[24] An example is *Pinellas Broadcasting Company v. Federal Communications Commission*, 230 Fed. 2d. 204 (1956), certiorari denied (1956).

[25] 9 Pike and Fischer, *Radio Regulation*, 1564 (1953). The FCC voted 4 to 3 on September 16, 1960, to permit continuation of option time but reduced it from a maximum of 12 to 10 hours per day. The majority decided that option time was necessary to the existence of the networks.

[26] Roscoe L. Barrow in a paper read at the National Symposium on Freedom and Responsibility in Broadcasting, Northwestern University School of Law, August 4, 1961, quoting FCC documents.

[27] *Broadcasting and Government Regulation in a Free Society*. Santa Barbara, California; Center for Study of Democratic Institutions, 1959, pp. 4–10.

[28] Newton N. Minow, in an address to the National Symposium on Freedom and Responsibility in Broadcasting, Northwestern University School of Law, August 4, 1961.

[29] *Ibid.*

[30] David Susskind is executive vice president of Talent Associates–Paramount, Ltd., New York. The changes of which he speaks came subsequent to mid-1960 when he was quoted extensively in two *New Yorker* articles by Thomas Whiteside, "The Selling Season," *New Yorker*, June 25, 1960, p. 39, July 2, 1960, p. 35.

[31] *Broadcasting and Government Regulation in a Free Society*, pp. 11–12.

[32] Edward P. Morgan, to the University of Wisconsin Student Association, Madison, February 16, 1960 (mimeographed).

[33] *Ibid.*

[34] Edward R. Murrow, address to the Radio and Television News Directors Association, Chicago, October 15, 1958 (mimeographed).

[35] Frank Stanton, statement to Federal Communications Commission, January 26, 1960, pp. 25–26 (mimeographed).

[36] Marya Mannes, with Robert Alan Aurthur, Evelyn Burkey, Rod Serling, Irve Tunick, Eric Goldman, Frank K. Kelly, and Robert W. Horton, *The Relation of the Writer and Television*. Santa Barbara: The Fund for the Republic, Inc., 1960.

[37] Sevareid, Agronsky, and Lyons, *op. cit.*, p. 12.

[38] Stanton, *op. cit.*, pp. 15–22.

[39] Frank L. Mott, *American Journalism*. New York: Macmillan Company, 1941, pp. 225–226.

[40] Gauvreau, *op. cit.*, p. 184.

[41] Donald M. Gillmor, "Mass Media and Cultural Decline," seminar paper, University of Minnesota, 1960.

[42] Ford Stewart, address to the Association for Education in Journalism, Northwestern University, August 30, 1956.

[43] William Miller, *The Book Industry*. New York: Columbia University Press, 1949, p. 61.

VI. *Freedom's New Community*

[1] Wilbur Schramm, *Responsibility in Mass Communication*. New York: Harper & Brothers, 1957, p. 57.

[2] Harold A. Innis, *The Bias of Communication*. Toronto: University Press, 1951, pp. 33–88; Harold A. Innis, *The Press, A Neglected Factor in the Economic History of the Twentieth Century*. London: Oxford University Press, 1949, pp. 35–41.

[3] See Paul F. Lazarsfeld and Robert K. Merton, "Mass Communication, Popular

Taste and Organized Social Action," in Lyman Bryson, editor, *The Communication of Ideas*. New York: Institute for Religious and Social Studies, 1948, pp. 95–118 (distributed by Harper & Bros.). The article may also be found in Wilbur Schramm, editor, *Mass Communications*. Urbana: University of Illinois Press, 1960, pp. 492–512.

[4] Robert Cooley Angell, *Free Society and Moral Crisis*. Ann Arbor: University of Michigan Press, 1958.

[5] *Ibid.*, pp. 34–38.

[6] *Ibid.*, p. 101.

[7] *Ibid.*, p. 98.

[8] *Ibid.*, p. 3.

[9] On this view of social organization, see Hans Gerth and C. Wright Mills, *Character and Social Structure*. New York: Harcourt, Brace and Company, 1953, *passim*; and David Riesman, Nathan Glazer, and Reuel Denney, *The Lonely Crowd*. Garden City: Doubleday and Company, 1953, pp. 250–257. The concept of the amorphous society and the quoted phrase are in Riesman, Glazer, and Denney, p. 251. In its political aspect, such a society is ordinarily characterized as the decentralized democratic state.

[10] For elaboration of this point, see Gerth and Mills, *op. cit.*, p. xv.

[11] Riesman, Glazer, and Denney, *op. cit.*, p. 32.

[12] Angell, *op. cit.*, p. 96.

[13] Howard R. Bowen, *Social Responsibilities of the Businessman*. New York: Harper & Brothers, 1953, p. 142.

[14] Angell, *op. cit.*, p. 23.

[15] Marquis W. Childs and Douglass Cater, *Ethics in a Business Society*. New York: Harper & Brothers, 1954, p. 90.

[16] Angell, *op. cit.*, p. 9.

[17] J. Whitney Bunting, "The Professionalization of Business," in *Ethics for Modern Business Practice*. New York: Prentice-Hall, 1953, p. 237.

[18] Erich Fromm, "Individual and Social Origins of Neurosis," *American Sociological Review*, Vol. 9, 1944, p. 380.

[19] Angell, *op. cit.*, p. 159.

[20] *Ibid.*, pp. 39, 40.

[21] *Ibid.*, p. 29.

[22] *Ibid.*, p. 30.

[23] *Ibid.*, p. 82.

[24] *Ibid.*, p. 83.

[25] Charles G. Ross, *The Writing of News*. New York: Henry Holt and Co., 1911, pp. 17–18.

[26] Nelson Antrim Crawford, *The Ethics of Journalism*. New York: Alfred A. Knopf, 1929.

[27] The canons may be found in any of the annual meeting volumes of ASNE (published under the series title *Problems of Journalism*) and the International Yearbook numbers of *Editor & Publisher* through 1959.

[28] Walter Williams and Frank L. Martin, *The Practice of Journalism*. Columbia, Missouri: E. W. Stephens Publishing Co., 1911, pp. 9–12.

[29] Ronald Shilen, "Concept of Objectivity in Journalism." Ann Arbor: University Microfilms, 1956, pp. 62–67.

[30] Robert Sinclair, *The British Press*. London: Home & Van Thal, 1949, p. 18.

[31] *Ibid.*, p. 29.

[32] *Ibid.*, pp. 39–40.

[33] *Ibid.*, p. 141.

[34] *Ibid.*, p. 226.

[35] Crawford, *op. cit.*

The Social Responsibility of the Press

[36] For details of the abortive election study proposal mentioned here, see *Editor & Publisher*, November 12, 1955, p. 9; December 3, 1955, p. 14; December 10, 1955, p. 15; January 28, 1956, p. 9.

[37] T. S. Matthews, *Name and Address*. New York: Simon and Schuster, 1960, pp. 252, 253, 255.

[38] *Ibid.*, p. 274.

[39] Commission on Freedom of the Press, *op. cit.*, p. 10.

[40] Royal Commission on the Press, *op. cit.*, p. 105.

[41] Commission on Freedom of the Press, *op. cit.*, pp. 17–18.

[42] *Ibid.*, pp. 18–24.

VII. *Professional Organization of Mass Communicators*

[1] Warren Breed, *The Newspaperman, News and Society*. Ann Arbor: University Microfilms, 1952, p. 123.

[2] *Ibid.*, p. 123.

[3] *Ibid.*, p. 151.

[4] *Ibid.*, p. 158.

[5] *Ibid.*, pp. 315–328.

[6] Royal Commission on the Press, *Minutes of Evidence*, day 3, p. 1.

[7] *Ibid.*, pp. 2–3.

[8] *Ibid.*, day 12, pp. 1–2.

[9] J. M. Clark, *Social Control of Business*. Chicago: University of Chicago Press, 1926, p. 47.

[10] Howard R. Bowen, *Social Responsibilities of the Businessman*. New York: Harper & Brothers, 1953, pp. 6–12.

[11] *Ibid.*, p. 19.

[12] N. S. B. Gras, *Casebook of Business History*. New York: F. S. Crofts and Company, 1939, p. 480.

[13] Bowen, *op. cit.*, p. 21.

[14] *Ibid.*, p. 103.

[15] *Ibid.*, p. 105.

[16] Abraham Flexner, "Is Social Work a Profession?" *School and Society*, Vol. 1, June 26, 1915, p. 904; A. M. Carr-Saunders and P. A. Wilson, *The Professions*. Oxford: Clarendon Press, 1933. Flexner's criteria may also be found in Morris L. Cogan, "The Problem of Defining a Profession," *Annals* of the American Academy of Political and Social Science, January 1955, p. 105.

[17] Carr-Saunders and Wilson, *op. cit.*, pp. 284–285.

[18] Commission on Freedom of the Press, *op. cit.*, p. 77.

[19] On the rationale of this section, see Angell, *op. cit.*, p. 15.

[20] *Journalism Quarterly*, Vol. 35, No. 4, Fall 1958, pp. 522–523.

[21] Roy W. Howard, editor of the New York *World-Telegram* and chairman of the executive committee of Scripps-Howard Newspapers, advised Sigma Delta Chi, of which he was honorary president at the time, to work for a system somewhat like that recommended here. He also suggested giving legal definition to the word "journalist" so that those who qualified to use it could obtain recognition and preferment for their work. "Howard Asks 'Levels' for Professional Rank," *Editor & Publisher*, November 12, 1955, p. 12.

[22] See the address of LeRoy Collins, president, National Association of Broadcasters, to the Conference on Freedom and Responsibility in Broadcasting, Northwestern University School of Law, May 3, 1961.

INDEX

BOWMAN LIBRARY
MENLO SCHOOL AND MENLO COLLEGE

070.11
G354